Jonah
The Reluctant Prophet

Erica Brown

JONAH
THE RELUCTANT PROPHET

OU Press
Maggid Books

Jonah
The Reluctant Prophet

First Edition, 2017

Maggid Books
An imprint of Koren Publishers Jerusalem Ltd.

POB 8531, New Milford, CT 06776-8531, USA
& POB 4044, Jerusalem 9104001, Israel
www.maggidbooks.com

© Erica Brown 2017

Cover image: "Jonah and the Whale," Alma Sheppard-Matsuo

The publication of this book was made possible through the generous support of *Torah Education in Israel*.

All rights reserved. No part of this publication may be reproduced, stored in a retrieval system, or transmitted in any form or by any means, electronic, mechanical, photocopying, or otherwise, without the prior permission of the publisher, except in the case of brief quotations embedded in critical articles or reviews.

ISBN 978-1-59264-485-8, *hardcover*

A CIP catalogue record for this title is available from the British Library

Printed and bound in the United States

*In loving memory of Irving and Beatrice Stone,
who dedicated their lives to the
advancement of Jewish education.
We are proud and honored to continue in their legacy.*

*Their Children, Grandchildren, and Great-Grandchildren
Cleveland, Ohio, USA*

This book is dedicated to my mother,
Tzipora Schoonmaker,
who taught her children never to run away
but to run toward God,
for in God's embrace
lies our truest strength.

Contents

Preface..ix
Introduction...xiii

PART ONE: JONAH'S RETREAT

Jonah's Theological Crisis..3
Jonah's Collapse into Silence..19
The Unity of Opposites: The Sailors, the Captain, and the King........37

PART TWO: JONAH ADRIFT

The Strange Fish that Trapped a Strange Man.........................57
The Liminality of Three Days and Three Nights.......................77
Jonah's Prayer: Things Said and Unsaid..............................91

PART THREE: RADICAL TRANSFORMATION

Nineveh: That "Great" City...119
Two Watery Tales of God's Sudden Compassion........................137
Destruction or Redemption?...159

PART FOUR: THE FINAL WORD

Job, Jonah, and the Power of God's Justice 181

*Nature as Teacher: A Hot Sun, a Blistering Wind,
   a Gourd, a Worm* 195

To End with a Question. 209

Epilogue: Jonah – Rebel or Revenant?. 223

Preface

My romance with the Book of Jonah began early. Its whimsicality and visuality, its brazenness, and its poignant emotional and philosophical landscape make this short book heady reading. I began studying the Book of Jonah most intensely during my very first year of teaching. Its riddles made an outstanding impression upon students, who never failed to wrestle with its language and theology. Only once did I encounter a student who turned away from its gripping plot. While teaching in a gap-year program in a seminary in Israel, I found that a young woman who was registered for the course on Jonah had dropped out before the first class. "I studied this book already in ninth grade," she sighed. Jonah is a biblical book that can fascinate a reader for an entire lifetime and still not reveal all of its secrets. Boredom handicapped this young woman's curiosity. She closed Jonah's pages much too early.

Every year we read this small book; it beckons to us from its place in the liturgy on our greatest Day of Awe, and the repetition might clue the listener in to its relevance. The words of the text do not change, but we do. We bring a new and ever-maturing self to the Book of Jonah each year, so that it yields new subtleties to us again and again if we keep its pages and our minds open.

Jonah

This particular book is organized as a series of three essays for each of the four chapters of the Book of Jonah, bookended by an introduction and epilogue. I make no claim for originality. There is nothing new under the sun, if not when Ecclesiastes was first written, then certainly not now, a few millennia later. What you will find on these pages is a melding of traditional exegetes, midrashic and other rabbinic literature, modern Bible scholars, and artists – all of whom, like me, fell under the spell of this book and were compelled to analyze it and swim in its dangerous and imaginative waters. Where classic medieval commentators are notably short on overarching explanations and tend more to a line-by-line reading than a holistic chapter-by-chapter approach, we will fill in the gaps using other scholars' writings.

For translation, I have relied predominantly, but not exclusively, on the Jewish Publication Society's *JPS Hebrew-English Tanakh*[1] and the *Koren Tanakh*.[2] I also relied upon the translation of relevant passages of *Pirkei DeRabbi Eliezer* rendered by David Stern and Mark Jay Mirsky in "Jonah and the Sailors from *Pirkei de-Rabbi Eliezer*"[3] and, in places, translations of standard medieval exegetes and Malbim from Steven Bob, *Go to Nineveh: Medieval Commentaries to the Book of Jonah Translated and Explained*.[4] In specific cases, I offer an alternative biblical translation of my own, usually scanning a variety of published and online translations – either in order to capture a specific meaning or when I felt that the translation needed to be more exact in context. When I refer to the biblical story, I use the past tense to describe acts and behaviors; however, I use the present tense when quoting commentators, even those who passed on hundreds of years ago, in order to render the ongoing, robust, and vibrant sense of continuity in commentary. The books are closed. The interpretation of the books remains open. Thus "Jonah fled" but "Rashi observes."

---

1. Philadelphia: Jewish Publication Society, 2003.
2. Second edition, Jerusalem: Koren, 2010.
3. In *Rabbinic Fantasies: Imaginative Narratives from Classical Hebrew Literature* (New Haven: Yale University Press, 1998), 59–66.
4. Eugene, OR: Wipf and Stock, 2013.

Preface

I am most grateful to Matthew Miller, Reuven Ziegler, Tomi Mager, Deena Glickman, Caryn Metz, and Avigayil Steiglitz of Maggid, who greatly improved upon the manuscript version, and give thanks to my Orthodox Union partners for their continued support. I also appreciate the insightful comments and edits of Jennifer Rubin Raskas and my husband, Jeremy Brown, and express my ongoing general appreciation – as always – to family, friends, and colleagues and especially to the two recent and beautiful additions to our family through marriage, Yoni and Rebecca. If books are our pleasure gardens and orchards, in the words of Yehuda ibn Tibbon, then thank you all for gardening with me.

Introduction

Prophetic Hesitation

The Book of Jonah, simply put, is misnamed. This is not an account of a prophet, although an unusual Hebrew prophet stands at its center. This is a book about God, a God associated with a particular nation, Israel, who expands His divine embrace to include non-Jews, animals large and small, and vegetation. Nowhere since the first chapters of Genesis do we find, in so few pages, mention of the world's totality and God's utter and urgent concern for the whole of creation. Jonah will serve as God's ultimate foil in this magical story, just as the sailors, the king of Nineveh, and the animals become foils for the prophet. Jonah's personal theological crisis will become the platform upon which God models divine compassion, urging Jonah to become more godly, more like his Creator. God serves Jonah as parent, friend, mentor, and teacher. God's props – from a fish to a storm to a gourd to a worm – are the teaching tools by which God patiently encourages the prophet to confront his ugliest self, predominantly his churlish disregard for a universe outside of his narrow, parochial concerns.

The world around Jonah is in constant flux. A group of sailors became a group of believers. A city and its king transformed themselves. A tree grew and died overnight. Everything and everyone changed, including God – but the prophet did not change. For this reason, we have no idea what happened to Jonah when the words written about him end, unceremoniously, as if in mid-sentence or mid-story. There are only so many chances given to a person who fails to believe in personal transformation, let alone radical collective change. But more than the transformations personal or collective that appear in the book, it was God's ability to change that was the source of Jonah's caustic resentment.

We read this book on Yom Kippur not because of Jonah but because of the God of Jonah. If God can change, we can change. If God recruits all of nature to fight human nature in the story of one individual, then surely, we can all overcome the barriers to compassion, the niggling resistance to being different than we are, and the narcissistic pull that keeps our own worlds small and limited. Jonah was unmoved, but perhaps we will read his book as his critics and be moved precisely because he was not. Maybe we will see in the God of Jonah, the God of each and every one of us, a God who cares for us intimately and personally, a God who marshals the world's resources for our reformation, who asks us questions that force introspection. Can we adjust, adapt, amend, refine, and modify who we are on this holiest of days because God also changes? Or are we, like Jonah, secret believers that nothing ever changes, least of all who we are? The God of Jonah changes; that should be motivation enough. It was not enough for Jonah. Will it be for us?

This book will travel through the four chapters of Jonah's story and divide them into four distinct phases of Jonah's mission. We will trace his call to leadership and then his intransigence, his momentary rise to duty and then his tragic resignation. We will conclude with God's ultimate lesson for him. We begin with Jonah's retreat from responsibility that culminates in his drifting at sea, a powerful metaphor for a prophet unanchored. Jonah will be released from this aquatic adventure to a city in the throes of a transformation, a city he inspires that fails to inspire him. Finally, we will see Jonah swallowed by a different force than a powerful fish: God's word. God will frame Jonah's experience and his conclusions through questioning and modeling compassion. God's prodding, His subtle hints, His overt directives, and His manipulation of events will still not change the prophet but, carefully read, may change the readers of Jonah's story.

Introduction

I have called Jonah the reluctant prophet. I could have called him the unchanging prophet, but we do not know how the story ends. Reluctance carries with it a sense of hesitation, the nod of the unwilling, the disinclined, the resistant, the oppositional, the unenthusiastic. All of these descriptors fit Jonah as he goes through different stages in his evolution as prophet. Even the few hints at his body language in the book are redolent with suggestion of helplessness and resistance: both his deep sleep in chapter 1 and his three days in the fish are often rendered by artists as a grown man in fetal position, hugging himself and making his world narrower and smaller. Whether tossed at sea or crouching under a gourd, our prophet lives alone. He cannot even stay in Nineveh long before leaving the city and building himself a booth for one far away. Jonah is the far-away prophet, always on the escape even when he is physically present.

THE JONAH ENIGMA

> Shipmates, this book, containing only four chapters – four yarns – is one of the smallest strands in the mighty cable of the Scriptures. Yet what depths of the soul Jonah's deep sealine sound! What a pregnant lesson to us is this prophet! What a noble thing is that canticle in the fish's belly! How billow-like and boisterously grand![1]

Father Mapple, the religious voice of repentance in Herman Melville's *Moby-Dick*, draws his congregants at the New Bedford Whaleman's Chapel to this small biblical book with its maritime themes. He knew his audience. No one could empathize with Jonah's plight more than his congregation of seamen. There was "a low rumbling of heavy sea-boots" heard as they shuffled into the church to hear his passionate plea for personal change: "We feel the floods surging over us, we sound with him to the kelpy bottom of the waters; sea-weed and all the slime of the sea is about us!" Like Ahab, Father Mapple was a believer in a singular truth – God's justice – that must be pursued at all costs. He saw Jonah

---

1. Herman Melville, *Moby-Dick* (London: CRW Publishing Ltd., 2004), 82.

ben Amitai, the son of truth, as the biblical protagonist who could best represent his message.

Perhaps Father Mapple picked Jonah as his subject for the same reason that we pick Jonah as an inspiring text to read at the end of the holiest day of a Jewish calendar year:

> But what is this lesson that the book of Jonah teaches? Shipmates, it is a two-stranded lesson; a lesson to us all as sinful men, and a lesson to me as a pilot of the living God. As sinful men, it is a lesson to us all, because it is a story of the sin, hard-heartedness, suddenly awakened fears, the swift punishment, repentance, prayers, and finally the deliverance and joy of Jonah. As with all sinners among men, the sin of this son of Amittai was in his wilful disobedience of the command of God – never mind now what that command was, or how conveyed – which he found a hard command. But all the things that God would have us do are hard for us to do – remember that – and hence, he oftener commands us than endeavors to persuade. And if we obey God, we must disobey ourselves; and it is in this disobeying ourselves, wherein the hardness of obeying God consists.[2]

Father Mapple asked the ultimate sacrifice of his congregation: the abnegation of self that true obedience demands – true obedience that Jonah himself was hard-pressed to provide. We obey God when we disobey a personal impulse to ignore duty. But when Father Mapple speaks of Jonah's deliverance and joy, we cannot help but wonder if the priest actually read the text before constructing his lesson.

Tumbling back many centuries from Melville's New England coastline, we find ourselves in Narbonne in the early thirteenth century. Rabbi David Kimche (or "Radak," 1160–1235) asked a question about the Book of Jonah: "And it could be asked why this prophecy is included in the Holy Scriptures."[3] Indeed, why? Radak puzzles over a book devoted to a "gentile nation of the world." He concludes that,

---

2. Ibid.
3. Radak to Jonah 1:1.

Introduction

it was written to be a moral lesson to Israel, for a foreign nation that is not part of Israel was close to repentance, and the first time a prophet rebuked them, they turned to a complete repentance from evil. And Israel, whom the prophets rebuke from dawn to dusk, still do not turn from their evil!

His comments sting with their truth. Radak, following in his critique, suggests that Jonah fled so as not to bring punishment on his people, thereby demonstrating more honor for the Israelites than he showed toward God.[4] He also mentions the *aggada* that Jonah received prophecy twice but not three times because of his obvious failings as a prophet.[5] Yet he softens the blow by adding another lesson based on Jonah's miraculous salvation in a fish belly twinned with God's compassion for Nineveh: "God, who is blessed, is merciful to those who repent from any nation and grants them mercy, even more so when they are many."[6] According to Radak, this book highlights both Israel's recalcitrance and God's expansive mercy. Yet these lessons are commonplace in the prophetic literature of the Hebrew Bible and told in ways far more believable than this fanciful tale. The oddity of the book offers its charms and, at the same time, its unlikely details can serve as a distraction from its deeper meanings. Before we begin an intensive study of the book's four chapters, we must deepen Radak's question rather than dismiss it: Why is this book included in the biblical canon?

To strengthen our question, we turn to the scholar Elias Bickerman, who included Jonah in his classic work, *Four Strange Books of the Bible*.[7] One wonders what he specifically had in mind in including Jonah in his exploration of "strange books." Was it God's unusual demand that a Hebrew prophet moralize to an important Assyrian stronghold, which was, not inconsequentially, a sworn enemy of the Israelites? Perhaps it was the absurd assumption that one can run away from the Almighty? Then there is the book's fairy-tale depiction of the great sea monster

---

4. This is based on the introduction to the comments in the *Mekhilta* to *Parashat Bo*.
5. See Yevamot 98a.
6. Radak to Jonah 1:1.
7. Elias Bickerman, *Four Strange Books of the Bible* (New York: Schocken, 1968).

that swallowed but did not consume the prophet and then conveniently dropped the prophet off on assignment. The outsized fish is not the only animal to make an appearance here. In contrast to the leviathan, there is the lowly worm that destroyed Jonah's precious gourd. There are also the beasts of Nineveh, pious animals that wore sackcloth and ashes to beg, as it were, for their own redemption. Nature too served as an odd conduit to God's will – from the midrashic reading that the tempest in chapter 1 happened only over Jonah's ship to the description of the harsh east wind and sun that provoked Jonah to ask for his own death in chapter 4. Sandwiched in between the negotiation between God and Jonah over his future is the mass conversion in chapter 3 of an entire city from the simple utterance of Jonah's five words. Never in the history of sacred literature could a prophet boast of such success, but still Jonah turned away, moved toward, and then turned away again from Nineveh. Is there anything that is *not* strange in the Book of Jonah?

All of these unusual elements mean that the Book of Jonah does not sit comfortably within any genre of typical epic hero legends or myths of antiquity. Jonah does not fit into Joseph Campbell's neat evolution of the protagonist; he did not accept great responsibility with enthusiasm nor did he face difficult trials of strength and patience.[8] He did not kill a beast in a string of events that prompted his self-actualization; instead, he was saved by a water beast making him, on some level, an antipode to the mythic Greek hero or perhaps even a parody of such figures. Judged by ancient Greek standards, Jonah was meek and cowardly, self-effacing and unsuccessful, even when he opted to accept God's challenge.

From a biblical perspective, however, the details and narrative arc of Jonah's story are not unusual. We find similar themes and linguistic parallels all over the Hebrew Bible, demanding intertextual treatment, the shaping of meaning through an understanding of the relationships between one text and another. Many of these relationships will be explored in depth on these pages. The scholar George Landes contends that the Book of Jonah has

---

8. See Joseph Campbell, *Hero with a Thousand Faces* (San Francisco: New World Library, 2008), particularly chapters 1 and 3 on departure and return.

Introduction

no fewer than sixty-three places in the text where the author's deliberate or inadvertent withholding of information poses at least some interpretive issue for the reader and, in addition, thirteen places where narrative features create a dissonance in the logic or coherence of the story.[9]

The narrative choices on the part of the author create abundant opportunities for rabbinic interpretation and the work of modern scholarship in filling in the gaps and in speculating on meanings and intentions.

Jonah's Movement: Ascent and Descent

Moving away from language, we find that on a visual level, Jonah's story shares beguiling horizontal and vertical dimensions with other biblical stories of ascent and descent. Jonah was told to rise and go to Nineveh. He did rise, but he went elsewhere. His ascent was the wrong ascent. Running away on a ship and being carried by a fish stimulate in the reader an impression of horizontal movement, particularly Jonah's sojourn aboard the ship. The horizon scanned against the water and sky creates an image of forward propulsion on the surface of existence. And yet there are also multiple vertical commands and rejections that take the form of ascents and descents. Jonah was told by God and the ship's captain to *get up*. But Jonah consistently *lowered* himself, as many traditional and modern scholars have pointed out. Jonah *went down* to Jaffa, *down into* the ship, *down into the recesses* of the ship, and then finally *down into a deep sleep*. Varying conjugations of Y-R-D suggest a continual movement downward. And because Jonah did not take the horizontal path to Nineveh, he would suffer the

---

9. George M. Landes, "Textual 'Information Gaps' and 'Dissonances' in the Interpretation of the Book of Jonah," in *Ki Baruch Hu: Ancient Near Eastern, Biblical and Judaic Studies in Honor of Baruch A. Levine*, ed. William W. Hallo, Lawrence H. Schiffman, and Robert Chazan (Winona Lake, IN: Eisenbrauns, 1999), 273–4. I am grateful to Stu Halpern for directing me to this essay. For more on textual omissions and discordances in the Hebrew Bible, see Meir Sternberg, *The Poetics of Biblical Narrative: Ideological Literature and the Drama of Reading* (Bloomington: Indiana University Press, 1985), chapters 6–7.

vertical descent to Sheol.[10] By the end of Jonah's prayer in chapter 2, Jonah was at the *very bottom* of the sea, on its sandbars: "I sank to the *base* of the mountains; the bars of the earth closed upon me forever" (Jonah 2:7). Jonah's reference to Sheol in his prayer suggests even greater depths, the pit or belly of the underworld, and a continuous and desired brush with death itself.

Yet God did not allow the prophet to pursue this descent. Once Jonah reached the very end of the known world, God rescued him, bringing him out of death waters and back to a life of purpose and service: "Yet You brought my life up from the pit" (ibid.). Once the descent and ascent were complete, the text moves back to its horizontal dimensions: "The Lord commanded the fish, and it spewed Jonah out upon dry land" (v. 11).

Several biblical narratives follow this similar descent/ascent pattern.[11] The most obvious are the narratives of Joseph who was thrown into a pit, rose out of it, and continued to rise in an almost meteoric upward gradient.[12] Later, after his seduction at the greedy hands of Potiphar's wife, he was thrown into prison. Lowering his rising star at this stage would have meant a sharp climb downward given the speed of his professional ascent. But Joseph, ever the favorite, managed to work his way back up in the graces of the court until he became the vizier of Egypt, second only to Pharaoh himself. His youthful dream of having

---

10. Sheol, as it is used biblically, refers to the grave or to the abode of the dead, appearing over seventy times in the Hebrew Bible. See, for example, Gen. 37:35; 44:29; I Kings 2:9; Ps. 88:4; 89:48; Prov. 1:12. Some believe it is the Hebrew equivalent of the Greek term "Hades."
11. In addition to the Joseph stories, note the rise and fall in Judah and Tamar's story in Genesis 38 and Naomi's fall and later ascent in the Book of Ruth. More to follow on Naomi's story below.
12. Genesis 39 uses excessive language to demonstrate Joseph's rise, "The Lord was with Joseph, and he was a successful man" (v. 2); "And when his master saw that the Lord was with him and that the Lord lent success to everything he undertook, he took a liking to Joseph" (v. 3); "The Lord blessed his house for Joseph's sake, so that the blessing of the Lord was upon everything that he owned, in the house and outside" (v. 5); "Joseph was well built and handsome" (v. 6). Is it a wonder that Joseph's fall, when it came, would be total and that his climb upward would be matched by a sharp slope downward?

Introduction

the sun and moon bow down to him meant that early on he regarded himself as a person who could soar vertically to heights unimaginable.

An additional important descent/ascent narrative with literary parallels to Jonah is present in another four-chapter book of the Bible, the Book of Ruth. The book opens with a small, intact family moving from the rocky terrain of Bethlehem, in the region of Judah south of Jerusalem, to the smooth plains of Moab during a famine. Yet as we travel with this family, we find that very quickly, its female protagonist Naomi suffered one loss after another: the loss of her people, her country, her husband, and her sons to Moabite wives, then childlessness (according to midrashic tradition), and then, finally, the death of her two sons. If we trace the opening five verses of Ruth, we find an inverted pyramid of loss and grief, plummeting Naomi into a personal descent she blamed on God's wrath: "The Lord has dealt harshly with me. Shaddai has brought misfortune upon me" (1:21). In one of the most extraordinary uses of the term *vatakom*, she rose to find her way back home (v. 6) – no easy task for a woman of the time who could simply have resigned herself to permanent mourning.[13] This rise informs the spirit of ascent that permeates the book, eventually culminating in the genealogy of King David.

Jonah, however, did not end his eponymous book on a vertical incline of success. He moved horizontally away from the book's supposed center. He moved eastward. Eastward is never a positive direction, biblically speaking; this is true from the very first chapters of Genesis.[14] Eastward suggests a movement away from goodness and

---

13. Yael Ziegler, in her excellent book, *Ruth: From Alienation to Monarchy* (Jerusalem: Maggid, 2015), discusses this verb and the feelings that inspired it: "Drawn after her husband's decision and constrained by circumstances beyond her control, Naomi must have been keen to return to her hometown. The first verb, *vatakom*, may imply especially avid action. If this verb alludes to the end of the mourning period, when the mourner 'gets up' from mourning the dead, then Naomi's return is undertaken at the first possible opportunity after her sons' death" (p. 133).
14. God planted the garden in the eastern part of Eden and created human beings there (Gen. 2:8). Ezekiel had a vision of people bowing to the east from the Temple (Ezek. 8:16) and gates of the Temple facing east (40:22). But when human beings sin, they move further and further away from this direction of God and goodness. When Adam and Eve were chased from the garden, they moved eastward and a sword-bearing angel was placed east of the garden to ensure they would not return

intimacy, from holiness and purposeful existence. It affirms that this is a book to be taken seriously as a theological struggle between human beings and their Maker.

Larger Than Life

Despite the sober nature of the material, modern Bible scholar Arnold Band contends that the Book of Jonah was originally conceived as a parody — and not only a parody but *the* parody of the Bible.[15] The outsized natural phenomena are meant to be noted as part of the conceit of an outlandish story,[16] as is the appearance of several *leitworts* — repeated words that offer thematic suggestions — and the distortion of serious themes present in earlier biblical works. These *leitworts* draw us again

---

(Gen. 3:24). After Cain murdered his brother, he too moved "east of Eden" (4:16). Lot journeyed eastward in the direction of Egypt when he separated from Abraham (13:11).

15. "If we are correct in our argument that the Book of Jonah was originally a masterwork of parody we are confronted with a literary phenomenon which has few parallels (I can think of none)," Arnold J. Band, "Swallowing Jonah: The Eclipse of Parody," *Prooftexts* 10 (1990): 177. Band is not alone. See John A. Miles, Jr., "Laughing at the Bible: Jonah as Parody," *The Jewish Quarterly Review*, new series 65, no. 3 (1975): 168–81; Baruch Halpern and Richard Friedman, "Composition and Paronomaisa," *Hebrew Annual Review* 4 (1980): 79–91; John C. Hulbert, "'The Deliverance Belongs to Yahweh!': Satire in the Book of Jonah," *JSOT* 21 (October, 1981): 59–81; and James S. Ackerman, "Satire and Symbolism in the Song of Jonah," *Traditions in Transformation*, ed. Baruch Halpern and Jon D. Levenson (Winona Lake, IN: Eisenbrauns, 1981), 213–46. For a critique of Miles's thesis, see Adele Berlin, "A Rejoinder to John A. Miles, Jr., with Some Observations on the Nature of Prophecy," *The Jewish Quarterly Review*, new series 66, no. 4 (1976): 227–35. Berlin writes that Miles is "implying that the canonizers of the Bible did not understand the message of the book" (p. 227), a position not helped by the fact that it was deemed appropriate by the sages for inclusion in the High Holiday liturgy, "hardly the appropriate occasion for a parody of the Bible" (ibid.).
16. Some might see in Jonah a comedic tale — as some other biblical books or narratives have been regarded — because of the strange natural phenomena. However, this is not indicated in content, only in the "props" of the story. For the role of humor in the Bible, see F. Landy, "Humour as a Tool for Biblical Exegesis," *On Humour and the Comic in the Hebrew Bible*, ed. Yehuda Thomas Radday and Athalya Brenner (Sheffield: Almond Press, 1990), 99–116, no. 23 in the Bible as Literature Series. Other helpful essays in the same volume include Athalya Brenner, "On the Semantic Field of Humor, Laughter and the Comic in the Old Testament," (pp. 39–58), and Yehuda T. Radday, "On Missing the Humour in the Bible: An Introduction" (pp. 21–38).

Introduction

and again to intentioned meanings, something lost on the reader without a grasp of Hebrew. They also point to the multivalent nature of the book. Translations often use synonyms to add sophistication to biblical verse but, in so doing, they can compromise the simplicity and value of a word written again and again, like a hammer knocking meaning into the reader. There are key words that appear several times in this book of only forty-eight verses – seventeen in the first chapter, ten in the middle two chapters, and eleven in the last.

The word that appears with the greatest frequency in the book is *gadol*, or "great"; it appears fourteen times in forty-eight verses, most frequently to describe the city of Nineveh itself. Its size, according to the book's second verse, seems to justify God's mission that Jonah make this city's reformation his chief task and responsibility. Being large in both size and population, Nineveh was worthy of God's attention and the time and energy of the prophet. This refrain repeats itself at the very end of the book as well, this time with an edgy jab at Jonah. God told him that He Himself invested in this city because it was an *ir gedola*, "a very great city," and then backed up this information with its numerical population of 120,000 people and their cattle. The fact that these were people who did not know their right from their left was not a reason to ignore them, God implied; rather, it was a reason for a more intensified divine investment. Whenever God mentioned the city, He added the adjective; in the narrator's description of Nineveh in chapter 3, an *additional* adjective is added with an ironic twist: "Nineveh was an enormously large city" (Jonah 3:3). This is a translation of a more complex description, *ir gedola leElohim*, meaning that it was "a city that was great to God" or for God. God is often referred to in liturgy as *HaGadol*, "the Great One"; thus the implication is that this city was large even by divine standards. This also offers a subtle wordplay: not only was this an expansive city; in this narrative, it was God's city. If it was God's city because it merited redemption and compassion then it must have been a large or great city to God's prophets. Jonah was not to be an exception.

Nineveh, the word most often modified by "large" in the Book of Jonah, is by no means the only element worthy of this adjective in the book's pages. The book tells us of a *great* wind, a *great* storm, a *great* fish. Nature in the book is outsized and daunting. To Jonah, who was trying to escape forces larger than himself, everything appeared as an overwhelming taunt to his powerlessness.

If the book seems unbelievable because of its dramatic expressions of size, it is far from the only biblical text that employs unrestrained imagination. The talking donkey in Numbers was wiser than her master (22:28–29). Two female bears killed forty-two children for ridiculing the prophet Elisha (II Kings 2:23–24). When David asked King Saul for permission to marry his daughter, the king, who did not desire the match, demanded a bride price of one hundred foreskins of his Philistine enemies; David showed up with two hundred (I Sam. 18:25–27). If the plot of Jonah seems fantastical, it is because it is, or at least, according to some modern Bible scholars, was meant to be:

> The storm at sea and the threat of death by drowning recall the Deluge; the brief oracle Jonah recites in Nineveh uses the fateful term used to portray the devastation of Abraham's pleading for Sodom. These three referents are from Genesis, as is what might be termed a burlesque of the Tree and Serpent story, Jonah's dejection over the eating of a gourd by a worm. Even a superficial reading, then, situates one familiar with the Hebrew Scriptures in a literary world which is extremely familiar.[17]

This pastiche of familiar tropes mashed together, according to Band, highlights the way the author of the book uses parody to show the absurdity of Jonah's proposition – that a prophet can flee from God. The facetiousness of a prophet sleeping while his boat was capsizing or a king who quickly responded to a prophet's words and even commanded animals to fast and wear sackcloth all point to a book ridiculing Jonah. How and why this book was transformed into the serious text it is today, according to this theory, represents a fascinating departure into the world of hermeneutics.

Another pair of scholars, one a theologian, the other a clinical psychologist, contend that Jonah was written as a criticism of the narrow-minded upper classes of Jerusalem, who saw in Israel the realization of God's exclusive love; it is "a protest against a well-to-do party in Jerusalem

---

17. Band, "Swallowing Jonah," 181.

in the fifth century BCE which abused its power in order to 'ghettoize' Judaism."[18] By demonstrating that the same God could care for the residents of the capital of the Assyrian Empire by sending them a Hebrew prophet, Jonah was dispelling this notion with his very person.

An Evolving Message

Whether regarded as parody, a cautionary tale, a testament to the power of repentance, or a narrative conveying the relational struggles of a Hebrew prophet with his God, the Book of Jonah continues to fascinate and challenge its readers. Four short chapters gave birth to over a millennium of debate and interpretation. In the canonization of the Bible, there was never a question, as there was with the Song of Songs or Ecclesiastes,[19] as to whether or not the Book of Jonah should be included because it relates the story of an intransigent or rebellious prophet. And yet, the book seems other-worldly; it is hard to wrap one's mind around the action and inaction of the prophet, the distractions of nature, and the speed of the city's transformation. The Book of Jonah begins and ends abruptly, with neither the genealogical and geographic markers typical of biblical

---

18. André Lacocque and Pierre-Emmanuel Lacocque, *The Jonah Complex* (Atlanta: John Knox Press, 1981), 24. This pair contends that the author of the Book of Jonah was likely influenced by the ancient satirical works of Menippus from Gadera (third century BCE). This point was also made by James S. Ackerman in "Satire and Symbolism in the Song of Jonah," *Traditions in Transformation: Turning Points in Biblical Faith*, F. M. Cross festschrift; ed. Baruch Halpern and Jon D. Levenson (Winona Lake, IN: Eisenbrauns, 1981), 227. George Landes argues against this view in "Textual 'Information Gaps' and 'Dissonances,'" 226–227.
19. See Mishna Yadayim 3:5 for the well-known debate about whether or not these two works have the same capacity to render one's hands impure:
    All the holy writings make the hands impure. The Song of Songs and Ecclesiastes make the hands impure. R. Yehuda says: The Song of Songs makes the hands impure, but there is a dispute about Ecclesiastes. R. Yose says: Ecclesiastes does not make the hands impure, but there is a dispute about the Song of Songs. R. Shimon says: Ecclesiastes is one of the leniencies of Beit Shammai [who say it does not make the hands impure] and one of the stringencies of Beit Hillel [who say it does make the hands impure]. R. Shimon b. Azzai said: I received a tradition from the seventy-two elders on the day when they appointed R. Elazar b. Azaria head of the court that the Song of Songs and Ecclesiastes make the hands impure.

Jonah

books nor an ending that offers, if not a satisfying denouement, then at least any ending at all. By concluding with a question asked by God, the text leaves the reader with no idea what ever happened to Jonah. And yet the story compels with its intrigue. Robert Alter suggests that Jonah, among other later biblical books, departs from the "stringent narrative economy" generally found in the Hebrew Bible and has been "replaced by a reveling in the sumptuousness of details."[20] He also offers a number of ways to view the story: "Jonah has variously been described as a parable, a Menippean satire, or a sailor's yarn."[21] Another scholar, stymied by the problem of its genre, calls it simply "a short story."[22]

What the book meant when it was originally written and what it came to mean in its later association with the High Holiday mood of atonement and transformation have changed over time. As Bickerman points out, because the book was likely written in the fifth century BCE, its author was "unlike the rabbis; for them prophesying was a thing of the past, having ceased, they believed with Haggai, Zechariah, and Malachi, that is, about 500 BCE."[23] The author, like others of antiquity, likely believed that prophets were foretellers of the future. As such, their predictions presented the humans who craved them with a "conditional fate." Once they learned of what might happen to them, they could choose to behave differently.

Richard Friedman contends that Jonah's story is only one of two in all of prophetic literature that features dramatic miracles. Its public nature is dampened somewhat because Jonah is the book's only named witness:

> In the prophetic books there are no more grand public miracles and few personal miracles. In all fifteen books, there are only two classic miracle stories. The first is the story of the fish that swallows Jonah. It is a personal miracle; no one witnesses it except Jonah himself.... After Jonah, probably the other most striking miracle in the books of the prophets is the story of Isaiah and

---

20. Robert Alter, *The World of Biblical Literature* (New York: Basic Books, 1992), 78.
21. Ibid., 77.
22. James S. Ackerman, "Jonah," in *The Literary Guide to the Bible*, ed. Robert Alter and Frank Kermode (Cambridge, MA: Belknap Press, 1987), 234.
23. Bickerman, *Four Strange Books*, 29.

Introduction

the shadow that turns back on the steps (Is. 38:7–8). This, too, is a personal miracle, with few witnesses.[24]

Friedman may be ignoring some of the miracles that took place in the books of Joshua and Judges, Samuel and Kings; on the other hand, he may be referring to the frequency of the miracles and the fact that Jonah's work was done with a gentile nation and its king, much the way Moses' miracles impacted Egypt and Pharaoh, its leader. Friedman believes that because there are so few public miracles in prophetic works, the textual emphasis shifts away from them and toward symbolism. While we have no small share of miracles in the Hebrew Bible, these seem to be largely relegated to the first third of the Book of Exodus. Egypt was a land of magic, a place where God contested Pharaoh's might using the cultural context that mattered there. After the Splitting of the Sea, this surfeit of God's intervention through fantastic and very public displays slowed down, almost to a halt, with future miracles largely limited to singular or private events. The Book of Jonah, however, seems to revisit that period of miracle-saturation; in it, God used one miracle after another to entrap Jonah and encourage a reluctant repentance.

Another mythical aspect of the book has to do with chronology. By the time the book was canonized, Nineveh no longer existed. Instead, it remained residually in the biblical imagination as a mythic city of great proportions, capable of great evil but also capable of great and rapid change. It would have been, in the ancient mind, the equivalent of a modern-day reference to a city of sin, much in the way that Sodom and Gomorrah became associated with immorality from the days of Abraham. Nineveh, however, was twinned with another association: belligerence. The very word "Nineveh" conjured trepidation among the enemies of the Assyrians. The city, first mentioned in Genesis 10 as part of Nimrod's empire,[25] was associated with a neighboring city great in size: "The first centers of his kingdom were Babylon, Erech, Accad, and Calneh,

---

24. Richard Friedman, *The Disappearance of God* (Boston: Little, Brown and Company, 1995), 63–64.
25. Nimrod was the great-grandson of Noah, the son of Cush: "Cush also begot Nimrod, who was the first man of might on earth. He was a mighty hunter by the grace of

Jonah

in Shinar. From that land he [Nimrod] went to Assyria, where he built Nineveh, Rehoboth-ir, Calah, and Resen, which is between Nineveh and Calah, which is the great city" (v. 10–12). Read in this light, the events in the Book of Jonah are less of a description of current events. The book is, perhaps, a cautionary tale about prophets who reject their mission. Or it might be the inspiring story of pagan sailors and the great and wayward people of Nineveh who reformed themselves and thus atoned for their sins, offering the hope that anyone can change.

The enigma or strangeness of the prophet and the story led contemporary scholar Avivah Gottleib Zornberg to conclude that Jonah may well be a mythic character:

> Essentially it stands alone. If this text tells of a largely unidentified figure who inhabits a world of great force, who flees from God and who ultimately speaks only to choose death over life, then perhaps it belongs to the mythic, or symbolic, rather than historical narrative.... And perhaps his story, in all its enigmatic force, is never to be finally decoded, its mystery resolved; but it is to evoke the elusive nature of narrative meaning, the internal silence at the heart of all stories.[26]

By singling out the uniqueness of Jonah, to the point of questioning the prophet's very existence, Zornberg minimizes the impact of the prophet's story, suggesting to the reader that such a rebellion could never have taken place. A story, however, can be both unique and real. Whereas the existence of Job was contested in the Talmud, Jonah himself was never regarded as a fictional character in traditional scholarship.[27] R. Shmuel

---

the Lord, hence, the saying, 'Like Nimrod a mighty hunter by the grace of the Lord'" (Gen. 10:8–9). He was described as ruling over the land of Shinar, with Nineveh as its capital or at least one of its most significant cities.

26. Avivah Gottlieb Zornberg, "Jonah: A Fantasy of Flight," in *The Murmuring Deep: Reflections on the Biblical Unconscious* (New York: Schocken, 2009), 81.
27. See Bava Batra 15a–b, where a number of talmudic scholars regarded the ellipses in the text as an opportunity to situate Job historically. R. Yehoshua b. Levi argues that Job lived in the days of Moses. R. Yoḥanan and R. Elazar contend that Job was one of the exiles from Babylonia. R. Yehoshua b. Korḥa states that Job lived in the

b. Naḥmani argued that Job could not have existed because of the supposition the story makes about God. Yet no such rabbinic debate exists concerning Jonah. Even among those not afraid to say that a biblical character was really a mythic figure, Jonah did indeed exist.

DATING THE PROPHET

Perhaps the oddity of the prophet is related to the time period in which he lived and the context in which he led. Jonah's composition dates roughly to the fifth or early fourth century BCE, reflecting on the slice of a prophet's life many centuries earlier. The first reference to it is among the Twelve Minor Prophets – minor only because of the length of these books – and it appears in the apocryphal work of Ben Sira (49:10), written approximately in 180 BCE. Jonah served as prophet during the reign of Jeroboam II, the fourteenth king of Israel. Jeroboam's reign in the eighth century BCE spanned over four decades and is referenced not only in the Book of Jonah but also in Hosea, Joel, and Amos. Jeroboam is often mentioned with disdain as a perpetrator of idol worship and a king of material excess at a time of great prosperity for ancient Israel – a fact that gave rise to a ruling class of merciless elites: "He did what was displeasing to the Lord; he did not depart from all the sins that Jeroboam son of Nebat had caused Israel to commit" (II Kings 14:44). It is immediately after this verse that we meet Jonah for the first time and sense the prophet's despair at ministering to a king who was evil and corrupt but who expanded the borders of the Kingdom of Israel:

> It was he who restored the territory of Israel from Lebo-hamath to the Sea of Arava, in accordance with the promise that the Lord, the God of Israel, had made through His servant, the prophet

---

time of Esther. Others believe he lived at the time of Jacob. These views may have to do with the rabbinic understanding of true tragedy; historically, the Jewish people confronted the theodicy as a real rather than abstract conundrum. There is also the sweeping statement that "Job never was and never will be" – a way of suggesting that God would never conceive of such a trial, to cause suffering to a human being and make him a pawn in a wager between God and Satan. Resh Lakish believed that Job was indeed a real character, but the events purported to him could never have happened (Genesis Rabba 57).

Jonah

> Jonah son of Amitai from Gath-hepher. For the Lord saw the bitter plight of Israel, with neither bond nor free left and with none to help Israel. And the Lord resolved not to blot out the name of Israel from under the heaven; and he delivered them through Jeroboam son of Joash. (II Kings 14:25–27)

This was a time of political mayhem for the Israelites; corrupt leadership often resulted in religious fissures. God mitigated this somewhat by restoring Israel to its earlier territorial expanse and by letting the people know, through Jonah, that despair as they might, God would not blot them out, echoing earlier promises.[28] Knowing this, we can appreciate Jonah's later hesitations even more; if God promised the Israelites that they would survive, then ministering to an enemy would put Jonah in a position of compromise with his people at a time when they were already suffering profoundly.

Josephus, the first-century historian of Jewish antiquity, included this time frame in Israelite chronicles in his account of early history, mentioning Jonah's relationship with the king:

---

28. More will be made later of the ample comparisons between the Noah and Jonah narratives. Focusing only on God's promise, we know that God first uttered a divine commitment never to destroy the world again in Genesis 9:8–17; this was regarding all of humanity. The notion that God can blot out a name represents the power to determine whose legacy will continue and whose will not. Excision, in this framework, was possibly worse than death; a name or reputation can continue after death, but when one is inexorably blotted out, even this cannot occur. The tone in verses that illustrate this principle is that of a total and irrevocable dismissal: "The Lord shall never be willing to forgive him, but rather the anger of the Lord and His jealousy will burn against that man, and every curse which is written in this book will rest on him, and *the Lord will blot out his name from under heaven*" (Deut. 20:29). In Nahum, we read: "Come, and let us wipe them out as a nation, that the name of Israel be remembered no more" (1:14). It can express itself in a wish: "Let his posterity be cut off; in the following generation *let their name be blotted out*" (Ps. 109:13). Enemies of Israel bent on this course are described in Psalms: "They have said, 'Come, and let us wipe them out as a nation, that *the name of Israel be remembered no more*'" (83:4). Contrast this with the promising future of the levirate marriage: "It shall be that the firstborn whom she bears shall assume the name of his dead brother, *so that his name will not be blotted out* from Israel" (Deut. 25:6). We find a similar reference to Ruth when her levirate marriage is established: "When you acquire the property from Naomi and from Ruth the Moabite, you must also acquire the wife of the deceased, *so as to perpetuate the name of the deceased upon his estate*" (Ruth 4:5).

Introduction

> In the fifteenth year of the reign of Amatzia, Jeroboam the son of Joash reigned over Israel in Samaria for forty years. This king was guilty of contumely against God and became very wicked in worshipping idols and in many undertakings that were absurd and foreign. He was also the cause of ten thousand misfortunes to the people of Israel. Now one Jonah, a prophet, foretold to him that he should make war with the Syrians and conquer their army and enlarge the bounds of his kingdom.[29]

Josephus helps us appreciate that the Book of Jonah may have been written not as the story of a failed prophet but as the story of a good king – the king of Nineveh. He atoned, as did his city, at a moment's notice, in contrast to the wicked Israelite king who rejected God. The king of Nineveh's behavior suggested that an entire enemy city could be redeemed while an Israelite prophet and his king languished. This reading may offer yet another reason for Jonah's refusal. Knowing that he answered to his own murderous king, Jonah may have been even less willing to face another of an enemy nation. Perhaps Jonah had simply exhausted his patience for evil by the time he was told to journey to Nineveh.

Jonah's Pedigree and Mission

It is in II Kings that we learn the scant details about Jonah's life. There his only stated task is the expansion of Israel's borders. Jonah was from Gath-hepher in the Kingdom of Israel, slightly north of Jaffa, the port town from whence he later set off to Tarshish. The city was located in the northern part of the land designated to the tribe of Zebulun, as we learn in the Book of Joshua.[30] This tribal association also links us with the water imagery of Jonah. Zebulun was a maritime tribe that traded on the high seas. Jacob gave this blessing to his son Zebulun before he died: "Zebulun will dwell at the shore of the sea, and he shall serve as a port

---

29. Josephus, *Antiquities*, 9.10.
30. "And the third lottery came out in favor of the children of Zebulun according to their families, and the border of their inheritance was as far as Sarid … and from there it went along the east to Gath-hepher" (Josh. 19:10–13).

for ships" (Gen. 49:13). Later, Moses continued the theme by blessing the descendants of Zebulun to rejoice on their journeys, suggesting, if not maritime travel, then at least continuous movement (Deut. 33:18).

If we read the Jonah story as one in which he was pushed by God into embracing a destiny from which he ran away, then the Zebulun connection makes that destiny multigenerational. Those from this tribe were adventure-seekers who got sustenance from the sea. They should have delighted in their travels, not feared the sea or become distraught at the thought of leaving dry land.

The Talmud records that Amitai, Jonah's father, who was from Zebulun, had a wife from the tribe of Asher (Eiruvin 96a). The combination of Zebulun and Asher is not insignificant, as we can see from the blessing Jacob bestowed on this son and his descendants: "Asher's bread shall be rich, and he shall yield royal dainties" (Gen. 49:20). The combination of travel and wealth was attractive. Zebulun's association with royalty appears in the penultimate chapter of the Pentateuch. Moses gave his blessing to the tribe of Asher: "And of Asher he said, 'Most blessed of sons be Asher; let him be the favorite of his brothers, and let him dip his foot in oil. May your door bolts be iron and copper, and your security last all your days'" (Deut. 34:24–25). Asher was to be beloved among the tribes. In contrast to many others given the tension rife in many biblical fraternities, this is a laudatory blessing. The oil and door bolts also signal a life of comfort and security. And yet Jonah was a man terribly alone in his journey; his life was characterized neither by comfort nor by security.

The comingling of the emblematic aspects of both tribes offers us a picture of leadership – indeed, a sense that those born to Zebulun and Asher were chosen for greatness, destined for oceanic travel, favored, and protected. But even a cursory reading of this book shows that Jonah firmly resisted this destiny and then tried, but failed, to accommodate it. Jonah was not to stay in one place; he was from a tribe of travelers who would always have powerful nautical associations. But he went to sea to leave God, not to fulfill the fate of his tribe. The sea was where he imagined he would finally die, covered by its raging waters. Jonah's calling was not a mission but a haunting death knell. He ran away from leadership. He was not beloved by others but feared and revered; his presence put the sailors in grave danger. When Jonah told the sailors that he was a

Hebrew and a worshipper of God, they were shocked: "The men were greatly terrified, and they asked him, 'What have you done?'" (Jonah 1:10). It must be noted that Jonah did not say that he was a prophet, only that he was a Hebrew, another way of denying or resisting his calling. When he told the sailors explicitly that he was running from the service of God, they had no idea how to treat him, so different was he from any other person they must have met. He was powerful enough to engender a storm at sea, oddly trying to run away from his God, even as he described himself as a worshipper of God.

That the prophet was busy literally expanding the boundaries of Israel further, from the entrance of Hamat to the Sea of Arava, is also significant as background information that sheds light on Jonah's refusal. The sea and dry land imagery appears in the first chapter: Jonah acknowledged to the sailors that his God did not rule over just one feature of nature, as was common among pagans, who had a god of thunder, a god of the moon, or of the sun. Jonah's God was master of *everything* seen and not seen, of every possible domain. His God, Jonah explained to those who inquired, was the God of sea *and* land. This may explain why Jonah ran away. He had partnered with God on a land-related project: the expansion of Israel. But when God threatened to help Nineveh repent, creating the possibility for Israel's possible demise at their hand, Jonah left for the sea thinking God could not give him prophecy if he physically left the Land of Israel. "He thought to himself that since the nations are easily brought to repentance, they would repent and The Holy One, Blessed Be He, would let out His rage on Israel."[31] Jonah had made an investment in his people and their land, an investment that would have been undermined if he helped a foreign nation that was also a devout enemy of the Israelites. What he had worked for in his early years would have been ruined and wasted. He did not want to see his own hard-earned successes end in misery. What good would expanding boundaries be should an enemy territory succeed and take over? It would mean giving the enemy even more.

This problem is more pressing when we internalize the last verse in the description of Jonah's prophecy in II Kings: "For the Lord saw the

---

31. Tanḥuma, Tzav 14.

affliction of Israel that it was very bitter: for there was not any shut up, nor any left free, nor any helper for Israel" (14:26). Jonah had no intention of adding to the bitterness, constraint, and alienation of this small nation surrounded by hostile tribes and afflicted internally by ruinous leaders who lacked the moral spine to stand up for the religious convictions of Israel.

What strikes us as ironic in the speech Jonah gave the sailors about his God is how little Jonah really understood his God. Jonah acted as God's representative but failed to see the way in which God operated in the universe. He was unable to change and to accept a God who changed. In that refusal, he re-fashioned the God that was for the God he wanted.

Jonah in Christian Literature

Even with every possible ounce of goodwill toward his people derived from II Kings, Jonah's decisions are difficult to exculpate in his eponymous book. The pagans serve as foils for his behavior and make the prophet only look worse in the eyes of his readers. This leads us to the polemical readings of Jonah where such contrasts abound – though these were generally ignored or unknown by the classic medieval commentators. Bickerman points out in great detail how Jonah was read by the Church fathers to demonstrate the intransigence of the Hebrews; even their own prophet ran away from God's word:

> The Church fathers accepted the Jewish interpretation but turned it against its authors. Theodore of Mopsuestia says Jonah was sent to Nineveh because the Jews refused to listen to the prophets, and the book about Jonah was written to teach a lesson to the stiff-necked people. Nineveh believed, says Jerome, but incredulous Israel persists in refusing to acknowledge Jesus. Ephraem describes how the saved Ninevites desired to learn righteousness from the holy people of their missionary. But Jonah feared lest they should see the iniquity of Israel. From the top of a mountain on the border of the Holy Land, the Ninevites, who accompanied the prophet home, saw with horror the abominations of Israel: graven images, the high places, the adoration of calves set up by Jeroboam (I Kings 12:29), and the public and private wickedness

castigated by the prophets. "Perhaps this people is going to be extirpated in place of Nineveh which has not been overthrown."[32]

Given such tendentious readings, what would be the purpose of this book other than to criticize Israel? Its inclusion in the canon becomes particularly troubling. James Smart contends that this story is a parable to highlight Israel's negative attitude to non-Jews.[33] "It has become customary to see Jonah as a petty, narrow-minded and stiff-necked representative of his stubborn people, and anti-Semites have always found in the book a fertile ground for their poisonous seeds."[34] Such polemical readings could only spell doom for the Jews and their lowly prophet. Using their own sacred Scripture against the Jews, Christian scholars of this view created an overlay of suspicion and a need for Jewish exegetes to defend Jonah or rationalize his waywardness. After all, it is not hard to arrive at such damning interpretations. It is not a linguistic stretch. This explains, as we will see, the rabbinic readings of Nineveh's repentance as shallow, superficial, and short-lived. How else could they counter the simple literal reading of the story but by interpreting between the lines?

The New Testament also alludes to Jonah in a strange and mysterious way. In the Book of Matthew, we read that people wanted Jesus to perform signs and wonders, but he refused and made an exception only when it came to paralleling the acts of the prophet Jonah:

> Then some of the Pharisees and teachers of the law said to him, "Teacher, we want to see a miraculous sign from you." He answered, "A wicked and adulterous generation asks for a miraculous sign! But none will be given it except the sign of the prophet Jonah. For as Jonah was three days and three nights in the belly of a huge fish, so the Son of Man will be three days and three nights in the heart of the earth. The men of Nineveh will stand up at the judgment with this generation and condemn it; for they

---

32. Bickerman, *Four Strange Books*, 16.
33. James D. Smart, *The Interpreter's Bible* (Nashville: Abingdon, 1956), 6:871.
34. Lacocque and Lacocque, *The Jonah Complex*, 4.

> repented at the preaching of Jonah, and now one greater than Jonah is here. (12:38–41)

Jonah here is leveraged as an odd antecedent to Jesus, with reference to his three days of suffering and incarceration in the fish as a prefiguration for Jesus' death and resurrection. Just as the fish opened its clutches and spat Jonah out, so too would Jesus enjoy a miraculous reprieve. As told by Matthew, Jesus would supersede Jonah in his ability to inspire repentance, another jab at the Hebrew prophet. It appears that according to Matthew, Jonah was the only one worthy of an overt sign in the form of a redeeming fish. This supposition is repeated four chapters later:

> The Pharisees and Sadducees came to Jesus and tested him by asking him to show them a sign from heaven. He replied, "When evening comes, you say, 'It will be fair weather, for the sky is red,' and in the morning, 'Today it will be stormy, for the sky is red and overcast.' You know how to interpret the appearance of the sky, but you cannot interpret the signs of the times. A wicked and adulterous generation looks for a miraculous sign, but none will be given it except the sign of Jonah." Jesus then left them and went away. (16:1–4)

Jonah was the only believable Hebrew who could interpret signs properly; others deemed less worthy by Jesus wanted God's comfort and presence through overt miracles without deserving them. This understanding credits Jonah with being a better reader of signs than he was in his own book, where even a large fish could not really motivate him to be different than he was or to think differently about God's world than he did.

Jonah is a natural locus for gentile inquiry since it is one of the few biblical books in which God shows an interest in the fate of non-Israelites. In fact, in the book God chastises a Hebrew prophet for his exclusive, narrow, and even merciless outlook. The length of the book itself is a condemnation. Isaiah is sixty-six chapters. Jeremiah is fifty-two. Ezekiel is forty-eight. Even with their long prophetic tenures and elegant biblical prose, none accomplished Jonah's feat of inspiring repentance – and certainly not in a mere four chapters. Isaiah's expresses a passionate vision of a future world in which all the nations of the world come together in faith:

> "And I, because of what they have planned and done, am about to come and gather the people of all nations and languages, and they will come and see My glory. I will set a sign among them, and I will send some of those who survive to the nations – to Tarshish, to the Libyans and Lydians (famous as archers), to Tubal and Greece, and to the distant islands that have not heard of My fame or seen My glory. They will proclaim My glory among the nations. And they will bring all your people, from all the nations, to My holy mountain in Jerusalem as an offering to the Lord – on horses, in chariots and wagons, and on mules and camels," says the Lord. "They will bring them, as the Israelites bring their grain offerings, to the Temple of the Lord in ceremonially clean vessels. And I will select some of them also to be priests and Levites," says the Lord. (66:18–21)

This future vision is far-reaching (including, ironically, Tarshish) and profound. God welcomes the foreign masses and is even prepared to have leaders from other nations serve as priests and Levites. This vision is not one in which God reaches out to the nations; rather, God invites them in. Jonah offered a radically different model of prophecy by not proselytizing to Nineveh but by merely adjuring them to leave their evil ways.

JONAH'S LITURGICAL USE

With all of the perils that Jonah presents, we may have imagined there would be a rabbinic tendency to overlook the book or tuck it away where its dangers are less glaring. But the very opposite occurred. The Talmud mentions the Book of Jonah's recitation as part of Yom Kippur liturgy many centuries after the book was canonized (Megilla 31a). This book was not shunned; it is read on the holiest Jewish day of the year, right before the fragile opportunity for the day's repentance is shut with the closing of the day's last gate: *Ne'ila*. Positioned here in the late afternoon

Jonah

service of Minḥa, the text cannot help but haunt and taunt its readers with one question: What are we to learn from the Book of Jonah?

Perhaps the miracles, the exaggerated details, the drama are only a platform for the larger theological pull of the story which confronts us on this most sober and intense day of the Jewish calendar. If repentance is predicated on returning to God, then Jonah becomes the ultimate model for the returnee: the one who could have gotten away but did not. Jonah is each one of us, afraid to fail, afraid to shine, fighting God's will for us, fighting ourselves.

Rabbi Abraham Joshua Heschel sees each of us in Jonah in a slightly different light. He does not blame Jonah for his recidivism. Rather, he looks at Jonah as a symbolic Everyman who runs away from social justice and obligation. "Jonah is running to Tarshish, while Nineveh is tottering on the brink. Are we not all guilty of Jonah's failure?"[35] He relates this failure to the casualties in Vietnam, to Hiroshima, and to the concentration camps dotting Europe during the Holocaust – all places where humanity did not live:

> The new situation in the world has plunged every one of us into unknown regions of responsibility. Unprepared, perplexed, misguided, the world is a spiritual no-man's land. Men all over the world are waiting for a way out of distress, for a new certainty for the meaning of being human. Will help come from those who seek to keep alive the words of the prophets? This is, indeed, a grave hour for those who are committed to honor the name of God.[36]

The prophet must be the one to see and hear injustice and alert all of us to it. But Jonah failed in this regard. He became just like the rest of humanity, which turned a blind eye to our responsibility toward others. Heschel points less to the intellectual faculties of the prophet and more to the prophet as a powerful advocate for justice, a person who

---

35. Abraham J. Heschel, *Moral Grandeur and Spiritual Audacity: Essays* (New York: Macmillan, 1997), 292.
36. Ibid.

has larger-than-normal ears and eyes, who hears and sees that which others refuse to hear and see:

> To us a single act of injustice – cheating in business, exploitation of the poor – is slight; to the prophets, a disaster. To us injustice is injurious to the welfare of the people; to the prophets it is a deathblow to existence: to us, an episode; to them, a catastrophe, a threat to the world.[37]

Naturally, this reading is most problematic when we consider Jonah's behavior. He was delinquent. He failed to recognize the importance of Nineveh's repentance and his stubborn rigidity in the face of God's mercy seems altogether puzzling. When faced with an opportunity to redeem the known world, he ran away – far, far away from his calling. His run reminds us of the powerful words of the polymath John Gardner:

> Human beings have always employed an enormous variety of clever devices for running away from themselves, and the modern world is particularly rich in such stratagems. We can keep ourselves so busy, fill our lives with so many diversions, stuff our heads with so much knowledge, involve ourselves with so many people, and cover so much ground that we never have time to probe the fearful and wonderful world within. More often than not, we don't want to know ourselves, don't want to depend on ourselves, don't want to live with ourselves. By middle life, most of us are accomplished fugitives from ourselves.[38]

To call Jonah a reluctant prophet is to understate his rejection of responsibility. God called out to him, inducing him to go out to an ancient and vast city first mentioned in Genesis. Yet he eviscerated God's word. He rejected responsibility once again when expressing happiness with a small tree that required none of his investment after leaving Nineveh

---

37. Abraham J. Heschel, *The Prophets* (New York: Perennial, 2001), 4.
38. John Gardner, *Self-Renewal: The Individual and the Innovative Society* (New York: W. W. Norton and Company, 1995), 13.

altogether in a fit of self-righteous indignation. He faulted God for His mercy. God's grace for others made life for Jonah unlivable – until he needed it himself:

> But Jonah was greatly displeased and became angry. He prayed to the Lord, "O Lord, is this not what I said when I was still at home? That is why I was so quick to flee to Tarshish. For I know that You are a compassionate and gracious God, slow to anger, abounding in kindness, renouncing punishment. Please, Lord, take my life, for I would rather die than live." (Jonah 4:1–3)

Since we only meet Jonah abruptly in chapter 1, we do not know about the conversation that we missed. What could Jonah have said while still at home? This is a critical detail to his story. Perhaps it does not matter if he did or did not say anything. What matters is that Jonah thought he had stated his case and that God felt that his self-defense was indefensible. If a prophet seeks death rather than life in a world in which God manifests grace through concern for the entire world then the prophet is doomed. Life and death ultimately become the same.

Nothing illustrates this concern more – both Jonah's self-concern and God's concern for the created universe – than the very last verse of the book:

> Then the Lord said, "You cared about the plant, which you did not work for and which you did not grow, which appeared overnight and perished overnight. And should I not care about Nineveh, that great city, in which there are more than 120,000 persons who do not yet know their right hand from their left, and many beasts as well?" (vv. 10–11)

There is God's world, and there is Jonah's world. This prophet desired his own personal comfort at a time of fragility and transformation for a very large city for which he had no genuine concern. He cared more about the temporality of a plant that he never nurtured. Not only did he lack concern for the people of Nineveh; he did not share the concerns of his Maker for the universe at large or beyond himself, a seminal feature of the Hebrew prophet. Pointing out the immediacy of Jonah's relationship with the gourd – "which appeared overnight and perished overnight" (v. 10) – God also tried to teach Jonah that his sense of urgency and disappointment, as well as his prior happiness over the gourd, were not justifiable feelings, neither for a prophet nor for a human being.

The Book of Jonah closes as strangely as it opens, bookending the text in mystery. Jonah, which opens abruptly and without the usual details that create context for the prophet's leadership, ends with a question, the only biblical book to do so. God, in His displeasure with the re-emergence of the prophet's refusal to serve, almost dared Jonah to judge divine compassion. Who was Jonah to deny compassion to an entire city and its cattle when the prophet's very purpose was to obey God's will and act in God's merciful image? This lingering question also stays with us at Yom Kippur's end, prompting our own self-reflection on justice and mercy and how far our compassion extends.

We have no idea what happened to Jonah. Perhaps he re-entered Nineveh in contrition and continued his task. Or perhaps he was punished for his recalcitrance and disappeared from the story, breaking down the small booth he built for his protection while mourning the loss of the impossible tree that rose and died in one day. In keeping with the strangeness of the book, this plant was Jonah's only source of happiness in the story. This is the only verse to use a variation of the Hebrew root word S-M-Ḥ, joy, amid the high tensions, the desperate pleas, and the fear and anger of everyone in the book – Jonah, God, the sailors, the king of Nineveh, and the city's citizens.

Alternatively, perhaps this strange ending, to be discussed at greater length in a later chapter, meant that Jonah was no longer needed because he had accomplished his task. The city repented. He had completed his assignment. It was time to go anyway. R. Akiva, referring to II Kings 14:25 where we first meet Jonah delivering a prophecy in the days of King Jeroboam, contends that God gave Jonah a mission only twice, once there and once here (see Yevamot 98a). The great sage is, in essence, suggesting that Jonah, son of Amitai, a prophet, was not to continue in the family profession. His resistance is a lesson to readers who doubt the power of God's word or who are overcome with a depth of self-doubt and unable to carry out God's calling. Twice and not three times, implies R. Akiva. There are prophets who engage in their duties over the course of a lifetime. Others may be needed to fulfill only one set of orders to achieve posterity. Those who fail are not asked again.

In some psychological interpretations of the book, the choice was not God's but ultimately Jonah's. While the prophet was able to stabilize himself and fulfill his task, he eventually sank back into the darkness that had engulfed him earlier:

> From a psychological vantage point, Jonah behaves like an acutely depressed person – hopeless, helpless, and feeling as if he were carrying a contagious disease. His injunction to the sailors to dispose of him is a gesture of suicide. "Despair expressed the feeling that time is short, too short for the attempt to start another life and to try alternate roads to integrity."[39]

Leaving Nineveh, constructing a booth to isolate himself, now burdened by natural forces that once pursued, cradled, and saved him, the prophet returned to an earlier self, too late to identify alternate roads to integrity. And yet, we read this book, with its open-ended conclusion, on Yom Kippur. The reading suggests that it is indeed never too late to identify alternate roads to integrity, authenticity, and intimacy with God, especially when God models change with His own behavior. We may give up on ourselves. God, however, does not give up on us.

---

39. Lacocque and Lacocque, *The Jonah Complex*, 48. The authors cite Rollo May, *Man's Search for Himself* (New York: W. W. Norton, 1953), 88.

Part One
Jonah's Retreat

Chapter One
Jonah's Theological Crisis

> The word of the Lord came to Jonah, son of Amitai: "Rise, go to Nineveh, that great city, and proclaim judgment upon it; for their wickedness has come before Me." Jonah, however, started out to flee to Tarshish from the Lord's service. He went down to Jaffa and found a ship going to Tarshish. He paid the fare and went aboard to sail with the others to Tarshish, away from the service of the Lord. (Jonah 1:1–3)

With these words a maritime adventure begins that tests a prophet and spotlights a theological conundrum. When God calls, what is the appropriate answer? It seems impossible to say no to God's command, so impossible that flight takes the place of words. So, who is this Jonah who leaves just when God calls? In the introduction, we offered the few biographical details available in the pages of the Bible, but such scant reference tells us little about what animates this prophet. Knowing him, if we can ever make such an audacious claim, will depend on how we understand what he did.

Rashi tells us on the second verse of the Book of Jonah that God did not give Jonah the actual word of his prophecy; He simply called him and told him the general nature of the assignment, to proclaim *something* – but that something was not detailed. The ambivalence of the task, heightened by the dangerous nature of the mission to the capital of an enemy nation would, no doubt, have shaken Jonah. A prophet cowed by fear or anger may not have been capable of understanding what it was that God wanted; perhaps he would have refused to answer a call that was not clear in its scope and intention. This might have been compounded by Jonah's larger philosophical problem: his rigidity in the face of change. Believing that neither God nor Nineveh were capable of change must have stymied the prophet.

Rashi continues, explaining that poor Jonah sought out Tarshish specifically because he wanted to leave the Land of Israel, naïvely believing that if he left his homeland, God's presence could not rest upon him. Thus, he would not have been responsible for God's proclamation. "He said, 'I will run away through the sea because the Divine Presence does not dwell outside the land. The Holy One, may He be blessed, said to him, 'By your life! I have agents like you whom I can send after you to fetch you from there.'"[1] Rashi's understanding of Jonah's strategy reminds us of a child's game of tag: identify a space where one cannot get caught and move with haste in its direction. Once there, safety prevails, like a force field that protects those in its grip. Rashi analogizes Jonah's experience to a servant of a priest who escapes from his master and enters a cemetery, knowing that because his master is a priest, the master is forbidden from entry. But the priest can easily deputize another to pull his servant from the cemetery. The servant's thinking, as Jonah's, is limited and flawed.

Abraham ibn Ezra (1089–1167) gives Jonah more credit:

> One wonders how there arose in the heart of a wise man, who knew God and His deeds, the thought to flee from before Him. For Jonah was in His hand and the world is filled with His glory. How did he reject the word of God since it is specifically stated earlier that he is "the prophet"?[2]

Ibn Ezra wishes to know how Jonah arrived at the thinking that he could escape God. He must have known cognitively, from his pre-existing knowledge of God, that there was nowhere God's presence was not felt. In answer, Ibn Ezra cites Saadia Gaon, who questions if there was

---

1. Rashi to Jonah 1:3.
2. A term used earlier in II Kings 14:25; Ibn Ezra to Jonah 1:1.

any real demand placed upon Jonah, since no words were offered with his calling. There was not yet a clear command – so Jonah, technically, was not running away from a mission. He merely heard an invitation and was free to refuse it. Ibn Ezra does not ultimately accept this reading because he believes that the receiving of a call is momentous in the life of a prophet. It is more than a mere recommendation to act but an intimate connection with the Divine that mandates action. The *Mekhilta*, which Ibn Ezra cites, suggests that Jonah was driven by a different logic: "He sought to protect the honor of the son above the honor of the father." Jonah disobeyed God, his Father, to protect the dignity of the Israelites who would look bad when their arch-enemies repented so quickly while they were chastised again and again to no effect. Ibn Ezra then offers an interesting insight into the nature of received wisdom:

> And now I will hint at a secret. There are those who create poetry by their nature without learning and there are those who require learning. And when he will receive prophecy, it is possible that he will not receive it. And it is easier for the latter than the earlier.[3]

If Jonah received prophecy without literacy or study, it is possible that he simply failed to understand what he was supposed to do. In this reading, Ibn Ezra suggests that prophecy, like poetry, is a word-based art that can exist on different levels, a primitive expression of feeling or an outgrowth of study, redolent with the elegance that this background contributes to language. Jonah was in the former category. Prophet, yes, but not a prophet with the intensity of experience or knowledge that would, like Moses, have involved an ear that could "turn quickly" to God.[4]

Ibn Ezra's reading adds another dimension of understanding to these initial, striking verses. Ibn Ezra suggests that fleeing in Hebrew – B-R-Ḥ – is always connected to the word "from" – P-N-Y.[5] Yet, in our book, Jonah runs not from God but from *before* God, similar to Cain

---

3. Ibid.
4. Ps. 31:2 reads, "Turn Your ear to me; rescue me quickly," a request that suggests an almost collegial intimacy with God.
5. See Ps. 139:7; Judges 11:3.

leaving God's presence.[6] When Jonah found himself in God's actual presence, he moved away. He was not prepared for this level of intimacy and responsibility. Being unready or unprepared or unwilling, Jonah stepped away from that kind of relationship with God, the closeness with the Divine Presence that would have occasioned prophecy. Ibn Ezra closes with this enigmatic line: "And the enlightened will understand"[7] – but perhaps even the most enlightened cannot imagine this moment, this black hole of acceptance that required the totality of the prophet's life and commitment that Jonah wished to sidestep altogether.

As we will see throughout this book, Jonah's theological beliefs become a persistent obstruction in his ability to become God's true servant. One indicator that theology drives the plot is the way Jonah is introduced to us, namely as the *ben Amitai*, "son of truth." The question of whether God, the world, and the prophet are more motivated by mercy or justice is offered up in this introduction: "The word of the Lord came to Jonah, son of Amitai" (Jonah 1:1). If God is driven more by compassion than strict and rigid truth, then the humans made in His image must also follow this path, suspending justice when grace offers the more tender option. This, however, seems impossible for a prophet introduced to us as the son of truth. In another powerful water story that pits truth against mercy, Herman Melville tells us in his novella *Billy Budd*, "Truth uncompromisingly told will always have its ragged edges."[8] Truth in Jonah's story has so many jagged edges that it drove Jonah to question his very existence, and to find himself at the brink of death not once but several times. Was Jonah a lost soul or an argumentative one? The dramatic polarities of this narrative are presented in the very first verses.

MOVEMENT IN THE BOOK OF JONAH AND THE BIBLE

In the second verse we encounter the call itself: "Rise, go to Nineveh" (Jonah 1:2). According to Ibn Ezra's reading, the first word of Jonah's prophecy carries with it immense potency. "Rise," God intoned, "go."

---

6. Gen. 4:16. Melville also cites proof texts from Gen. 4:14; Is. 2:21.
7. Ibn Ezra to Jonah 1:1.
8. Herman Melville, *Billy Budd* (New York: TOR Books, 1992), 109.

God first offers Jonah a direction, perhaps sensing that before any utterance, Jonah has to commit to moving out of his land and beyond his normal constituency. Movement first; words later. Abraham too was told that to build a nation, he must leave a familiar space. The foreignness of new territory would serve as a stimulus to constitute a new people. In the Book of Jonah, leaving his familiar place would serve as an impetus to reform a nation. And Jonah did rise, but he rose to turn away; he did not say, "*Hineni*," "I am fully present and in a state of obedience," the typical response of the prophet to a call. Nor did he refuse to go, another less typical but appropriate response and one which would have allowed him to express his reservations openly to his God, as did Moses and Jeremiah. Instead, Jonah rose, intimating that he was prepared to go – and then turned in another direction. Robert Alter notes: "For a brief moment, he might seem to be heeding God's command to get up and go to Nineveh, but this momentary illusion is broken by the infinitive 'to flee.'"[9] The movement is stunning. The nerve of the prophet astounds us.

Later we hear the same word from the ship's captain: "Rise, call upon your god" (Jonah 1:6), but here no action was forthcoming; attention is suddenly turned to the sailors, who suggested casting lots to determine the cause of the storm. We do not know if Jonah ever rose to pray; we suspect not, given his anti-authoritarian tendencies. What we do know is that Jonah's momentary possible ascent – "rise and go" – was followed by multiple descents that ended with him sinking to the sea floor. He first descended (*vayered*) from Gath-hepher to Jaffa, descended into a ship, descended into the recesses of the ship, and then fell into a deep sleep – also linguistically related in Hebrew to descent. Finally, by the chapter's end, Jonah began what started off as a climb upward only to move further and further down, further inward, and out of the story by trying to escape life itself. Zornberg describes it thus: "There is a suicidal desire in Jonah's flight that is intimated in the insistent verbs of *descent* that carry him downward into a posture of regressed stupor."[10]

A later change of movement signals promise on the horizon. In the belly of the fish, Jonah was no longer moving vertically. As noted in

---

9. Robert Alter, *Strong as Death Is Love* (New York: W. W. Norton & Co, 2015), 139.
10. Zornberg, "Jonah: A Fantasy of Flight," 78.

the introduction, movement is critical in understanding Jonah's repentance trajectory. He was transported horizontally, vertiginously, an indication of a much-needed stabilization. This created the conditions wherein the prophet could rethink, but not negotiate his willingness to accept his mission. Much has been written on the second calling that opens chapter 3, with God repeating the command to rise and proclaim to Nineveh – though, again, without any specific words given: "The word of the Lord came to Jonah a second time. 'Go at once to Nineveh, that great city, and proclaim to it what I tell you'" (vv. 1–2). Just get there, God adjured, and then "proclaim to it what I tell you." The absence of the prophetic formula again highlights the message of *movement* over *language*. If Jonah could physically get himself to Nineveh, then the proclamation would be forthcoming. Jonah got up, finally. The three demands for Jonah to rise – from God, the captain, and then God again – highlight his resistance, a spiritual or moral lassitude or torpor that calls for outside intervention. His resistance is contrasted to the last appearance of the word "to rise" in the Book of Jonah. The king of Nineveh heard the news and rose unprompted from his throne to remove his robe, don sackcloth, and then sit in a pile of ash. Before he descended into the travail of the moment, the king ascended: ascended to responsibility, ascended to atonement, ascended to authority in a time of crisis. The king was not told to rise. He rose of his own initiative. The king's *vayakom* is a direct taunt of the prophet, who failed to rise even when told directly to do so by his God.

JONAH AND ELIJAH: BIRTH AND REBIRTH

Understanding this mystery prophet who got up and went in the opposite direction leads us to an unlikely context created by the sages, namely the identification of Jonah with another enigmatic minor biblical character. One midrash identifies Jonah as the son of the widow whom Elijah the prophet assisted,[11] making Jonah an even more puzzling biblical figure, pulling us to Jonah's childhood in the hunt to make his adulthood make sense. To understand the midrash and its implications, we must first turn to the text itself.

---

11. See I Kings 17.

Elijah told King Ahab that there would be no rain in the land. Rain was a gift from the heavens. Bad behavior on the part of Israelite leaders would impact the course of nature, just as flood waters destroyed humanity and the land of Canaan spat out its inhabitants in earlier texts. Ahab was angry. He was indignant. God warned Elijah of impending doom and told him to go into hiding, to flee from Ahab; powerful men in high places do, in fact, kill the messenger. Elijah was instructed to hide in a wadi east of the Jordan where he would be fed by ravens and drink from the wadi. Elijah's eastward direction, away from the central action, reminds us of Jonah's move to the east of Nineveh (Jonah 4:5). But then Elijah's wadi dried up and, because there was no rain, he was parched. God instructed him to go to a new destination: Zarephath of Zidon. He was to be fed by a widow who lived there. And thus our story continues:

> So he went to Zarephath. When he came to the town gate, a widow was there gathering sticks. He called to her and asked, "Would you bring me a little water in a jar so I may have a drink?" As she was going to get it, he called, "And bring me, please, a piece of bread." "As surely as the Lord your God lives," she replied, "I don't have any bread – only a handful of flour in a jar and a little jug of oil. I am gathering a few sticks to take home to make a meal for myself and my son, that we may eat it and die." (I Kings 17:10–12)

Overcome by hunger, thirst, and fear, Elijah asked this unnamed woman for a display of generosity of which she was incapable. She did not hesitate to get him water, even though this too was a difficult request, but when Elijah asked this widow for bread, she confessed to him that she was about to have her very last meal. Elijah gave her an enigmatic set of instructions:

> Elijah said to her, "Don't be afraid. Go home and do as you have said. But first make a small cake of bread for me from what you have and bring it to me, and then make something for yourself and your son. For this is what the Lord, God of Israel, says: 'The jar of flour will not be used up and the jug of oil will not run dry until the Lord gives rain on the land.'" (vv. 13–14)

Elijah boldly asked her to take her last flour to make him a small loaf of bread. She agreed. Although Elijah never introduced himself as a prophet, perhaps the widow sensed something holy or different about this stranger's presence.

> She went away and did as Elijah told her. So there was food every day for Elijah and the woman and her family. For the jar of flour was not used up and the jug of oil did not run dry, in keeping with the word of the Lord spoken by Elijah. Some time later the son of the woman who owned the house became ill. He grew worse and worse and finally stopped breathing. She said to Elijah, "What do you have against me, man of God? Did you come to remind me of my sin and kill my son?" "Give me your son," Elijah replied. He took him from her arms, carried him to the upper room where he was staying and lay him on his bed. Then he cried out to the Lord, "O Lord my God, why have You brought tragedy also upon this widow I am staying with, by causing her son to die?" Then he stretched himself out on the boy three times and cried to the Lord, "O Lord my God, let this boy's life return to him." The Lord heard Elijah's cry, and the boy's life returned to him, and he lived. Elijah picked up the child and carried him down from the room into the house. He gave him to his mother and said, "Look, your son is alive." Then the woman said to Elijah, "Now I know you are a man of God and that the word of the Lord from your mouth is the truth." (vv. 15–24)

Ironically, this woman praised Elijah for being truthful – where Jonah criticized God for being a God of truth (Jonah 4:2) – yet this story demonstrates the limits of trust. The widow enjoyed the material generosity of Elijah's presence over an extended but unspecified period of time. Yet the instant her son's health failed, she saw this as the prophet's doing, unwilling to give him the benefit of the doubt even as he kept them alive for much longer than she had anticipated. Rather than correct her, Elijah rose to show her the extent of God's power in responding to his cry: His ability to bring the dead back to life. And with this, the narrative ends on a flourish of certainty. Now the widow understood that the prophet spoke the truth, not fully believing him until put to a harder test.

Who was the child in this tale who was brought back to life? "This," one midrash contends, "is Jonah ben Amitai, and he was a completely pious one."[12] In the biblical text, the widow and her son have no names and are only identified by place. But the midrashic style does not leave biblical characters anonymous. If they appear in the Hebrew Bible, then they must be worthy of a name.

How did the rabbinic imagination arrive at this particular identification? If we read the last line again – "Now I know you are a man of God and that the word of the Lord from your mouth is the truth" (v. 24) – we realize that this child was reborn "in truth." Jonah was the son of truth, *ben Amitai*, a son who was himself born and reborn and finally born once again when he accepted the prophetic role he originally resisted. As such, he is an excellent candidate to make his appearance elsewhere.

This fiction is carried into an even more elaborate fiction, as the midrash continues: "He was consumed by a fish and sea water but did not die and entered the Garden of Eden with honor."[13] On the surface, this conclusion seems odd. Rather than view Jonah as someone who ran away from God and failed to complete his mission, this midrash sees the fact that he survived near drowning and life inside the belly of a fish as a spiritual accomplishment that merited a return to paradise itself. This brave underwater traveler could take short-cuts beneath the surface of the sea and travel not only through space, but through time itself, bringing him back to the place where all humanity and nature were born.

In order to understand why this midrash identifies Jonah as the nameless boy in the I Kings narrative, we must also establish some similarities between Elijah's story with the widow and its strong parallels to II Kings 4, where Elisha revived the child of an unnamed Shunamite woman who asked that the prophet not deceive her. Uriel Simon contends that these two narratives are "built of the same basic elements":

> A woman deserves assistance from the man of God by virtue of having hosted him (in the first half of the story); the child dies suddenly; the mother informs the man of God of the disaster

---

12. *Midrash Shoḥer Tov* 26:7.
13. Ibid.

(albeit in very different ways); the man of God locks himself up with the child's corpse in the upper room, prays for him, and treats him; and, finally, the child revives and is returned to his mother.[14]

Simon insists, however, that Elijah's is the superior story, having happened at an earlier stage of Elijah's career than did Elisha's. As in the career of Moses and Joshua, the prophet's successor does many of the same heroic acts with a slightly different flavor, indicating that this leader is indeed a worthy spiritual heir. In Elijah's story, the widow's difficulties and her resistance pushed the prophet to actualize his full prophetic capacity. He solved a problem, earned her trust, and then brought her child back to life with a shocking degree of familiarity bordering on intimacy. In the Elisha narrative, the death of the child was regarded as a punishment for the prophet's brazen gift of a child without his ever having prayed to God. Subsequently, we as readers are unsure if the child would have a miraculous resurrection and feel, when he sneezed and came back to life, that everyone – he, his mother, and the prophet – was given a second chance. In Elijah's resurrection, the child's illness had nothing to do with the prophet, except in the mind of his mother, and was likely the result of the difficult physical conditions in which they lived.

Why not then identify the Shunamite woman's child as Jonah? If the stories are so similar then it is difficult to understand why the sage behind this midrashic tradition picked one over the other. There seem to be two aspects, one practical and the other theological, that may have driven the identification. In Elijah's story, the child was not born miraculously but born normally; at least we have no indication that his was a miracle birth. Jonah's introduction in II Kings offers no suggestion that his was anything but a normal childhood; at least, it was not one worth textual attention. It is what happened to Jonah later that makes his story leap off the page. In Elisha's tale, the birth, death, and rebirth all have to do with the prophet; in one instance Elisha is overreaching his prophetic arts, in the next, paying the price in loss for

---

14. Uriel Simon, *Reading Prophetic Narratives* (Bloomington, IN: Indiana University Press, 1997), 255.

the bold intervention in God's handiwork, and finally acting with an affection that showed the prophet to be completely committed to that which he created.

Having Jonah come from relatively simple stock in this midrash belies the fact that the text which mentioned him by name in II Kings (14:25) suggests otherwise; Jonah's father was a prophet who thereby gave his progeny spiritual status. Only mothers and not fathers are mentioned in these two other comparison narratives. More to the point, the widow makes an association for the reader. When the prophet brought the child back, she finally believed that Elijah was telling the truth. He was a holy man of God endowed with special gifts and powers. In this sense, the child himself was literally the son of truth – just as Jonah is called in verse 1 of his eponymous book.

But Jonah, unlike Elijah, though born in truth, needed to relinquish some of the rigid truths to which he adhered in order to actualize the gifts and prophetic powers he had but worked hard to repress. Born in truth, he had to be reborn into prophecy. His truth allowed no room for transformation. Beyond that, the closeness shared by the prophet and the child, the sense of the prophet's total investment in another human being, prefigured the way that God as a divine Being invested completely in the rebirth of the prophet.

Rebirthing imagery is a highlight of chapters 2 and 3 of Jonah. Within the use of all of nature as a tool for Jonah's reformation, Jonah is placed in the belly of a fish; the womb-like associations of being spat out remind us of the birthing canal that brings life. This too was picked up on obliquely in midrashic tradition in the change from male to female references to the fish. Chapter 2 opens with a *dag gadol*, a "great fish," which is male. But the second verse refers to the creature as a *daga*, "a female fish." This leads the *Mekhilta*, cited by Rashi and others, to conclude that the fish that saved Jonah was male but because there was so much cavernous space inside it, Jonah did not feel the literal squeeze to change. "The Holy One," in Rashi's words, "spoke to the male fish and it spat him out into the mouth of the female, which was full of embryos. There he was stressed and he prayed there as it says, *mim'ai hadaga*."[15]

---

15. Rashi to Jonah 2:1.

He prayed from the belly of the female fish. In this scenario, the crowding of Jonah among female organs behaving as they should was sufficiently suffocating to inspire repentance – unless, of course, this was not a matter of suffocation. It was Jonah joining the mammalian world of reproduction, being reborn in a place so foreign as to force him to contemplate death and then life and then to choose life when signs of emerging life were all about him.[16]

IDENTITY AND TRANSFORMATION

Jonah, it is important to bear in mind, also identified himself. He tells us who he is in telling the sailors who he is. The sailors, anxious to know who caused the storm that might bring about their deaths, questioned Jonah after the lot fell on him. Ibn Ezra disagrees with Rashi, who contends that they wanted to know Jonah's nation lest there be a decree against this particular nation that would explain the storm. If the fugitive left his city, Ibn Ezra[17] observes, then he cleared himself of their fate. "Why, then," he writes, "should they be frightened?" And perhaps this is why the sailors did not act immediately after the lot was drawn and fell upon the prophet. If God or gods or a moral enemy were after Jonah, this would not lead to the injustice of ridding the ship of everyone. The sailors asked Jonah what we want to ask him: Who are you? They sought this knowledge the way we commonly cull identification: from what a person does and from a person's origins: his country and his people. These should give clues, if not a helpful background. Rashi writes that if the sailors could ascertain Jonah's job, he might share with them sinful behaviors that may have happened in the practice of his trade, which would have occasioned the storm.[18] As Ibn Ezra states: "It is the way of most people to have a trade. The trade of a person teaches us about his situation and why he might go to a particular place since there are places where most people are good.

---

16. Ibn Ezra spoils this romantic vision with his comment on the "gender" switch in Jonah 2:2: "There is a person who says that the female fish swallowed him from the male fish. There is no need for this. *Dag* and *daga* are nouns without gender, like *tzedek* and *tzedaka*."
17. Ibn Ezra to Jonah 1:8.
18. Rashi to 1:8.

And this is well known."[19] What is well known is the reputation that the residents of a particular place have. The sailors thought they could ascertain something about Jonah's personality or crime if they knew his surrounding culture. Yet in Jonah's case, his answers were so unconventional that they only deepened the mystery:

> They said to him, "Tell us, you who have brought this misfortune upon us, what is your business? Where have you come from? What is your country, and of what people are you?" "I am a Hebrew," he replied. "I worship the Lord, the God of heaven, who made both sea and dry land." The men were greatly terrified, and they asked him, "What have you done?" And when the men learned that he was fleeing from the service of the Lord – for so he had told them… (Jonah 1:8–10)

Jonah did not tell them he was a prophet. This may have been an identity to which he never personally subscribed. He had the qualifications but lacked the calling or drive. Perhaps he was riven with impostor syndrome. Describing himself as a prophet to these strangers may have suggested a relationship to God, to wisdom, and to insight that he could not assume, one that he thought he could not achieve. He described himself with only one momentous word: "Hebrew," *ivri*. In this, he covered his profession, his people, and his country. This one word, *ivri*, suggests a transitional identity. *Laavor* is "to cross over"; an *ivri* is one who crosses over. Jonah was a crosser, one who used to be one thing and then, through a transformative act, became another. The king "took off," *vayaaver* (3:6), his robe when transitioning from royalty to penitent.[20] But the same root word also conveys the notion of sin. An *avera* is a transgression; one might cross the line, so to speak, or break through an acceptable boundary.

Typically, in biblical history, the transformation by which we earned our collective name came from crossing water – the Jabbok, Reed Sea, the Jordan. This horizontal identity was not sufficiently descriptive

---

19. Ibn Ezra to 1:8.
20. Jennifer Rubin Raskas pointed out this linguistic connection to the king, which parallels the usage in chapter 1.

Jonah's Retreat

in Jonah's case. His transition also involved water – not crossing over it but being tossed into it. He was a Hebrew, a worshipper of God, and a fugitive. And in this he described the self that he saw and the self that he wished to shed.

Ibn Ezra believes that *ivri* is a term describing the descendants of Eber (Gen. 10:21), who was an ancestor of Abraham's, pulling the genealogical line back several generations. Perhaps without realizing it, Ibn Ezra is drawing us back to Genesis 11 where both Nineveh and Eber are also mentioned. Jonah thus takes us to where the first polarities of the post-diluvian world were established. In using this singular word, Jonah may have been suggesting that he was just as old as Nineveh. Or he might have been saying the polar opposite, explaining or justifying to himself, or God, or these strangers why he was on the ship in the first place.

Don Isaac Abrabanel (1437–1508) reads Jonah's response differently. Jonah was not going back in time to ancient days but to his own recent past. He was a sinner:

> It means to say, what you asked, are my misdeed and my sin against the land or against my people, and that, as a result of it, I have been sentenced to death? And against whom have I sinned is known and seen because *ivri anokhi* – I am a Hebrew. There the intent is not to indicate that he was from the land of the Hebrews but rather he sinned [A-V-R] against the commandment of his God.[21]

This wordplay, pregnant in meaning, is in keeping with Jonah's answer to the sailors' next question: "What have you done?" We know not Jonah's exact response, but it is clear that he did not hide his intransigence: "And when the men learned that he was fleeing from the service of the Lord – for so he told them..." (Jonah 1:10).

Jonah did not tell the sailors much because there was no detail more important than one. He was a sinner. Place, people, trade are all mere details in an ordinary life. But Jonah's was no ordinary life. In not answering their questions in more than a few words he indicated to them

---

21. Answer to Abrabanel's fourth question to Jonah, chapter 1.

and to himself that there was one label that mattered in the context of this terrifying journey. Jonah, who journeyed and descended, who was born and reborn, regarded himself not so much a prophet as a sinner. His identity as the son of a prophet, the very son of truth, the miracle child of Elijah in a midrashic treatment, the prophet whose mission was the subject of debate and deliberation for centuries, would have meant nothing to him. Jonah believed his life was characterized by one act: his sin, his rejection of God's task, and thereby, his rejection of God. For this, there is no chance for redemption. In Jonah's mind, atonement is neither a possibility for all nor a possibility for him.

Jonah mistakenly believed that if he left God's supposed aegis in the Land of Israel, the rules of God would not apply. But God would soon give Jonah a different message in the form of his capture. No place is free of God. No being, place, or person is free of change. That message is inescapable.

Chapter Two

Jonah's Collapse into Silence

> The word of the Lord came to Jonah, son of Amitai: "Rise, go to Nineveh, that great city, and proclaim judgment upon it; for their wickedness has come before Me." (Jonah 1:1–2)
>
> The word of the Lord came to Jonah a second time: "Go at once to Nineveh, that great city, and proclaim to it what I tell you." (3:1–2)
>
> But Jonah was greatly displeased and became angry. He prayed to the Lord, "O Lord, is this not what I said when I was still at home?" (4:1–2)

Jonah is a book of words and pauses. Jonah's escape was one of silence, punctured only intermittently by speech. His words were few and mysterious. And even his singular prophetic sentence: "Forty days more and Nineveh will be overturned" (3:4), lacked the verbal heft and poetic expression of other prophets, thin as it was on content and detail and entangled as it was in ambiguous consequences. Søren Kierkegaard points to the great irony of silence within the realm of the holy, the paradox of the divine and the demonic: "For silence is both of these. It is the demon's lure, and the more silent one keeps, the more terrible the demon becomes, but silence is also divinity's communion with the individual."[1]

---

1. Søren Kierkegaard, *Fear and Trembling* (New York: Penguin, 1986), 115.

Thinking about the role of language and its absence in Jonah's story demands that we pause from straightforward exegesis to address more fundamental issues about the nature of biblical prophecy in general.

The fact that Jonah spoke so infrequently confers greater weight on each word, and gives the reader occasion to stop and consider the layering of denotations possible with each utterance. With this in mind, when we turn to Jonah, we find that he did not embody God's words nor did he find his own words to reject God's task. Whereas a prophet's job revolves around words, Jonah's relationship to God is characterized instead by a deafening silence. Instead, he used his body, a corporeal defense, to run away. The sensory and material rather than oracular or audible quality of Jonah's life continued to plague him from chapter to chapter. He ran. He slept. He was cast into the sea. He described the seaweed that encircled his head as he descended past the breakers and into the heart of the sea. He was spat out. He walked. He entered Nineveh. He left. He built a hut. He suffered a chafing sun. He wanted only to die.

Jonah did not reconcile his body and his words with God's words because he never took ownership of them. They passed through him without moving him. Jonah abided in an alienating silence while his body suffered the torments of an unyielding natural world, a world that in his mind was conspiring to hurt him – although in God's mind, if you will, nature's actions were meant to save him.

RELUCTANT PROPHETS

In the introduction to his two-volume work *The Prophets*, titled "What Manner of Man Is the Prophet?" Heschel observes that the prophet's relationship with the word is critical to the prophet's calling. Like God in the first chapter of Creation, the prophet creates and can potentially destroy worlds with words. The prophet's entire profession is wrapped in language – that which he receives through divine transmission and that which he disseminates in his attempt to chastise his constituents, bring justice, and repair the broken relationship of the wayward Israelites with their God:

> Authentic utterance derives from a moment of identification of a person and a word; its significance depends upon the urgency and magnitude of its themes. The prophet's theme is, first of

all, the very life of a whole people, and his identification lasts more than a moment. He is not only one with what he says; he is involved with his people in what his words foreshadow. This is the secret of the prophet's style; his life and soul are at stake in what he says and in what is going to happen to what he says. It is an involvement that echoes on.[2]

There is an ongoing resonance between the prophet's word and his enduring relationship with those he serves. The prophet must embody God's words, live them, and then continue to live them while actualizing them in the lifeblood of his people. Jonah, however, lacked the authenticity that Heschel attributes to the master prophets who *were* their words.

In deciding with his body that he did not want to serve, Jonah also had a choice. He could have found words, in the prophetic tradition, to refuse his calling. Comparisons to other rejections of prophecy are important in understanding a "permissible" biblical approach to hesitation or self-doubt. This was true for the two most well-known biblical rejections of prophecy: Moses and Jeremiah.

Moses' initial rejection of the prophetic calling was, not unlike Jonah's, also about language: he feared repeatedly that he could not muster the courage for the words, that he was slow of speech, that the Israelites would not listen to his words. And even were he to find the right words, he observed, a compelling description of God eluded him. First Moses questioned his own identity and then he questioned God's. "Who am I that I should go to Pharaoh and free the Israelites from Egypt?" (Ex. 3:11). God assured him, just as He did Jeremiah later on, that He would be with him. But this was not enough for the reluctant prophet. "Moses said to God, When I come to the Israelites and say to them, 'The God of your fathers has sent me to you,' and they ask me, 'What is His name?' what shall I say to them?" (v. 13). This hesitation was likely not helped by God's vague description as "One who will come into being" (v. 14). For someone looking for clarity in communication, Moses seemed to feel that God's opacity would limit his success even further.

---

2. Heschel, *The Prophets*, 7.

This dance of hesitation mired in language continues into chapter 4 of Exodus. There it takes a downward spiral of specific language-based obstructions in a very famous passage from Moses' early leadership:

> But Moses said to the Lord, "Please, O Lord, I have never been a man of words, either in times past or now that You have spoken to Your servant; I am slow of speech and slow of tongue." And the Lord said to him, "Who gives man speech? Who makes him dumb or deaf, seeing or blind? Is it not I, the Lord? Now go, and I will be with you as you speak and will instruct you what to say." (4:10–12)

One senses that God was accommodating Moses' angst while also tiring of Moses' excuses; thus He lashed out with an existential retort. If God created a handicap and gave a mission to the very same person, obviously it was because God felt that the mission was entirely within the range of possibility. And yet, even with this strong remonstration, Moses continued to plead his case: "Please, O Lord, make someone else Your agent" (v. 13). God did not take kindly to this naïve recommendation: "The Lord became angry with Moses" (v. 14). And even so, God's willingness to partner with Moses on this large-scale project of redemption was not offset by these minor obstacles. God gave Moses his brother to serve as spokesman with the additional promise that God's presence around the word would hover continuously: "You shall speak to him and put the words in his mouth – I will be with you and with him as you speak, and tell both of you what to do – and he shall speak for you to the people" (vv. 15–16). If Moses was indeed tangled of speech, it is odd to think that Moses would provide the words to Aaron – and, if this were so, then why did God need to be with them both? The process of revelation and transmission sounds almost transactional – word deposits were to be transferred from One – God – to another. And yet the reader can appreciate that the word of God must have been freighted with so much meaning and expectation that each word needed judicious selection, crystallization, and hardening before becoming fully formed and ready to be passed on to those destined to receive each one.

The second well-known refusal to prophesy in the Hebrew Bible involved youth. In the first chapter of Jeremiah, this prophet rejected his task because he thought he was too young to speak. God ignored Jeremiah's self-imposed limitation with an unusual reference to Jeremiah's in utero existence:

> Before I created you in the womb, I selected you;
> Before you were born, I consecrated you;
> I appointed you a prophet concerning the nations. (1:4–5)

This sense of the purpose-driven birth only exacerbated Jeremiah's anxiety about this post:

> I replied: Ah, Lord God!
> I don't know how to speak,
> For I am still a boy. (v. 6)

If his aborted tongue were because of his age, God needed to make Jeremiah grow up into the recognition that a person dedicated to service from the womb would be metaphysically prepared for any calling God assigned. Age matters little. God will speak through the prophet. God will provide the words. Youth is a problem from which people generally recover:

> And the Lord said to me: "Do not say – I am still a boy – but go wherever I command you. Have no fear of them, for I am with you to deliver you" – declares the Lord. The Lord put out His hand and touched my mouth, and the Lord said to me: "Herewith I put My words into your mouth." (vv. 7–9)

God demonstrated that age was not a problem for Jeremiah by asking him to unpack the meaning of an almond tree branch that the prophet saw in a vision. When Jeremiah did this successfully, God was able to persuade Jeremiah that he was not too young for prophecy.

In both these accounts, God took the prophets' personal leadership conflicts seriously enough to address their concerns, giving them both practical assistance in the form of words and a larger psychological understanding of the mission from which neither was existentially free. This is the argument of destiny, and it is powerful.

JONAH: FLEEING FROM WORDS

The process of negotiation present in the Moses and Jeremiah narratives is notably absent in the Book of Jonah. Jonah had so few words that he did not even have enough to tell God that he had no intention of going to Nineveh. Naturally, the absence of this confession created no room for God to interject, to offer help, or even to provide exhortation.

One could make the case, however, that Jonah's assignment was not fully articulated in the first verse, although the Book of Jonah begins with a suggestion that the word *would* be sent: "The word of the Lord came to Jonah, son of Amitai: 'Rise, go to Nineveh, that great city, and proclaim judgment upon it; for their wickedness has come before Me'" (1:1–2). As noted, God spoke but did not give Jonah the words to be spoken. If this was a man ill-equipped for a life in words, God made it no easier. In fact, not giving the words may have provoked the prophet to flee to Tarshish. His assignment was first about body and then about mind: Go to Nineveh and then proclaim judgment. Left to his own devices, Jonah experienced the impossibility of the task and reversed the order. His body simply went elsewhere.

When he heard that Nineveh was a "great city" – large, old, and a perpetual thorn in Israel's side – like Moses, Jonah could have responded with "Who am I?" But instead of a question of humility, for Jonah it may have been a question of incompetence or paralysis – as if to say, "I cannot tackle this enemy. I am a small being, an insignificant foreigner with no personal interest in their repentance."

Many medieval commentators read this escape differently. They are of the view that Jonah fled precisely out of fear that he would be so successful that the residents of Nineveh would repent, be forgiven, and then, as a result of their complete moral transformation, become God's favored agents in waging war with the Israelites for their malfeasance. Jonah did not want this long-term outcome to be on his head. He would be known in posterity as the prophet who made an Israelite decline possible. Much of the book pits short-term and long-term thinking in a disturbing relationship with each other. Forgiveness in this text is immediate. But the consequences of forgiveness can take years to unravel. The prophet views his work in terms of long-range change, seeing far into the future less for purposes of prediction than for preparation.

This reading coheres with Jonah's words in chapter 4, when he supposedly accused God of lacking a firm commitment to justice and extending His mercy too graciously, even randomly. Pity would only hurt God's chosen ones in Jonah's limited view. Jonah's only recourse was to go where he believed words would not find him. He fled. Again, for some medieval exegetes, flight out of the Land of Israel – from the port city of Jaffa to Tarshish – was not Jonah's escape route from God; no one can run away from God. Rather, it was Jonah's attempt to escape from God's word. Perhaps the prophet believed that prophecy could only be given in the Land of Israel, some contend. If holy words can only be transmitted in the Holy Land, then Jonah reckoned that he could run away from the word and be spared the assignment. God spent the rest of the book disabusing Jonah of this notion. The word is everywhere: in the heart of the ocean and on the dry land, in Israel and in foreign cities, and even in enemy territory. If Jonah was to learn a lesson, it was this.

But what if Jonah ran away not because God gave him the word but because God *did not* give him words? Without first giving him the words to say, but merely telling Jonah to go and proclaim his own judgment, God may have paralyzed Jonah's mission from the outset. Jonah may have felt incapacitated to rise to this challenge of language. He was not hiding from God but hiding from language. Hiding, by its very nature, requires silence. Without silence, there is no chance of concealment. By boarding a foreign ship where sailors spoke other languages, Jonah was enabling his own silence. There was no expectation of speech where he was going, even though this is ironically the chapter that contains the most dialogue. Jonah's inability to face the demon of language would not be relieved in another country or among those who did not share his tongue. After all, he was asked to go to another country to proclaim judgment. There is no mention in the text of simultaneous translation.

The French novelist André Malraux writes, "Man is not what he thinks he is. He is what he hides." In running from words into a net of silence, Jonah hid from the very thing that always accompanied him: speech. This may also explain why Jonah entered the ship and descended into its bottom-most chamber and fell into a deep sleep at the oddest and most inappropriate moment. The ship was being tossed about the sea in a raging storm. The sailors on board were all frenetically trying to save the ship and themselves. They all called out to their gods – in other words, they all spoke to their gods, while this strange man left the decks to withdraw into himself so deeply that he was lost in a place of no language, no words:

> But the Lord cast a mighty wind upon the sea, and such a great tempest came upon the sea that the ship was in danger of breaking up. In their fright, the sailors cried out, each to his own god; and they flung the ship's cargo overboard to make it lighter for them. Jonah, meanwhile, had gone down into the hold of the vessel where he lay down and fell asleep. (Jonah 1:4–6)

Asleep, we humans stop speaking. We speak in dreams and subconscious torments, but this happens only in our own heads. There is no revelation. There is only concealment. There may not even have been the dimmest recognition of this process, especially because Jonah's sleep is described as thick and regressive. When the captain confronted Jonah and demanded that he pray, the text proffers no response, as if to suggest that even with this sardonic or incredulous prompting, Jonah could not summon words.

Even when Jonah accepted the task upon himself, he never enunciated the one word most common in the acceptance of a difficult prophetic challenge: *Hineni*, "I am fully present in this moment to serve." When "the word of the Lord came to Jonah a second time" in chapter 3 (v. 1), "Jonah went at once to Nineveh in accordance with the Lord's command" (v. 3). Jonah's silent "no" in chapter 1 when he fled God's word was just as loud as his silent "yes" when he finally went to Nineveh. The failure to use words at these two critical junctures prevented him from negotiating his discomfort in chapter 1 and preparing himself mentally in chapter 3. Unlike Moses and Jeremiah, who each respectively rejected God's call for different reasons but articulated their hesitations and self-doubt, Jonah's failure to use words, propelling his body in one direction or another instead, meant that he could not properly come to terms with the immense responsibility before him. It is no wonder that he could not fully complete his mission.

WHAT MAKES A PROPHET?

Words are crucial to the prophetic enterprise because prophecy is not politics. The words of a prophet have a chiseled quality to them. They

Jonah's Collapse into Silence

drop hard like stones and have immense staying power, captured in their ongoing resonances. They both describe and shape experience, and they matter. While the words may fit the situation and context of a larger political scenario – the succession of kings or the downing of enemies – they are regarded chiefly as transcendent and universal. They are words that suit the times but ultimately go beyond time. In modern parlance, however, we tend to regard leaders and their relationship with language differently. We have become accustomed to political leaders and business titans using words expediently and in a self-serving manner; when the political climate changes, the language changes. Words become almost instantly disposable, replayed to the leader in moments of weakness and vulnerability to highlight hypocrisy. In such cases, both the leader and the follower understand that no harm is really meant because language is a game. In this game the winner matters, especially the temporary winner – because in business and politics, all is temporal. We assume that the prophet's task is ineluctably different, not only because of the prophet's language but because of the prophet's character.

Here we pause again to ask about the moral quality or disposition of our prophet. Jonah's very existence prompts readers to ask questions about the general nature of prophets, feeding the curiosity present in Heschel's seminal essay, "What Manner of Man Is the Prophet?" If we ask that question in earnest, we could direct it only at Jonah: What manner of man is *this* prophet? To answer this we must create a context for the characterization of prophets in the broadest sense. Kugel defines a prophet as "a messenger sent by God to speak on His behalf."[3] We have numerous instances in the Bible, James Kugel points out, where the word of God without any human intervention is too dangerous, too frightening, or too much for people to bear.[4] The prophet was an important go-between, traversing the liminal space between the human and the Divine. In the words of Heschel: "[A prophet's] true greatness is his ability to hold God and man in a single thought."[5]

---

3. James L. Kugel, *How to Read the Bible: A Guide to Scripture Then and Now* (New York: Free Press, 2007), 439.
4. See Gen. 32:30; Ex. 20:18–21; 33:20; Deut. 18:16–18; Judges 13:22.
5. Heschel, *The Prophets*, 25.

The prophet as messenger was deputized to give moral admonition to the people, to offer criticisms of kings and dignitaries, or to warn of upcoming events, often of a tragic nature. The prophet was decidedly not a fortune-teller for the Israelites, the way that oracles or auguries often functioned in the ancient Near East, even though Samuel was referred to as a "seer."[6] It appears that this term was used more liberally in the days that predated Samuel, as indicated in the following verse: "Formerly, if someone went to inquire of God, they would say, 'Let us go to the seer'" (I Sam. 9:9). This term seems to have fallen out of fashion, perhaps because it created an impression of the prophet that was not accurate to the job description and one too redolent of pagan soothsayers.

The prophet, according to Maimonides (1135–1204) and others, was supposed to be a morally upstanding role model. How does our prophet, Jonah, measure up to Maimonides' high expectations of character? Maimonides in both *Guide of the Perplexed* and the *Mishneh Torah, Hilkhot Yesodei HaTorah*, dissects the nature of revelation and how it takes place. He also offers an elemental definition in his Thirteen Principles: "God communicates to human beings through prophecy." This does not imply that the morality of the prophet is in question. Yet, in *Guide of the Perplexed*, Maimonides presents three opinions regarding prophecy that clearly state that the character of the prophet is a key element in his capacity to receive God's word:

---

6. The honorific "seer" may have specifically been used because of the role that Samuel played in identifying the location of Saul's lost donkeys. A three-day search yielded nothing but a kingship. Saul could not even "see" or identify the very seer he sought to give him guidance on his herd's location. "When they reached the district of Zuph, Saul said to the servant who was with him, 'Come, let's go back, or my father will stop thinking about the donkeys and start worrying about us.' But the servant replied, 'Look, in this town there is a man of God; he is highly respected, and everything he says comes true. Let's go there now. Perhaps he will tell us what way to take'" (I Sam. 9:5–6). They were using the gifts of the prophet for a prosaic task beneath the prophet's dignity, a sure indication that Samuel would not be impressed by this future king and his judgment. This uncertainty about Saul's worthiness and readiness was, no doubt, enhanced by their first meeting, when we have the following verse: "Saul approached Samuel in the gateway and asked, 'Would you please tell me where the seer's house is?' 'I am the seer,' Samuel replied" (vv. 18–19).

> The first opinion – that of the multitude of those among the pagans who considered prophecy as true and also believed by some of the common people professing our Law – is that God, may He be exalted, chooses whom He wishes from among men, turns him into a prophet, and sends him with a mission.[7]

Maimonides discredits this view of prophecy because it means that any individual can be given prophecy by God, regardless of intelligence or age. He then adds one caveat:

> However, they also posit as a condition his having a certain goodness and sound morality. For up to now people have not gone so far as to say that God sometimes turns a wicked man into a prophet unless He has first, according to this opinion, turned him into a good man.[8]

With his next approach, the prominence of character is amplified and can never be discounted from an understanding of who the prophet is and what he does:

> The second opinion is that of the philosophers. It affirms that prophecy is a certain perfection in the nature of man. This perfection is not achieved in any individual from among men except after a training that makes that which exists in the potentiality of the species pass into actuality, provided an obstacle due to temperament or to some external cause does not hinder this, as is the case with regard to every perfection whose existence is possible in a certain species.[9]

In this view of the prophet as philosopher, any flaw of the prophet can result in the obstruction of revelation; this may be due to an inherent character blemish or a temporal flare-up of emotion, like anger. In this

---

7. Moses Maimonides, *The Guide of the Perplexed*, trans. Shlomo Pines (Chicago: University of Chicago Press, 1963), 360 (II:32).
8. Ibid., 360–361.
9. Ibid., 361.

understanding of prophecy, it is even harder to justify the choice of Jonah as prophet, unless the second act of revelation in the book came after Jonah's complete repentance. This repentance would have to be assumed, as it is nowhere stated.

Maimonides' third opinion is based on his understanding of the second. There are individuals who are worthy of prophecy because of their personal excellence in matters of the intellect and the spirit but do not serve as prophets because God does not will it:

> For we believe that it may happen that one who is fit for prophecy and prepared for it should not become a prophet, namely, on account of the divine will. To my mind this is like all the miracles and takes the same course as they. For it is a natural thing that everyone who according to his natural disposition is fit for prophecy and who has been trained in his education and study should become a prophet.... As for its being fundamentally with us that the prophet must possess preparation and perfection in the moral and rational qualities, it is indubitably the opinion expressed in their dictum: Prophecy only rests upon a wise, strong, and rich man.[10]

Maimonides is not basing his views on the worthiness of the prophet's philosophical notions but uses as a proof text a rabbinic statement that prophecy can only take hold of an individual of great wisdom and character (see Shabbat 92a; Nedarim 38a). The very idea that a person can achieve a state of prophecy even though he does not receive revelation caused considerable problems for Maimonides, who believed as a tenet of his perfect faith that revelation was not only the gift of divine communication but also could rest upon those who had achieved greatness of their spiritual and intellectual faculties. This implies that one could have, in his days and beyond, reached that level and that the prophetic tradition had not closed with the Book of Malachi; in principle if not in practice, prophecy is ongoing. Nevertheless, it is evident from his categorization that a person must be morally worthy to be a prophet.

---

10. Ibid., 361–362.

The moral characterization of the prophet is problematic from a biblical survey of various prophets. Of course, Heschel is correct in his assessment that so many biblical prophets led with a boldness for truth and the audacity to challenge power, but perhaps we need a more morally neutral understanding of prophecy that has room for a prophet like Jonah on its list.

The character or description of the prophet or the receiver of revelation, it would appear, was not as significant as the message. Many who received God's revelation did not, at least on the surface, seem worthy of the divine word. Individuals like Manoah's wife (Judges 13), to whom an angel of God spoke, did nothing to show particular merit. She and her husband seem unlikely recipients of the special news that they would have a son after many years of barrenness. Balaam, to whom God spoke directly, seems not deserving of prophecy, if we regard it as reward for superior moral judgment and behavior. In these instances, the human being is a pure conduit of God's intentions, a pass-through without the agency to resist.

This forces us to ask a difficult question: Why was Jonah's prophecy not operative in the same way? Jonah had the power to run away. And the de-emphasis on the moral character of the prophet helps us understand that Jonah could do his task and was able to receive revelation even if his relationship with God and his fellow humans lacked sufficient empathy, if he did not communicate particular holiness or a willingness to serve. Jonah's flawed thinking and behavior did not mean that God found him unworthy of prophecy, if we understand that a prophet had to deliver words and did not have to be a moral exemplar.

The Talmud has a principle that appears many times in its pages: "There is a presumption that an agent performs his assigned agency."[11]

---

11. This is discussed regarding an agent for the delivery of a bill of divorce. See Gittin 64a and R. Yitzḥak's position regarding this principle, when it comes to both betrothal and marriage. If we assume, as the Talmud does, that "a man's agent is like himself" (for examples, see Mishna Berakhot 5:5, Kiddushin 42a, and Bava Metzia 96a), then we must assume that if a person desires to perform a particular action, he can count on his agent to fulfill his request just as he himself would. This principle also means that the agent must be particular in the exact execution of this task, according to the will of the one who appointed him – as Maimonides in the *Mishneh Torah* writes, "to

Jonah's Retreat

When someone agrees to perform a task, we naturally assume that he or she will execute it as demanded. Perhaps this explains the dictionary definition of an agent as both a vehicle or conduit and an emissary or proxy. These definitions are divided by a common understanding. As an instrument of someone else, an agent merely channels the will of the one who appointed him. As a representative of someone else, an agent acts in place of another. In the first definition, the agent has little personal imprint on the task assigned. In the second, the agent tries to understand the intent and concerns of the one who appointed him and act accordingly. In considering the role of the ancient Hebrew prophets, one assumes that at times, a prophet merely delivered the exact words that he received from God and at other times he paraphrased or used his own creativity and intelligence to intuit what God would want him to communicate in various situations. For example, Rashi notes on Exodus 19:3 that Moses was to deliver the exact words he heard from God based on the doubling of verbs, suggesting precise repetition: "And Moses went up to God. The Lord called to him from the mountain, saying: 'Thus shall you *say* to the house of Jacob and *declare* to the children of Israel.'"[12] As God's agent in the delivery of the Ten Commandments, Moses was to represent God with fidelity to the message, with exactitude. This became even more critical slightly later in this narrative when the people, in their fright, refused to hear the rest of the Ten Commandments from God and insisted that Moses deliver them instead: "'You speak to us,' they said to Moses, 'and we will obey; but let not God speak to us, lest we die'" (Ex. 20:16). This verse alone helps unearth why God needed an agent in the first place. The intensity of holiness in the moment of encounter between God and humans could easily deter an ordinary mortal from contact with the divine.

This intensity explains, according to Kugel in his essay, "The Moment of Confusion," the appearance of angels in the Bible that

---

uphold and not to depart from the mandate" (*Hilkhot Sheluḥin* 1:3; see also *Shulḥan Arukh* 182:2). For a general discussion of agency in Jewish law, see Israel Herbert Levinthal, "The Jewish Law of Agency," *Jewish Quarterly Review* 13, no. 2 (October, 1922): 117–191.

12. Rashi, basing himself on the *Mekhilta* to this verse, writes, "with these exact words and in this order."

play intermediary roles. God "overly existed." God's presence so overwhelmed humans that God had to temper communication and minimize its perceived dangers:

> When God wished to speak to people, He normally did so by sending an angel, that is to say, a humanlike stand-in. The most common Hebrew word for "angel" (*malakh*) seems to come from a root meaning "send" – and this would confirm the general impression that scholars have of the angel's role in the Bible's most ancient parts. An angel, it would seem, was essentially an emissary used by God to represent Him among human beings. (The same word, *malakh*, was sometimes used of ordinary, human messengers, such as those sent by Jacob to his brother in Genesis 32:3.)[13]

Prophets, like Moses, functioned in largely the same way as angels, delivering messages from a netherworld as those who could mediate the spaces between the divine and the human.

Maimonides, in *Hilkhot Yesodei HaTorah*, observes that a prophet could receive God's word from an angel or in a dream or visionary state

---

13. James Kugel, *The God of Old: Inside the Lost World of the Bible* (New York: Free Press, 2003), 6. Kugel begins the essay with this basic assumption and goes on to describe that this explains an odd phenomenon in the biblical text, namely, that angels often appear randomly, bearing personal information about an individual's actions or character and a prediction for the future – but this is never commented on as odd by those present in the encounter. This is perhaps best illustrated by Judges 13, where Manoah is highly aware and skeptical of the confusion of revelation and thus believes that his wife, Samson's mother, is being tricked by a human being. These moments of confusion, Kugel contends, demonstrate something essential about the landscape of the Bible: "The spiritual is not something tidy and distinct, another order of being. Instead, it is perfectly capable of intruding into everyday reality, as if part of this world. It is not just 'in here'; it is also out there a presence, looming" (p. 36). Kugel continues this theme in a later work, a meditation on his illness, recovery, and study of Bible, *In the Valley of the Shadow: On the Foundations of Religious Belief* (New York: The Free Press, 2011). In his essay, "The Eerie Proximity" (pp. 115–129), Kugel observes that God dissolves into the human form of angels, creating confusion and even, as in the case of the Burning Bush, what appears to be illusions to signal God's presence.

that altered his physical bearing. Such a prophet could be "sent to one of the nations of the world or to the residents of a specific city or kingdom, to prepare them and to let them know what they should do or to prevent them from behaving in their evil ways."[14] In this capacity, a prophet, according to Maimonides, would need to perform a wonder or give a sign so that his constituents would believe he was sent by God. This then devolves into the next set of concerns, namely a discussion of false prophets who fooled with signs and wonders but were not on a divine mission:

> Not all who perform signs and wonders should be treated as prophets. Only one who is worthy of prophecy and this is understood beforehand (the individual in question has a reputation as a prophet), meaning that his intelligence and his superior deeds exceed those of others around him. If he adheres to the holy paths of prophecy and separates himself from this-worldly concerns and then performs a sign or wonder and says that he was sent by God, then it is a command to listen to him, as it states explicitly: "Listen to him." (Deut. 18:15)[15]

The message and its delivery had to be consistent with a set of values and with the character Maimonides expected from God's most intimate servants. Moral lassitude was an indication that a prophet was false. But if a prophet was merely a conduit for words then character becomes less of an issue. This makes us wonder where Jonah fits in. Without being a moral exemplar but merely a conduit, Jonah may have been able to function as a prophet, but he seemed uninterested in either function – or ideologically opposed.

The other salient and similar aspect threading through all the Hebrew prophets according to Heschel is the prophet's relationship to God. Here too Jonah seems an unlikely choice. Prophetic theology, Heschel contended, is based on involvement, attentiveness, and concern.[16] This surfaces from the prophet's intimate relationship with God:

---

14. Maimonides, *Mishneh Torah, Hilkhot Yesodei HaTorah* 7:6.
15. Ibid., 7:7.
16. Heschel, *The Prophets*, 619.

> Prophetic religion may be defined, not as what man does with his ultimate concern, but rather *what man does with God's concern* (italics in the original).
>
> He whose thinking is guided by the prophets would say: God's presence is my first thought; His unity and transcendence, my second; His concern and involvement (justice and compassion), my third. Upon deeper reflection, however, he will realize that all three thoughts are one. God's presence in the world is, in essence, His concern for the world. One word stands for both.[17]

If a prophet is measured by the way that a human being channels God's desire for the world He created, then it leaves Jonah cold and isolated among prophets. God, in the book's lingering question, implied that Jonah did not care for God's creatures, 120,000 people and their cattle.

By the book's last chapter, Jonah's words, previously eclipsed by his silence, came out in a torrent of anger and frustration. They became accusatory, slippery, and careless, careless enough that God was forced to ask the prophet more than once if, indeed, he meant them. With the pounding of a verbal drumbeat, we hear God confront Jonah:

> "Are you that deeply grieved?" (4:4)
> "Are you so deeply grieved about the plant?" (v. 9)
> "Should I not care about Nineveh?" (v. 11)

When no words became hostile words and then God questioned their very sincerity, Jonah retreated into the silence that characterized him throughout. He never answered God's expansive moral questioning. He never got the last word. His story ends with what he never said. Debilitated and humiliated by a majestic God whose compassion seemed boundless, the narrow Jonah narrowed himself further into the silence that begins our story and closes it. Sometimes in the face of a theology you cannot accept, silence is the only authentic response.

---

17. Ibid.

Chapter Three

The Unity of Opposites: The Sailors, the Captain, and the King

> In their fright, the sailors cried out, each to his own god; and they flung the ship's cargo overboard to make it lighter for them. Jonah, meanwhile, had gone down into the hold of the vessel where he lay down and fell asleep. The captain went over to him and cried out, "How can you be sleeping so soundly? Rise, call upon your god! Perhaps the god will be kind to us and we will not perish." The men said to one another, "Let us cast lots and find out on whose account this misfortune has come upon us." They cast lots and the lot fell on Jonah. They said to him, "Tell us, you who have brought this misfortune upon us, what is your business? Where have you come from? What is your country, and of what people are you?" "I am a Hebrew," he replied. "I worship the Lord, the God of heaven, who made both sea and dry land." The men were greatly terrified, and they asked him, "What have you done?" And when the men learned that he was fleeing from the service of the Lord – for so had he told them – they said to him, "What must we do to you to make the sea calm around us?" for the sea was growing more and more stormy." (Jonah 1:5–11)

Jonah's Retreat

The pre-Socratic philosopher Heraclitus (535–485 BCE) created a theory called the unity of opposites. A thing can only properly be understood through contrast with its oppositional object. Objects are formed and changed through a confrontation with their opposites. Heat exposed to cold makes an object colder. Something dry exposed to moisture becomes wetter. This is true not only for objects but for ideas and emotions. Later philosophers, Hegel in particular, believed that ideas are shaped and sharpened by their dialectic opposites. Light requires darkness in order for one to understand either state. An identity can best be understood through both its similarity and its contrast to an opposing idea. This tension is dynamic.

The Book of Jonah is filled with characters who provide opposition to Jonah as a way for him to refine his own self-understanding. The prominent presence of gentiles in the Book of Jonah has been noted by scholars ancient and modern as figures who serve as Jonah's foils. These characters also provide the oppositional contrasts necessary to help us understand Jonah's non-normative behavior through their acceptable responses to crisis. In their concern for life, for example, the sailors spotlighted Jonah's disregard for it. In his concern for authority, the captain exposed Jonah's lack of it. In his rapid and intense repentance, the king of Nineveh showcased Jonah's incapacity to apologize or take full accountability for his own wrongdoing. But such a reading, with its surface appeal, makes the appearance of these righteous gentiles seem like an illustration of character rather than a matter of theology. These characters represent an appositional religious worldview, one riddled with fear and uncertainty regarding the higher forces that guide their polymorphic universe.

Much of this sentiment can be captured in language used by all three in contrast to the theologically charged language that Jonah used to describe his situation and his future. This pivots on the use of the Hebrew root word Y-D-A, to know or not to know. Jonah seemed to know the way God worked, in contrast to the sailors, the captain, and the king, who seemed unsure and ambivalent: "I *know* that it is my fault that this great storm has come upon you" (Jonah 1:12); "for I *know* that You are a compassionate and gracious God" (4:2).

The Unity of Opposites

The only moment of confusion that Jonah confessed to was in his prayer, when he was uncertain if he would drown and not be able to make future pilgrimages: "I thought I was driven away, out of Your sight: Would I ever gaze again upon Your holy Temple?" (2:5). There is, of course, irony, in his reflexive verb choice – being driven away as opposed to driving himself away[1] – but nevertheless, he understood at that moment that his future was unclear. The difference is that in this instance his doubt was regarding his material existence rather than the formulation of his religious views.

In contrast, the sailors asked Jonah questions, ceding to him authority over his situation rather than casting him overboard when the lot fell on him. The unnamed sailors in chapter 1 acted with alacrity, responsibility, and humanity during a punishing storm. They serve to highlight Jonah's flawed behavior: his resistance to authority, his seeming carelessness about the lives of those around him, and his lethargy when it came to his own self-preservation.

THE SAILORS AND THEIR LOTTERY

The Hebrew term for sailors used in the Book of Jonah, *hamalaḥim*, is defined by Rashi as "those who steer a ship."[2] Ibn Ezra uses a similar explanation of *yo'atzei hasfina*, "those who guide the ship."[3] These two understandings lead us to regard these men as captains or leaders rather than mere oarsmen. Radak calls them the oar holders, knocking them down in the hierarchy of boat steerage. This accords with the literal definition; the term implies a stirring or plowing of water, the movement that sailors use each time they dip their oars in the sea. We find a similar usage in the Book of Exodus referring to the mixing of ingredients for the frankincense: "Make them [various herbs] into incense, a compound expertly blended, mixed [*memulaḥ*], pure and

---

1. Compare this verse to the opening of chapter 2 of Esther: "Some time afterward, when the anger of King Ahasuerus subsided, he thought of Vashti and what she had done and *what had been decreed against her*" (Est. 2:1). This is written as if the king had not been the one to make the decree against Vashti in the first place. This verb form vitiates personal agency and is an invitation to blame.
2. Rashi to Jonah 1:5. For this usage in rabbinic literature, see Ketubbot 85a.
3. Ibid.

sacred" (30:35). The term appears elsewhere as a specific reference to sailors (Ezek. 26:9; 27:27). The difference in these interpretations lies in the seniority of those who confronted Jonah. Making the sailors into leaders would imply that once again Jonah resisted those in positions of authority: God, the captain of the ship, and these officers. The latter understanding implies that Jonah had imperiled simple and innocent men who followed directions, just as he himself should have. Even the visual image of them all rowing in the same direction – which we see later in the chapter as they tried desperately to avoid taking Jonah's life – suggests a collective cooperation to achieve a particular goal. This is in stark contrast to Jonah who we might imagine would row, if handed an oar, in the opposite direction.

Uriel Simon observes that in three places the word "sailors," *malaḥim*, is replaced by "men," *anashim*, moving from their professional expertise to the common existential status of human beings in fear for their lives.[4] Even though the words are spelled differently, the word for sailors and angels are homophones in Hebrew. Because the Hebrew Bible's aural quality was important, particularly in the days before mass printing and universal literacy, a listener to this story would have heard the term and perhaps made the association that these sailors were indeed angels in the way they treated Jonah and in their leading questions which created a forced self-reflection for someone fleeing and sleeping.

To focus on the language of the text, we repeat the passage that opens this chapter:

> The men said to one another, "Let us cast lots and find out on whose account this misfortune has come upon us." They cast lots and the lot fell on Jonah. They said to him, "Tell us, you who have brought this misfortune upon us, what is your business? Where have you come from? What is your country, and of what people are you?" "I am a Hebrew," he replied. "I worship the Lord, the God of heaven, who made both sea and dry land." The men were greatly terrified, and they asked him, "What have you done?" And

---

4. Uriel Simon, *Mikra LeYisrael Ovadia Yona* (Tel Aviv: Am Oved Publishers/Magnes Press, 1992), 48. See Jonah 1:10, 13, 16.

when the men learned that he was fleeing from the service of the Lord – for so had he told them… (Jonah 1:7–10)

How did Jonah conceive of the idea to have himself thrown overboard and get responsible sailors to agree?

> …they said to him, "What must we do to you to make the sea calm around us?" for the sea was growing more and more stormy. "Pick me up and throw me into the sea," he replied, "and it will become calm. I know that it is my fault that this great storm has come upon you." (vv. 11–12)

We have ancient mariner myths about individuals thrown overboard to placate the gods. In fact, we find one such story in the New Testament, with similarities to the Jonah narrative (Acts 27). Paul and a number of prisoners boarded a ship sailing from Adramyttium, an ancient city in Asia under Roman jurisdiction, to Rome. Winds tossed about the ship, making travel difficult. Paul warned of the impending disaster but the captain pressed on, further endangering the crew and passengers. Ignoring Paul's advice was unwise, and the ship faced a perilous storm. After a violent battering, the crew threw cargo overboard on the third day – another parallel with the Jonah narrative – and gave up hope of being saved. Paul urged the sailors to eat and keep up their strength since, he announced, the boat would be destroyed but its passengers would all be spared. Paul had encountered an angel the night before who foretold their salvation. Again, in parallel to the Jonah story, a holy man on a ship of heathens confronted a storm and predicted deliverance. It took an additional fourteen days for the 276 men aboard to see land. But as they did, the ship confronted disaster and ran aground. The soldiers on board, hoping to propitiate the gods, wanted to kill the prisoners, perhaps believing that they were the cause of the problem. Paul insisted their lives be spared or all would suffer death. Everyone reached land safely. Here, the religious leader directed the actions on board the ship to save lives. Jonah also did this – but only under duress and with a caveat: saving them required sacrificing him.

Jonah's sailors, however, spoke more. They were not only men of action but also men of introspection. They asked Jonah several questions that revealed their own confusion about the situation and their desire to do right by this stranger. The lottery itself is an indicator of the world of chance that they occupied. Again, ironically, they drew lots "to *know* on whose account this misfortune has come upon us" (Jonah 1:7); knowing can never be ascertained this way in the world of reason. The lottery, a central feature of chapter 1, suggests randomness, possibility, and hope, the very same conditions or emotions wrapped up in the captain's word "perhaps" – "Perhaps the god will be kind to us" (v. 6) or the "may" in the mouth of the King of Nineveh – "Who knows but that God may turn and relent?" (3:9). Radak questions why the sailors would even call for a lottery since every ship was being tossed by the same tempest. He then cites *Pirkei DeRabbi Eliezer*, as do Rashi, Ibn Ezra, and many others. The midrash suggests that their ship was the only one to be caught in the storm, leading them to the conclusion that someone on their boat must have been responsible for the problem.

The sailors' lottery reminds us of the most famous one in the Hebrew Bible, the one that Haman created to determine the most auspicious day to annihilate the Jews in Ahasuerus' vast empire. It is important to note that these two lotteries were not conducted by Jews, not only because of the rabbinic aphorism that "Jews are not subject to astrological forecasting" (see Shabbat 156a–b; Nedarim 32b) but because this reliance on arbitrary factors is counter to the monotheistic belief as to how God operates. This rabbinic expression has biblical roots in the story of Balaam and explains why his curses on the Israelites were not effective: "For there is no enchantment with Jacob, neither is there any divination with Israel" (Num. 23:23).[5] Belief that a lottery – rather than

---

5. There are numerous biblical references to wise men who served as court astrologers. See, for example, Gen. 41:33, 39; Dan. 2:27; Is. 44:25; 47:10–15; Jer. 50:35; 51:57; I Chr. 12:32. The narrow rationalist view that Jews did not believe in astrology has been trounced by many scholars. See, in reference to Bible commentary in particular, Y. Tzvi Langermann, "Some Astrological Themes in the Thought of Abraham ibn Ezra," *Rabbi Abraham ibn Ezra: Studies in the Writings of a Twelfth Century Polymath*, ed. Isadore Twersky and Jay Harris (Cambridge, MA: Harvard University Press, 1993), 28–85. For example, Ibn Ezra on Exodus 33:23 writes on the expression, "There is no *mazal* in Israel" that "Whatever the configuration of stars existing at birth has decreed for an individual will surely befall him, unless he be protected by a power superior to the stars. If he attaches himself to it, he will be saved from the

human behavior – can alter God's decrees suggests a universe guided by chaotic forces that can be easily manipulated. Repentance, on the other hand, demands personal accountability and transformation. For those who do not wish to put in the effort, a lottery can seem like an immense psychological relief. George Orwell masterfully captured the magnetism of a lottery in *1984*, describing the millions of proles, or working-class members, who bought into it:

> The Lottery was the principal if not the only reason for remaining alive. It was their delight, their folly, their anodyne, their intellectual stimulant. Where the Lottery was concerned, even people who could barely read and write seemed capable of intricate calculations and staggering feats of memory.[6]

Orwell helps us understand the seduction of the lottery; it allows its participants to renege on decision-making and accountability, particularly when facing sensitive and difficult problems.

There were clearly lotteries in the Hebrew Bible conducted by Jews, and one even conducted by the High Priest on Yom Kippur, the holiest day of the year. Leviticus 16 recounts the ritual (whose details are much discussed in Yoma) of the lots that were placed on two identical goats, one to be sacrificed for the atonement of the people and another to be led to its death in the wilderness: "Aaron shall take the two he-goats and let them stand before the Lord at the entrance of the Tent of Meeting and he shall place lots upon the two goats, one marked for the Lord and the other marked for Azazel" (v. 7). The other well-known lottery appears in the eighteenth chapter of the Book of Joshua, where lots were drawn to determine the apportionment of the Land of Israel among the tribes. The chapter concludes: "These are the portions assigned by lot to the tribes of Israel by the priest Eleazar, Joshua son of

---

decrees…. This is what the Sages have said, 'Israel has no planets (*mazal*)' [that is] as long as they observe the Torah. But if they do not observe it, the stars will rule over them…" (Langermann trans., p. 50). This assumes that astrology is predictive and accurate but that Torah observance will shield the believer from its determining and deleterious forces.

6. George Orwell, *1984* (New York: Signet, 1961), 85.

Nun, and the heads of the ancestral houses before the Lord at Shiloh, at the entrance of the Tent of Meeting" (18:51).

It is no coincidence that both these lotteries were performed by or in the presence of the High Priest and before the "Tent of Meeting." These were not random activities to change God's mind. These were opportunities, symbolic or real, for human beings to actualize the next step in their own autonomous lives. The goat was a symbolic expiation for the people, but it had to be accompanied in rabbinic literature by confession, contrition, and a commitment for future change. It could not accomplish all the work of atonement but could inspire the penitent to move in the direction of repentance, changing personal will rather than God's will. This is even more the case in the lottery to determine tribal allotments in the era of Joshua. The land had been given by God but only a random selection of the actual lots would accomplish a sense of fairness in the difficult apportionment of property since not all of the parcels were evenly sized or similarly comprised. Some had more fertile soil or more territory but inferior soil quality and other differences that may have been the subject of resentment had the division not occurred by lottery. Lotteries can accomplish the same outcomes as choice and selection but without the perceived favoritism that often accompanies selection.

In the case of Jonah, the lottery used to determine the storm's cause was not the final arbiter. The sailors followed up with a series of questions and, in exchange, they received one piece of definitive knowledge connected to Jonah: "And when the men *learned (yadu)* that he was fleeing from the service of the Lord – for so had he told them..." (Jonah 1:10). They only knew this because Jonah chose to share this information with them. Jonah's short autobiographical revelation inspired terror in them.

Theodor Gaster offers this insight into the sailors' questions: "It is a common superstition that *it is dangerous to sail with an impious or wicked person,* since his presence aboard will inevitably provoke an outraged god to embroil the sea and possibly wreak the ship."[7] To substantiate this, Gaster quotes Aeschylus who declares, "The pious man who on a ship embarks/ with hothead crew or other villainy/Goes to his doom with that god-hated

---

7. Theodor Gaster, *Myth, Legend and Custom in the Old Testament* (New York: Harper and Row, 1969), 652.

brood."[8] Gaster even cites a modern example of this thinking. When Olive Schreiner was going to be lowered into a lifeboat to escape the wreck of the Titanic, some objected, saying that she was an atheist and would bring harm to them.[9] What the sailors seemed sure of was their precarious position as a result of this fugitive.

Jonah, on the other hand, seemed sure of the way God worked, in sharp contrast to those who confront the *mysterium tremendum* with humility and uncertainty. This becomes most evident when the verses that convey this are presented together: "'I am a Hebrew,' he replied. 'I worship the Lord, the God of heaven, who made both sea and dry land.' The men were greatly terrified" (Jonah 1:9–10). The sailors' insecurity surfaced even when they were assured by the prophet that God wanted only Jonah's demise. When we pay careful attention to Jonah's absolute surety of his crime and the sailors' uncertainty we also see how this dissonance impacted their self-understanding:

> "Pick me up and throw me into the sea," he replied, "and it will become calm. *I know* that it is my fault that this great storm has come upon you." Nevertheless the men rowed hard to regain the shore, but they could not, for the sea was growing more and more stormy about them. Then they cried out to the Lord, "Please, Lord, do not let us die for taking this man's life. Do not hold us accountable for killing an innocent man, for You, Lord, have done as You

---

8. Gaster cites Aeschylus, *Septem contra Thebas*, 602ff.
9. See *The Times Literary Supplement*, Dec. 13, 1957. There was a popular legend that a passenger on the Titanic yelled, referring to Olive Schreiner, "Don't put her in here. She is an atheist and will sink us." This legend is cited in the *Times Literary Supplement* and quoted by R. G. Ussher, *The Characters of Theophrastus* (London: Macmillan, 1960), 211. It also makes an appearance in David Ladouceur, "Hellenistic Preconceptions of Shipwreck and Pollution as a Context for Acts 27-28," *The Harvard Theological Review*, vol. 73, no.3/4 (1980): 440, #11. The only problem is that Olive Schreiner was never on the Titanic. Schreiner's letters include one dated April 24th, 1912, suggesting that she learned of the ship's sinking and had a friend on the boat and was not a lover of sea travel: "We have just got the full news of the loss of the Titanic, & dear old Stead's passing. You know I've never loved the sea as I have the land & the sky, the dear, wonderful sky." See https://www.oliveschreiner.org/vre?view=collections&colid=39&letterid=14.

pleased." They took Jonah and threw him overboard, and the raging sea grew calm. At this the men greatly feared the Lord, and they offered a sacrifice to the Lord and made vows to Him. (vv. 12–16)

Jonah "knew" the reason for the storm, but even when he told them this, their uncertainty pushed them on to high ground as they searched for dry ground. Had they shared Jonah's smug surety, they may have casually tossed him overboard without hesitation. Doing what they were told was God's will from His assumed representative, they still never assumed they would not be held accountable; thus their heartfelt prayer. It was only after the sea actually calmed that they acquired knowledge through experience. The men, nevertheless, did their best to row back to land. They could not. The sea grew even wilder than before.

In *Pirkei DeRabbi Eliezer*, we find a lengthy disquisition on Jonah that adds yet another overlay of decency to the sailors' efforts. This late midrashic work, usually dated to the eighth century, opens with a discussion of Creation and events that occurred on each day of Creation but that are not mentioned in the biblical text. The fifth day of Creation is an apt platform for a discussion of Jonah because it was on this day that God created fish (Gen. 1:20–21). The great fish these sages describe has even more magical powers than the one that appears in Jonah. This also allows the authors of this midrashic collection to discuss other aspects of the book, most notably the behavior of the sailors:

> They took Jonah and lowered him up to his knees into the ocean, and the sea quieted from its storm. But when they drew him back, the sea raged again. So they lowered him until his navel, and the sea's storm grew still; but when they lifted him out, it raged again. They lowered him up to his neck, and the sea quieted; but again, as soon as they had raised him, it raged. Finally, they lowered Jonah's entire body into the ocean. Immediately, the storm at sea ceased.[10]

---

10. See David Stern's translation in "Jonah and the Sailors from *Pirkei DeRabbi Eliezer*," in *Rabbinic Fantasies: Imaginative Narratives from Classical Hebrew Literature*, by David Stern and Mark Jay Mirsky (New Haven: Yale University Press, 1998), 64.

CERTAINTY AND UNCERTAINTY IN THE BIBLE

Jonah was right, but he was also wrong. He knew that God was after him but he thought that God wished him dead. That was where he erred: God was after him because He wanted a living prophet and was prepared to move the natural world to save and prepare Jonah for His mission.

The gentile "un-knowingness" in the Book of Jonah is amplified by the question the captain voiced, "Perhaps the god will be kind to us and we will not perish" (1:6), and then again when the King of Nineveh had a similar query: "Who *knows* but that God *may* turn and relent? He *may* turn back from His wrath so that we do not perish" (3:9). This question flies in the face of Jonah's declarative statement when he entered Nineveh: "Jonah began by going a day's journey into the city, proclaiming, 'Forty days more and Nineveh will be overturned.' *The Ninevites believed God.* A fast was proclaimed, and all of them, from the greatest to the least, put on sackcloth" (vv. 4–5). Jonah's prophecy was harsh and direct. It was neither couched in typical prophetic lyricism nor pillowed in metaphor or parable; it again reflected Jonah's general surety. Interestingly, his proclamation was not followed by a belief in Jonah but rather by the Ninevite belief in God. It was also followed by Ninevite action: "Let everyone turn back from his evil ways and from the injustice that is in his hands" (v. 8). They did not merely speculate on a changed fate but believed that they, like God, also needed to change their ways to affect their destiny. They had a singular strategy: pray and act, just as the sailors did. In contrast, Jonah persisted in his stubborn and misguided belief that he knew God's ways and, therefore, his own ways remained unchanged throughout. His prayer was not one of contrition but one of basic thanksgiving. Jonah did not undertake any atonement in action or in thought.

It appears that God wanted Jonah to question his own sense of certainty, his vehement understanding of the way that God works in the world. This is exemplified by Jonah's outrageous leave-taking from Nineveh, sure the city would be destroyed even though God explicitly set out to save it. In so doing, Jonah suggested that he was more all-knowing and powerful than God Himself. Yet God renounced His punishment in chapter 3, and when we open chapter 4 and turn our attention back to the prophet, we see that Jonah's response was disappointment and anger at God's generosity:

> But Jonah was greatly displeased and became angry. He prayed to the Lord, "O Lord, is this not what I said when I was still at home? That is why I was so quick to flee to Tarshish. For I *know* that You are a compassionate and gracious God, slow to anger, abounding in kindness, renouncing punishment. Please, Lord, take my life, for I would rather die than live." The Lord replied, "Are you that deeply grieved?" Now Jonah had left the city and found a place east of the city. He made a booth there and sat under it in the shade, until he should see what happened to the city. (4:1–5)

God, through the gentle instrument of the rhetorical question, tried to guide Jonah to a place of self-reflection, to judge his own anger and find it wanting, perhaps to create a sliver of empathy for this city. Instead of answering with words, Jonah, as expected, answered with his body. With the same silence that spoke so loudly in chapter 1, Jonah turned away from God's question and made himself a personal shelter. Much like Noah, to whom we will compare Jonah more fully later on, he created an ark-like structure for self-containment – but his only had room for one. The prophet became increasingly isolated as a result of the way he understood God and God's world. At this point in time, after the prophecy, Jonah also knew that at most, he could retreat. There was no place he could run. That option was now exhausted, its strategy flawed. This meant that his only resort was a temporary shelter until God took his life, as he begged. What Jonah did not realize was that the prophet too required mercy from God's wrath.

Jonah's unshakable confidence about the rigidity of God's world was incorrect. God was indeed capable of changing or commuting a sentence. In fact, some have argued that the notion that repentance changes divine wrath is not unique to Jewish texts and the Israelite ethos. The voices of "maybe" in the Book of Jonah are authentic to pagan traditions: "The divine mercy was no privilege of Israel. Gods of the nations, too, were compassionate and relenting from evil.... The pagan gods often delayed the punishment of the wicked in order to allow them time to change their way of life."[11] The captain and the king in Jonah were seeking

---

11. Bickerman, *Four Strange Books*, 42.

The Unity of Opposites

to delay divine retribution by convincing their followers that God/the gods could change. Theirs was not simple insecurity or uncertainty. They were certain that some things were uncertain.

The Hebrew *ulai* that appears in Jonah 1:6 as a word of possibility does not appear frequently in the Bible. Sarah uttered it to Abraham when she conceived of the idea of surrogacy as the path to creating an heir for Abraham with a solution that would include her rather than dismiss her from the annals of Jewish history. After Abraham was told explicitly that his heir would not be Eliezer, the household servant, God added that the child would be his very own: "That one shall not be your heir; none but your very own issue shall be your heir" (Gen. 15:4). This puzzling expectation is rendered in the Hebrew using a rhyming and challenging wordplay: *asher yetze memei'ekha, hu yirashekha,* "out of your belly, shall be your heir." Abraham, gifted as he was, was incapable of giving birth to an heir, so directing attention to his loins instead of Sarah's may have indicated to the couple that she would not be included in the fulfillment of this promise. Sarah may have overheard this interchange or it may have been shared with her in a moment of reflection or confusion on Abraham's part. This, it seems, may have prompted Sarah's surrogacy idea: "And Sarai said to Abram, 'Look the Lord has kept me from bearing. Consort with my maid; *perhaps* [*ulai*] I shall have a son through her'" (16:2). Sarah did not give her maid to Abraham so that Abraham's dream could finally be fulfilled. Perhaps she understood that this would indeed happen but that she would not be part of the master plan and believed that with this solution she could be built up.

Instead, Sarah's plan paradoxically reduced and diminished her. When Hagar conceived, she immediately began to belittle her former mistress: "and when she saw that she had conceived, her mistress was lowered in her esteem" (v. 4). The situation that Sarah created inadvertently became an unbearable emotional weight for her and eventually led to violence and the banishment of Hagar and Ishmael from Abraham's household. Although Abraham listened to Sarah and banished his second wife and their son, it caused him profound suffering. Sarah's plan led to ruination for Hagar and Ishmael and, on some level, for her. From this point onward, we hear nothing more from or about Sarah until her death in Genesis 23. The *ulai* she pondered was a possibility, but not one that made sense, had she considered all of the emotional fractiousness it could and did create for herself and her family. Unlike the *ulai* in the Book of Jonah which did materialize for the good, Sarah's *ulai* was not the "maybe" that resolved itself in happiness or salvation.

The different type of "maybes" should also be noted. When Jonah and Sarah used the term, they took charge of the situation and leveraged the ambiguity. The captain and king in the Book of Jonah, however, left the "maybe" up to God or gods. They prayed and propitiated the Hebrew God, deposited their faith in the graces of a higher authority, and provoked or inspired others to do the same without assurance that change would happen. All they could do was work as hard as they possibly could to deserve a change of fate. Sarah did no such thing. She did not pray to God to help her find her way or ask if this was indeed a desirable strategy to gain an heir. Neither did she review the possible consequences of her decision. Her "maybe" felt flippant and not weighty, as if her strategy might or might not solve her problem without sufficiently coming to terms with the emotional entanglement it could create if her solution failed. Most importantly, her "maybe" was about saving herself, not ultimately about saving others or, more specifically, about bringing a resolution to Abraham's dilemma. There was a narcissistic desperation to Sarah's sense of possibility, and it backfired, causing her deep personal anguish.

How different this is from the other *ulai* in the Abraham narratives. When Abraham implored God to spare the righteous in Sodom, he did not state unequivocally that there were definitely righteous individuals living there. "Abraham came forward and said, 'Will You sweep away the innocent along with the guilty? What if there should be fifty innocent within the city; will You then wipe out the place and not forgive it for the sake of the innocent fifty who are in it? Far be it from You to do such a thing" (Gen. 18:23–25). And the drumbeat of *ulai* continues in Abraham's outcry: "What if [*ulai*] the fifty innocent should lack five? Will You destroy the whole city for want of five?" (18:28).

These famous "maybes" do not exhaust the possibilities of the one who founded our faith. Twice in the Eliezer story of matchmaking do we find this word again: "And the servant [Eliezer] said to him [Abraham], 'What if [*ulai*] the woman does not consent to follow me to this land?'" (Gen. 24:5). His anxiety at this momentous task, to represent his master

The Unity of Opposites

faithfully in the search for Isaac's bride, continued even when Eliezer found Rebecca, as he repeated to Bethuel, her father: "What if the woman does not follow me?" (24:39). In this second rendering, questioning gave way to bewilderment that he had indeed identified a match for his master's son.

A different and troubling "maybe" appears some chapters later. Jacob said to Rebecca upon her creation of a ruse for Jacob to appear as Esau to a blind father: "If [*ulai*] my father touches me, I shall appear to him as a trickster and bring upon myself a curse, not a blessing" (27:12). Even were Isaac to be fooled, Jacob may have felt himself to be an impostor who deserved his father's curse. Later, this haunted him when he uttered another *ulai*. When Jacob prepared to encounter Esau and his forces, he told his representative to say the following: "And you shall add, 'And your servant Jacob himself is right behind us,' for he reasoned, 'If I propitiate him with presents in advance and then face him, maybe [*ulai*] he will show me favor'" (32:21). No one suspected failure in this meeting more than Jacob, who knew that he had created this traumatic sibling mess. Had he acted conservatively when he first said *ulai*, he would never have had to utter the word again.

One more *ulai* appears in Genesis in relation to sibling difficulties. Jacob, once again but at a much later stage of his life, told his sons when they traveled back to Egypt to beseech the still-disguised Joseph: "And take back with you double the money, carrying back with you the money that was replaced in the mouths of your bags; perhaps [*ulai*] it was a mistake" (43:12). In each instance, Jacob's *ulai* reflects a family fissure that could have been avoided with better judgment.

While the word "*ulai*" can be found in many other places in the Bible, the preponderance appears in Genesis.[12] At the beginning of our

---

12. The other notable examples outside of Genesis include Num. 22:33; Josh. 4:12, 9:7; I Sam. 6:5; I Kings 18:27; Hos. 8:7; Lam. 3:29. Specifically in the Balaam story, the word "maybe" underlines the surety that Balak had the power to defeat the Jews; though the gentile prophet thought he could control Jewish fate through astrology, Balak, as quoted by his messengers, realized that control was out of Balaam's purview: "Come then put a curse upon this people for me since they are too numerous for me; perhaps [*ulai*] I can thus defeat them and drive them out of the land. For I know that he whom you bless is indeed blessed and he whom you curse is cursed" (Num. 22:6).

origin story, we are unsure how history will play out: if a family can survive in Canaan fighting famine and infertility, if a small tribe will become a nation, if a larger tribe in Egypt will return to Canaan, if families broken by deceit can heal, if humans can live up to a covenant with God, and if God can again dwell within a world He once destroyed by floodwaters. Yet, every *ulai*, every pregnant pause of Genesis, is limited to human interaction. While we might find some similarities with the *ulai* in the Book of Jonah, these Genesis "maybes" do not represent theological bewilderments. They are interpersonal questions. But there is another *ulai* in the Bible that speaks to Nineveh's royal "maybe."

There is a tender moment in the opening chapter of Job where *ulai* is used in a way that foreshadows the entire book:

> When a round of feast days was over, Job would send word to them [his children] to sanctify themselves, and, rising early in the morning, he would make burnt offerings, one for each of them; for Job thought, "*Perhaps* [*ulai*] my children have sinned and blasphemed God in their thoughts." This is what Job used to do. (1:5)

Job wanted to preempt punishment in the event that one of his children had sinned in a moment of frivolity or impulse prompted by excessive feasting. But Job's gambit is problematic from our understanding of sacrifices and what they accomplish. One cannot seek expiation for someone else's crime or misdemeanor. A parent may feel partly responsible for the behavior of his or her adult children but cannot repent on their behalf. Repentance must be self-determined. This *ulai*, thoughtful as it was on one level, demonstrated a certain lack of understanding on Job's part of the way that God works. It minimized human autonomy and judgment in favor of God's elasticity and capacity to change without any human intervention. A sacrifice could never accomplish this, which explains why the prophets so often railed against the empty offerings of Israelites seeking God's favor without any of the underlying commitments to change that would have made them effectual in the first place. As we read in Hosea: "For I desire mercy, not sacrifice, and acknowledgment of God rather than burnt offerings" (6:6).

The Unity of Opposites

Sometimes "maybe" is a word we toss into the ether on the very rare and random chance that something totally out of the ordinary will happen. This is the "maybe" of a lottery ticket, the slim and mathematically unlikely chance of something audacious and exceptional taking place. But sometimes "maybe" is a word that helps us create new possibilities and move in new directions, preparing ourselves for a transformation that we can anticipate but cannot guarantee, a more certain uncertainty. This is the "maybe" of Nineveh, a "maybe" that requires change, contrition, and action to create a new type of existence, one anticipated but not guaranteed.

The captain and the king serve as Jonah's foils; their behavior was meant to communicate to Jonah that his was flawed. Moreover, the "maybe" of the captain and the king highlights the possibility of change on behalf of another – in this instance, God – because of their own change. They could not control God. They could only control their own actions, and so were determined to do just that. Once they controlled their actions and moved toward transformation, they created a ground that was fertile for shared change. Jonah, on the other hand, convinced that he knew exactly how God worked and arrogantly implied that they did not, swam or walked away from the possibility of redemption. But his surety was not at all what God wanted. God was more satisfied with a humility that prompted action than a certainty that prompted inaction.

At the close of chapter 1, Jonah's theological struggle was about to meet its climax in the sea. Only there, when he was adrift in the waters, did his certainty come under challenge.

Part Two
Jonah Adrift

Chapter Four
The Strange Fish that Trapped a Strange Man

> But the Lord provided a huge fish to swallow Jonah, and Jonah was inside the fish three days and three nights. Jonah prayed to the Lord his God from the belly of the fish.... The Lord commanded the fish, and it spewed Jonah out upon dry land. (Jonah 2:1–2, 11)

"I have spoken of Jonah, and of the story of him and the whale. – A fit story for ridicule, if it was written to be believed; or of laughter, if it was intended to try what credulity could swallow; for, if it could swallow Jonah and the whale it could swallow anything." Thomas Paine (1737–1809) had a rather unkind assessment of the prophet Jonah and his fairy-tale story in *Common Sense*.[1] What could be more fantastical than a man swallowed by a fish, if not a fish that acts as refuge, sanctuary, and transportation for the reluctant prophet? It is no wonder that the revolutionary Paine, author of *The Age of Reason*, had little patience for a tale of unrestrained imagination as he explicated the foundations of rationality. Common sense leaves no room for a biblical figure so odd in character and behavior. Jonah is a perfect illustration of Paine's assumption that instead of "the recitals of miracles as evidence of any

---

1. Thomas Paine, "Common Sense," *Thomas Paine: Collected Writings*, ed. Eric Foner (New York: Library of America: 1995), 584.

system of religion being true, they ought to be considered symptoms of its being fabulous."[2] It would have been more of a miracle, Paine wrote, had Jonah actually swallowed the whale.[3]

Paine was hardly the only one to trivialize the Book of Jonah because of the strange fish. But classic commentators and the faithful believed they had no choice but to accept as historical fact the plot and details of biblical tales, as Theodor Gaster explains:

> In ages less enlightened than our own, when it was considered blasphemous to see in the stories of the Bible anything but the record of historical fact, commentators and ecclesiastics were often put to considerable pains to "authenticate" our bizarre narrative, and wondrous and ingenious were some of the explanations they propounded. What troubled them especially was that the more common type of whale or shark does not in fact possess a gullet wide enough to swallow a human being whole.[4]

Thus real-world considerations made it difficult to explain away odd details in Jonah's narrative. Among the fantastic explanations Gaster collected to make common sense of the story is that "Great Fish" was the name of the ship that God provided to save Jonah or that there was an image of a fish on its prow. "Alternatively, could not *Great Fish* have been the name of an inn at which Jonah put up when he reached land?"[5]

These writers and thinkers are not trapped by a fish but trapped by their literal understanding of the fish. They fail to see in it the great metaphor that it is. It is the monster of the deep, the fear-inducing tool of self-confrontation. Jonah could have stayed on the surface of the water, flailing for his life; the sea would have also been an apt metaphor for his drowning. Instead, the fish became the terrifying source of his deliverance in the guise of a threatening creature. It represents the in-between, liminal space that trapped Jonah for three days, allowing him

---

2. Ibid., 529.
3. Ibid., 528.
4. Gaster, *Myth, Legend and Custom in the Old Testament*, 655.
5. Ibid.

The Strange Fish that Trapped a Strange Man

to either die in the leviathan or emerge and be reborn. As readers, we must peruse the text with innocence and exist in that space and time with our poor prophet as he contemplates what has just happened to him and what might yet happen.

CONTEXTUALIZING THE GREAT FISH

To contemplate Jonah's great fish is also to situate it within its ancient Near Eastern context.[6] To comprehend this book and its "props," it is critical to understand the kind of idol worship that Jeroboam – king, idol worshipper, and father of the king to whom Jonah ministered – may have favored, which would have been popular at the time of the story. Dagon, a popular Semitic fish-god among the Philistines, was regarded as the head of its pantheon of gods and worshipped along the eastern Mediterranean coast. Dagon is referred to in several places in the Hebrew Bible,[7] and his image has been found in artifacts and ruins in the area, often as part-man and part-fish or a man wearing a fish. In one of the Maccabees' most successful battles they destroyed the temple of Dagon, as recorded in I Maccabees: "But Jonathan set fire on Azotus, and the cities round about it... and the temple of Dagon, with them that were fled into it, he burned with fire" (10:84). Gustave Doré captures this battle in incredible detail in his etching of the scene. Jonathan stands with arm and sword outstretched in the middle of a glut of soldiers, whose shields do not protect them, as another Maccabee hacks away at a lion statue. Doré perhaps did not realize that Dagon was not the strong lion but the less belligerent fish.

Since the region was heavily fished, the mysteries of the sea and its power over the fiscal fate of many in the region would, no doubt, have made Jonah's story far-fetched to modern sensibilities but compelling for those who lived during that time. It is no coincidence that the

---

6. Sam Summers, in *Situations Matter* (New York: Riverhead Books, 2011), argues that one should study the science of situations; they greatly impact behaviors and offer us indicators of how to predict more accurately how others will act and how to navigate and maximize success in encounters. Later commentaries that fail to take into account the likely biblical setting – weather, clothing, manners, expectations, topography, etc. – but instead overlay an ancient story with the vernacular, often miss critical details and meanings in biblical stories.
7. See Judges 16:23–24; I Sam. 5:1–7; I Chr. 10:8–12.

Hebrew for fish is *dag* and the word for grain is *dagan* since Dagon was both the god of human fertility and grain. There was the abiding hope in Dagon's worshippers that both would multiply.

God's sending a fish to save and move the prophet suggests that even such a large and frightening creature as the great fish – one that was worshipped as a manifestation of a pagan god – was nothing more than a tool in the much more powerful armament of the Israelite God. This subtle message takes an unsubtle turn in a biblical story that predates the Book of Jonah and supports this sentiment. In I Samuel, in a most dramatic encounter that pits the two cultures – Israelite and Philistine, God and Dagon – against each other, it is not only war that requires triumph but religion as well:

> When the Philistines captured the Ark of God, they brought it from Eben-ezer to Ashdod. The Philistines took the Ark of God and brought it into the temple of Dagon and they set it up beside Dagon. Early the next day, the Ashdodites found Dagon lying face down on the ground in front of the Ark of the Lord. They picked Dagon up and put him back in his place; but early the next morning, Dagon was again lying prone on the ground in front of the Ark of the Lord. The head and both hands of Dagon were cut off, lying on the threshold; only Dagon's trunk was left intact. That is why, to this day, the priests of Dagon and all who enter the temple of Dagon do not tread on the threshold of Dagon in Ashdod. (5:1–5)

While the Book of Jonah illustrates the fish's powerlessness to exert its autonomy, this narrative demonstrates that in an explicit face-off between Dagon and God, there was no contest. If the Philistines thought that their god fell accidentally, by the passage's end, there was no question about God's capacity to incapacitate. The Philistines, terrified of this presence in their midst, gave back the Ark of the Lord with haste.

Rashi observes that Dagon was "a statue made in the image of a fish."[8] Radak offers a more detailed description based on a midrash; Dagon "from his navel below was the image of a fish and was, therefore,

---

8. Rashi to I Sam. 5:2.

called 'Dagon,' and from his navel upward he had the shape of a man," which explains how his hands could be severed in this text.[9] Fish, of course, do not have hands. Therefore, Radak concludes, all that remained of this god after the Israelite God amputated his arms and decapitated him was the shape of a fish: a powerless creature that travels indistinguishably in schools and is tossed aimlessly by the sea.[10]

There is also a Greek myth from the days of antiquity that has parallels to our story. Heracles, son of Zeus and Alcmene, who was known as Hercules in Rome, was a paragon of strength. He fought beasts of great might. In one caper, he saved the Trojan princess Hesione. Apollo and Poseidon were angry at Hesione's father, King Leomeden of Troy, and threatened to send a sea monster to devour the city. An oracle promised the king he would save the city if Leomeden would give the sea monster his daughter Hesione as an offering. The king tied his daughter to rocks at the shore's edge to ready her as a gift; when Heracles returned from a sea journey, he saw Hesione and courageously saved her for a promising reward. In some versions of this story, Heracles hacked at the sea monster for three days, the time it took him to kill the beast. Sadly, the king did not come through with Heracles' reward.

This story, which floated in the ancient world of sea tales, has some of the mythical elements of Jonah and the three-day time period – but Jonah's fish reverses this story. Jonah's fish is an object of salvation that transports him to safety in three days. Heracles' fish is a destroyer that took three days to be destroyed itself. There the parallels end.

In a similar story, Heracles spotted a group of men ready to offer a young maiden, Deianeira, as a sacrifice to a water god. Heracles saved her, and then, on a later adventure as the two journeyed to Troy, a mystery figure summoned a sea serpent to swallow them both. The fish saved them,

---

9. See Radak to I Sam. 5:4; *Midrash Shmuel* 11:5.
10. We find a parallel story that smacks of revenge in I Chronicles: "The next day the Philistines came to strip the slain, and they found Saul and his sons lying on Mount Gilboa. They stripped him and carried off his head and his armor and sent them throughout the land of the Philistines to spread the news to their idols and among the people. They placed his armor in the temple of their god, and they impaled his head in the temple of Dagon" (10:8–10).

but Heracles killed the fish from its inside.[11] Again, this water tale involves violence, specifically aggression toward an animal that was an instrument of deliverance. Jonah never thanked the fish that swam him back to safety, perhaps because he was preparing himself for an even greater danger once out of the fish's secure protection. There is nothing like layers of blubber to separate a prophet from the perils of a task to which he never really acquiesced – one which he arguably never truly completed.

THE PARADOX OF JONAH'S FISH

One modern scholar has observed that Jonah's fish is only mentioned in the text three times, yet it dominates the thinking of those who are quick to dismiss one of the most psychologically[12] and theologically charged books in the Bible.[13] The fish is hardly the main character. It plays a minor role – the supporting actor, if you will, alongside all of the other conduits of nature that God sent to Jonah to reform him and to force self-confrontation. Those who pay too much attention to the

---

11. Bickerman refers readers to the Greek poet Arion (625 BCE) who jumped into the ocean to escape from seamen; a dolphin was said to carry him back to land. See *Four Strange Books of the Bible*, 11. One can imagine many such tales and fantasies surfaced in maritime communities so that the blend of fact and fiction blurred and embellishments to reality flourished.
12. This book does not deal with psychological readings of Jonah per se. Interested readers can consult Bruno Bettelheim, *The Uses of Enchantment* (New York: Knopf, 1976); Hyman Fingert's strange interpretation in "The Psychoanalytical Study of the Minor Prophet Jonah," *The Psychoanalytic Review* 41 (1954): 55–65; Joseph More, "The Prophet Jonah: The Story of an Intrapsychic Process," *American Imago* 27 (1970): 3–11; and Erich Fromm, *The Forgotten Language* (New York: Grove Press, 1937), 22.
13. See Terrence E. Fretheim, *The Message of Jonah: A Theological Commentary* (Eugene, OR: Wipf and Stock Publishers, 2000), 13. Fretheim argues that too much attention has been focused on the fish by those who have only a fleeting understanding of the deeper meaning of the story: "The miracle of the fish plays only a relatively minor role in the story." Those who do overemphasize this most unusual aspect of Jonah's narrative, betraying "minimal acquaintance with the book as a whole, shift attention from the more significant aspects of the book and the question of its message then and now." The "Jonah syndrome," as defined by Lacocque and Lacocque, designates "distorted human behavior prompted by cowardice before life, refusal to make a commitment, fear of success, narcissism, parochialism, greed, envy" (see *The Jonah Complex*, xv).

fish's presence often ignore the significance of the story in an attempt to disprove its historicity.

Humans catch fish. Sometimes they throw them back when fishing is practiced for sport. When fishing for food, the stakes are different for the fish. Jonah's case inverts the paradigm, creating a raucous upside-down sense of the food chain; the fish caught the man and, instead of killing him, protected him, delivered him safely to his mission, and deposited him on the shores of Nineveh. This feat of transportation made rejecting the mission or revoking Jonah's new pledge of commitment much harder to do. It also must have provoked introspection. If a fish that could have killed him instantly instead gave him a reprieve, then the oddity of it all must have made him realize that God did not seek his death for running away – a natural conclusion for rebellion and for calming of a storm. God desired that the prophet live.

The fish accomplished something far greater than mere protection. In its jaws, Jonah not only did not die, he finally repented. What died was Jonah's tenacious resistance to God's will. It could only disappear when that which could have killed him gave him life. The fish was not an accidental prop in this story but an intentional vehicle for transformation. Heid E. Erdrich, in "Origin of a Poem," takes us into the watery imagery that describes the potency of a fishing metaphor, that life soon gives way to death. But in our story death gives birth to life:

> We fish our own waters
> green and layered
> weedy and warm –
> Nothing rises.
> No ripples, but we wait.
> All we want is the tug –
> something deep, alive, on the line.[14]

The paradox of wanting the tug on the line, the sign of life that soon would be for naught, is not lost on the reader. Nothing happens on the surface of

---

14. Heid E. Erdrich, "Origen of Poem," *Fishing for Myth* (Minneapolis: New Rivers Press, 1997), 14.

the water, but the potential for a surprise pull of life deep under the surface offers an unusual sense of hope for the person and not for the fish – the one tugging, not the one tugged. In Jonah's case, life is finally found deep under the water, when he had already reached the sand bars at the sea floor. New research demonstrates that the Cuvier beaked whale can dive up to ten thousand feet (three thousand meters) under the sea, far deeper than any other mammal.[15] Jonah's tug of life was not on the surface where humans can live but far below where there are no signs of human life.

"But the Lord provided a huge fish to swallow Jonah" (Jonah 2:1). Radak interprets the word *vayeman* (provided) to mean "to prepare" or "to invite." M-N-H is an act of intention or appointment.[16] Radak continues in his explication – thus far, no different from other medieval commentators – and mentions the famous statement credited to R. Tarfon from *Pirkei DeRabbi Eliezer*, namely, that this fish was tasked to swallow Jonah from the very first six days of Creation:

> R. Tarfon commented: The fish that swallowed Jonah had been assigned this task since the six days of Creation, as it is said, "The Lord provided a huge fish to swallow Jonah." Jonah entered its mouth the way a man enters a large synagogue. He stood there, and the eyes of the fish shone down upon him like two skylights.[17]

More than intention, this verb communicates predeterminism. Jonah entered the fish's mouth, the aggadic passage states, just as a man enters the great synagogue, and he stood. The two eyes of the fish were like windows of glass giving light to Jonah. Not only was this fish sent to save Jonah from the immediacy of death, it was to serve as a place of awe and

---

15. See Jane J. Lee, "Elusive Whales Set New Record for Depth and Length of Dives among Mammals," http://news.nationalgeographic.com/news/2014/03/140326-cuvier-beaked-whale-record-dive-depth-ocean-animal-science.
16. This is similar to the usage in Daniel 1:10: "The chief officer said to Daniel, 'I fear that my lord the king, who allotted (*mina*) food and drink to you, will notice that you look out of sorts.'"
17. See the translation of *Pirkei DeRabbi Eliezer* in David Stern and Mark Jay Mirsky, "Jonah and the Sailors from *Pirkei de-Rabbi Eliezer*," *Rabbinic Fantasies: Imaginative Narratives from Classical Hebrew Literature* (New Haven: Yale University Press, 1998), 64.

reverence, according to this fanciful rabbinic view, a place where Jonah had light in the blackness of the sea, signaling that all was not lost and gone. The miracle of the fish's arrival is imbricated with the miracle of the fish's very design so that Jonah would know instantly that this fish was sent to him by God, not as punishment but as an act of love.

Contemporary artist Simon Carr, in his 2005 oil painting "Jonah and the Whale," captures a very different emotion than does R. Tarfon. In his painting, the fish's mouth is outsized compared to its body. Its eyes are luminescent and bulging. Half the prophet's body flails outside the fish's gaping mouth, showing the prophet in a hopeless tussle with a force far greater than himself. In the dark background of multiple shades of blue and black, we see the silhouette of the ship Jonah left behind. Safety appears only in the distance, a distance too great for Jonah to traverse, stuck as he is in the mammoth jaws of this sea monster. The large size of the canvas (sixty-four by sixty-four inches) and Carr's compositional choice to cut a diagonal moving from the bottom right to the top left has the effect of the fish jumping out and snapping the prophet in its mouth, much the way we expect it might in nature. This is no synagogue with its welcoming doors and slivers of light, a place where Jonah can sit in quiet repose and contemplate events. This is the food chain, natural, elemental, and absolutely brutal. Not until Jonah sinks into the belly of the fish will it be evident that this fish was sent to save him. At first glance, Jonah is nothing more than lunch.

But this view is not accurate to the story or at least to the way in which the story continues. Classical medieval commentators argue about how to view the fish's behavior and Jonah's perception of it. Was Jonah's prayer because the fish saved him from death or was his prayer uttered because the fish spat him out? In other words, commentators want to know if the fish was salvation or terror to the prophet. Jonah's prayer in this later view was an expression of passionate thanksgiving that he was saved from the leviathan and not that he was saved from the sea. This argument might seem tendentious, but in actual fact, it is quite profound. By the end of chapter 1, it appears that Jonah's death wish has been granted. Tossed into the sea by unwilling sailors, he expressed no desire to live. "Pick me up and throw me into the sea...and it will become calm. I know that it is my fault that this great storm has come upon you"

(v. 12). Jonah was so passive he did not even take his own life. He asked others to do it for him, failing to take initiative to accomplish the one thing he repeatedly desired, to leave his task by leaving the world. And yet he said this with great certainty, the certainty mentioned earlier that characterizes Jonah's speech and acts generally.

GOD'S MESSENGERS

The verb M-N-H discussed several pages ago repeats itself to show God's use of nature as a conduit for divine will. *Veyeman* means that God "sent" or "provided." There is no coincidence here in the way natural forces appear. All is intentional. All is for one purpose: Jonah's repentance.

In chapter 2, the *dag* served as God's agent. It was commanded to swallow and commanded to expel the prophet: "The Lord *provided* a huge fish to swallow Jonah" (v. 1); "The Lord *commanded* the fish, and it spewed Jonah out upon dry land" (v. 11).

In chapter 4, the *kikayon*, "a miraculous gourd," grew overnight and died overnight – ostensibly as a lesson in compassion: "The Lord God *provided* a ricinus plant, which grew up over Jonah, to provide shade for his head and save him from discomfort" (v. 6). Suddenly God sent a "small worm" to destroy the gourd tree He had created. "But the next day at dawn God *provided* a worm, which attacked the plant so that it withered" (v. 7).

God also sent a storm, a sultry east wind, and a burning sun, harnessing animal and plant life and climate forces to shape and change Jonah's destiny. The term *vayeman* is used four times; other terms with similar meanings include *hetiel*, "to cast" or "to send," and *vayomer*, "to speak," sometimes translated as the infinitive "to command." The three verbs in conjunction communicate God's paternal interest in the reformation project of the wayward prophet. But it is not only the verbs that matter theologically. It is the subject of the verbs and the way that each powerful force is guided and manipulated willingly by God. This is also true for the unnamed human beings in the story who responded to God's call. The entire unquestioning universe surrounding Jonah revolved around a divine centrifugal force without oppositional forces pushing back. In this picture, only Jonah stands in opposition. God too sent him on a mission just like He sent every other thing mentioned in the book, yet Jonah acted independently of these forces, exercising the free will to disobey that was imprinted in the Garden of Eden long, long before him.

Just as in chapter 1 God *hetiel*, "sent," a great storm, so, too, did the sailors *vayatilu*, "cast," their utensils overboard when the storm hit (1:5). Ibn Ezra adds a specific purpose in God sending the storm: it was necessary to push the ship beyond a comfortable distance to return easily to dry land in the event of danger, a detail confirmed several verses later that the sailors "rowed hard to regain the shore, but they could not, for the sea was growing more and more stormy about them" (1:13). The *Metzudat Tzion* (Rabbi David Altschuler, 1687–1769) on 1:5 defines *vayatilu* as "hurl," using as a cross-reference the appearance of the verb in the Book of Jeremiah: "Therefore, I will hurl you out of this land to a land that neither you nor your fathers have known" (16:13). The proximity of these two uses of the same verb gives us a fresh perspective on the sailors who, like God, cast objects away to achieve a particular end – in this case their urgent salvation. In an act of *imitatio Dei*, human beings can also use their own agency to shape their circumstances, something that Jonah failed to understand in the first chapter, when he slept through a situation that demanded his active resistance. In other words, he failed to submit to God's will the way that the rest of the animate and inanimate characters that populate the book did; he also failed to act in ways that would have demonstrated a principled stand against God, in the shadow of biblical figures like Abraham and Moses.

Pirkei DeRabbi Eliezer, in yet another surprising midrashic twist, presents the fish expressing gratitude to Jonah for saving him. The fish was apparently destined in the food chain for the jaws of the leviathan when God assigned it to swallow Jonah, sparing its life. Jonah, in the midrash, then begins an intriguing conversation with the fish that explains why Jonah prayed from the fish's belly. The answer requires patience as we delve into the convoluted rivulets commonly found in midrash: "Jonah then said to the fish, 'See! I have saved you from the mouth of Leviathan. Now show me everything in the depths of the ocean.'"[18]

Here, instead of expressing gratitude, Jonah bargained with the fish for reciprocity, as if to say: I saved you; now you owe me. In actuality,

---

18. Ibid., 64–65.

this is hardly reciprocity. It was already a quid pro quo exchange, since each saved the other in the midrashic view. And the midrash continues:

> The fish showed him the great river bearing the waters of Oceanus, as it is said, "The deep engulfed me" (Jonah 2:6). Then it showed him the Reed Sea that the Israelites had crossed, as it is said, "Weeds twined around my head" (v. 6). It showed him the places where the sea breaks, from which the waves depart, as it is said, "All Your breakers and billows swept over me" (v. 4); and the pillars of the earth and its foundations, as it is said, "The bars of the earth closed upon me forever" (v. 7); and Gehenna, as it is said, "You brought my life up from the pit, O Lord my God" (ibid.); and the nethermost underworld, Sheol, as it is said, "From the belly of Sheol I cried out, and You heard my voice" (v. 3). The fish showed Jonah the base of God's Temple, as it is said, "I sank to the base of the mountains" (v. 7) – from this verse we can deduce that Jerusalem is built upon seven mountains. And finally, the fish brought Jonah to the foundation stone of the world, set in the depths beneath the Temple of God, the place above which the sons of Korah stand and pray. "Jonah," the fish said, "you are now standing directly beneath God's Temple. Pray, and your prayers will be answered." Jonah responded, "Wait here, right where you are, while I pray."[19]

The fish, in this midrash, was more than savior to Jonah. It served – almost as a precursor to Dante's underworld travels – as Jonah's undersea tour guide, pointing out stops that would be critical to Jonah's eventual spiritual ascent. For those who read Jonah's prayer and wonder why it happened or why Jonah mentioned Jerusalem, this midrash explains all. Each verse of the prayer corresponds to a place in the water that Jonah traveled to inside the fish. The fish wanted Jonah to pray so it took him to Jerusalem. The base of the mountains mentioned in the prayer is naught but the mountains of Jerusalem, the city of God, the city of prayer. Korah's sons may be mentioned because their father was a Levite with priestly ambitions and also

---

19. Ibid.

because the rebellion of Korah was redeemed by the service of the sons. But it was not enough to take Jonah to the place of prayer. The fish had to explicitly command Jonah to pray by, in effect, dropping him off at the place most likely for God to hear Jonah's prayers. And, like a waiting taxi, the fish was told by the prophet to stay near him, ready to take Jonah in the direction of his mission when his prayer and his healing had been effectuated. "Jonah," the midrash continues, "was not answered until out of his mouth came this promise, 'What I have vowed I will perform'" (Jonah 2:10). At that point, God signaled to the fish to deliver the prophet to dry land. The fish's arduous work was complete. The fish mentored Jonah, spoke to Jonah, and served, in the rabbinic imagination, as Jonah's complex navigational system.

This reading does not require a particularly vivid imagination as there is precedent in the Hebrew Bible itself for talking animals; these usually know the way forward for their masters better than the masters do themselves. Animals appear elsewhere in the Hebrew Bible as agents of God's will. The most renowned animal in the Pentateuch to serve this purpose was Balaam's donkey, the subject of much textual and artistic curiosity. When God told Balaam not to curse the Israelites at King Balak's demand, he paid no heed:

> He was riding on his donkey with his two servants alongside when the donkey caught sight of the angel of the Lord standing in the way with a sword drawn in his hand. The donkey swerved from the road and went into the fields and Balaam beat the donkey to turn her back onto the road. The angel of the Lord then stationed himself in a lane between the vineyards, with a fence on either side. The donkey, seeing the angel of the Lord, pressed herself against the wall and squeezed Balaam's foot against the wall, so he beat her again. Once more the angel of the Lord moved forward and stationed himself on a spot so narrow that there was no room to swerve right or left. (Num. 22:22–26)

Up until that point the donkey was, unsurprisingly, stubborn under Balaam's harsh direction but had no power to fight divine will. The donkey was able to see the angel that Balaam was unable to see and could not pass by the sworded figure who actively obstructed their path. Finally, the poor donkey sought refuge under her merciless master:

> When the donkey now saw the angel of the Lord, she lay down under Balaam; and Balaam was furious and beat the donkey with his stick. Then the Lord opened the donkey's mouth, and she said to Balaam, "What have I done to you that you have beaten me these three times?" Balaam said to the donkey, "You have made a mockery out of me! If I had a sword with me, I'd kill you." The donkey said to Balaam, "Look, I am the donkey that you have been riding on all along until this day! Have I been in the habit of doing this to you?" And he answered, "No." Then the Lord uncovered Balaam's eyes. (23:22–31)

The story then takes a very strange turn. The donkey spoke, something that does not happen in any of the other animal stories. More than speaking, the donkey talked back to its master – again breaking convention. And the donkey did not say what we, the readers, expect it to say. It did not tell Balaam that it was unable to move because there was an angel blocking the narrow path. Instead it made an argument of mercy more than once. It questioned Balaam's actions, although it was not abnormal for a rider to whip its obstinate charge. Balaam responded with even greater cruelty. For not following his instruction, the donkey should have been killed.

What stings is the argument of fidelity that the donkey threw Balaam's way. She had been a loyal animal, steadfast in her service, thus any diversion from her fidelity should have been excused. Balaam responded that she had indeed not been an obstreperous animal. Then the dialogue ended. Balaam's eyes were opened, and he was able to see the total picture, a context he lacked before but not one he sought, in his arrogance. There was no apology from master to animal, no moment of tenderness when he realized his mistake, even after the angel pointed out Balaam's violence toward the animal.

Balaam's anger flew against one of the created purposes of animals. The relationship of humans to animals is established in the first few chapters of Genesis: "Let us make man in Our image, after Our likeness. They shall rule the fish of the sea, the birds of the sky, the cattle, the whole earth, and all the creeping things that creep on the earth" (1:26). This is a role of dominance, different from the portrait offered in the next chapter of Genesis. There is a distinct move from service to companionship as the narrative continues:

> The Lord God said: "It is not good for man to be alone, I will make a fitting helper for him." And the Lord God formed out of the earth all the wild beasts and all the birds of the sky, and brought them to the man to see what he would call them; and whatever the man called each living creature, that would be its name. And the man gave names to all the cattle and to the birds of the sky and to all the wild beasts but for Adam no fitting helper was found. (2:18–20)

When God, rather than Adam, observed that man was lonely, the first solution pursued was to identify a partner from the animal kingdom. In naming the animals, Adam realized that the essence of each creature was not in harmony with his own. He made an anatomical observation when the woman was finally created: "This one at last is bone of my bones and flesh of my flesh" (v. 23). The anatomic similarity that drew Adam and Eve together displaced the animal as partner, but the residual impact of the text remains. Animals are not only for human service. They are also for companionship because they are loyal, steadfast, and, unlike humans, unable to dissemble.

The Balaam plot continues. The interaction between man and beast ends, leaving the reader unsatisfied. An obvious reading pointed out by ancient and modern commentators alike is that the donkey ironically saw what the seer could not see, and that the animal was a foil for the human's inadequacies. But this answer does not explain the dialogue between the two and why, at that moment, God opened Balaam's eyes. Balaam, like Jonah, was a prophet. He was supposed to see for a living. Seeing can become a means of invoking mercy. When we open our eyes, it often leads to opening our hearts. Closed eyes cannot take in pain. Balaam looked straight ahead at his task, bullying his way to its service while ignoring the one that served him, the one suffering at his hand. Later, when Balaam waxed lyrical on a hilltop overlooking Israelite tents, he quipped of himself, "Who beholds visions from the Almighty, prostrate but with eyes unveiled" (Num. 2:4) – even though his eyes were veiled at the story's beginning. God's eyes, however, are not like this, as we read in I Samuel: "God sees not as man sees, for man looks at the outward appearance, but the Lord looks at the heart" (16:7). Job too reminds us that God sees all: "For His eyes are upon the ways of a man, and He sees all his steps" (Job 34:21).

The central animals serving two prophets had an innocence and a fealty that shows up the inadequacies of those they serve. God merely had to command the great fish, and it rushed to Jonah's service. But a similar command met its human objection in Jonah, a prophet constrained by justice who lacked the mercy that is a requisite of the truly great prophet. The dichotomy reminds us of a talmudic teaching that sums up our story:

> It was taught: R. Shimon b. Elazar says: In all my days, I have not seen a deer drying figs, a lion carrying burdens or a fox as a shopkeeper, yet they are sustained without trouble. No, they were created only to serve me, and I was created to serve my Maker. Now if these, who were created only to serve me are sustained without trouble, how much more so should I – who was created to serve my Maker – be sustained without trouble? But it is because I have acted with evil and destroyed my livelihood, as it is stated: "Your iniquities have turned away...these things and your sins have withheld the good from you" (Jer. 5:25). (Kiddushin 82b)

Humans cause their own misfortune. Animals serve their masters "without trouble." R. Shimon b. Elazar ponders whether or not humans could do the same.

STABILITY INSIDE THE SEA

In the midrashic tradition, the fish was both a sanctuary and a conveyer for Jonah. In the text, it appears to be merely a conduit. And yet, it created for Jonah a place of dry land within the sea, emblematic of stability in an inherently unstable place. When Jonah summed up his identity in the curious phrase: "I am a Hebrew...I worship the Lord, the God of heaven, who made both sea and dry land" (Jonah 1:9), he put together these two sharp natural contrasts in describing God. This same God had created a fish to swallow Jonah and then, after Jonah prayed and reconciled himself with his mission, "it spewed Jonah out upon dry land" (2:11). From dry land to dry land, the fish provided the closest experience to dry land that Jonah could have experienced in the midst of the sea.

This dialectic combination of sea and dry land can be traced all the way back to Genesis 1: "God said, 'Let the water below the sky be gathered into one area, that the dry land may appear.' And it was so. God called the dry land earth, and the gathering of the waters, He called seas. And God saw that it was good" (v. 9). Sea and dry land, once a singular unit, were separated in the creation of two distinct earthly topographies. Later, Noah's raven, the one he sent out on a search expedition to know if he could release his family and the animals he stewarded, "went to and fro until the waters had dried up from the land" (8:6). But the process of the earth drying took much time: "The waters began to dry from the earth; and when Noah removed the covering of the ark, he saw that the surface of the ground was drying. And in the second month, on the twenty-seventh of the month, the earth was dry" (8:13–14). It was then that God told Noah it was time to leave the ark. Earth and water had to be separated and distinct yet again for a new and improved universe to emerge.[20]

Both the ark and the fish are images of dry land within water. They were containers, much like Moses' basket on the Nile, that served as temporary modes of protection against the dangers of the sea. They were, metaphorically speaking, the stable dry land amidst the unstable sea. God, Jonah's God, is the God of both dry land and the sea. He too is a place (*Makom*) of stability in a world of instability, a spiritual anchor in chaos. Redemption is predicated on the capacity to make oneself temporarily unstable for the sake of greater future stability.

This colludes with a repeated biblical expression around redemption that appears several times in Exodus 14 and 15 in the sea-splitting narrative and its aftermath; "the sea on dry ground" shows both the miracle of how a wet place can be dry and how waters which can be

---

20. The ideas in the next several paragraphs have been excerpted and developed from a personal "Weekly Jewish Wisdom" blog post called "A Stable Instability," April 28, 2016 (http://www.ericabrown.com/new-blog-1/2016/4/28/stable-instability).

destructive can also be redemptive. This expression is chanted with a different musical notation that alerts us to pay attention and be swept away musically, much the way our ancestors were in the heady moment of a final act of freedom:

- "Then Moses held out his arm over the sea and the Lord drove back the sea with a strong east wind all that night and *the sea turned into dry ground*" (Ex. 14:21).
- "The waters were split, and the Israelites went into *the sea on dry ground*, the waters forming a wall for them on their right and on their left" (14:22).
- "The Israelites marched through *the sea on dry ground*, the waters forming a wall for them on their right and on their left" (14:29).
- "For the horses of Pharaoh, with his chariots and horsemen, went into the sea; and the Lord turned back on them the waters of the sea, but the Israelites marched *on dry ground in the midst of the sea*" (15:19).

Many biblical books later, when the Israelites crossed the Jordan rather than the Reed Sea, we find a repeated image of dry land in the midst of the sea. God told Joshua to command the priests transporting twelve stones representing the tribes across the Jordan to come out of the water, after the Israelites had already crossed: "The feet of the priests stepped onto the dry ground and the waters of the Jordan resumed their course, flowing over its entire bed as before" (Josh. 4:18).

This expression can simply highlight the miraculous nature of the event – the astonishing fact that the nation could go through water on dry land, a contradiction not unlike other plagues that had opposing natural forces in combination, like the hail that contained fire. This would surely augment the capacity for a miracle within each miracle. Yet in the repetition of this almost incomprehensible refrain – *the sea on dry ground* – we are aware not only of the wonder at the miracle but the risk it took to make the miracle happen, the invitation to instability where both strength and vulnerability had to exist in exquisite balance. The American martial arts expert and actor Bruce Lee once said, "If you want to learn to swim, jump in the water. On dry land, no frame of mind is ever going to help you."

The Strange Fish that Trapped a Strange Man

Jonah, suspended for days within a fish, experienced instability, a state that enhanced his vulnerability while at the same time creating the proper conditions for commitment, an act of stability. But such a precarious and delicate balance was to be very hard to maintain when the fish spat him out on dry land.

Unquestionably, the great, strange fish played a remarkable role in the life of the reluctant prophet, so unusual that it is one of only two creatures in the Hebrew Bible with which God communicated. A midrash states that God spoke to animals in only two places – in Genesis God spoke to the snake and in Jonah God spoke to the fish.[21] The snake was punished for disobedience. If the fish was ever rewarded for obedience, we will never know. The fish worked hard to put the prophet on track. But outside of being a remarkable conveyance, it could not do the prophet's inner work. For this, the prophet needed time. With three days and nights in the fish's belly, he could strategize about who he wanted to be when he left its monstrous innards.

---

21. Genesis Rabba 20:3.

Chapter Five

The Liminality of Three Days and Three Nights

> But the Lord provided a huge fish to swallow Jonah, and Jonah was inside the fish three days and three nights. (Jonah 2:1)

> Nineveh was an enormously large city, a three days' walk across. Jonah began by going a day's journey into the city, proclaiming, "Forty days more and Nineveh will be overturned." (3:3–4)

There are two three-day periods mentioned in Jonah: the three days and nights Jonah spent in the belly of the fish and the three days' journey to traverse the city of Nineveh. The repetition of this time frame in such a short biblical book demands that we pay attention to the book's pacing, which seems fast and momentous. Three days seems to signal a period of anticipation and preparation for radical transformation. We as readers will never know if Jonah's change of heart was a true and lasting change. The same holds true for the people of Nineveh. When such serious change happens within such a short framework of time, it is hard to believe that it will be authentic and enduring. We know what happened to the Ninevites in three days, but what happened to Jonah in the belly of the fish?

There are so many appearances of threes in the Hebrew Bible that they are, ironically, hard to count: Noah rebuilds the world with his three sons (Gen. 9); there are three patriarchs in Genesis; three men announce to Abraham that his wife will bear a son (chap. 18); Moses is hidden for three months before his mother sets him out on the Nile in a basket (Ex. 2); holiness is mentioned by seraphim or angels three times in Isaiah (6:3). The threes in the Book of Jonah involve time, rather than objects or persons – most similar then to the Moses story. Closer to Jonah's experience, the earth was separated from the waters on the third day of Creation: "God said, 'Let the water below the sky be gathered into one area, that the dry land may appear.' And it was so. God called the dry land Earth, and the gathering of waters He called Seas" (Gen. 1:9). Water, the very water that Jonah used to plot an escape, was created on the third day of Creation.

But why three days? As it happens, "Three Days Grace" is also the name of a Canadian rock band formed in Ontario in 1997. Its lead singer, Adam Gontier, explains the name this way: "The name came from when we had day jobs. Brad (the band's bassist) was going to be an accountant, and he'd heard the term 'three days grace period' to pay off a debt."[1] Gontier also suggests that the name offers a sense of urgency. Could someone change something in their life if they had only three days to do so? Good question. Ask Jonah.

Jonah was in a fish for three days and nights before he prayed to God. This chronology of events is established as we open chapter 2. From the moment the prophet's body hit the waves, his story took a remarkable twist involving a fantastical sea creature serving as his new sanctuary. There for a few days, Jonah finally found the strength, courage, and audacity to pray. The act of prayer in this place and in these strange circumstances was not simple. Turning toward God when you have turned away from Him in such an extreme fashion demands a depth of humility and contrition. If we render the verb form used here, *vayitpallel*, as a reflexive way of saying that Jonah "judged himself" through his words to God, we understand that we have entered the most transformative and private moment of a reluctant prophet.

Radak takes a different approach. It was a great miracle, he says, that Jonah was able to survive three days and nights in the stomach of a

---

1. Michael Montes, "Interview with Adam Gontier of Three Days Grace," *Florida Entertainment Scene*, 2004.

The Liminality of Three Days and Three Nights

fish; it was also miraculous that despite his location, he did not faint but "was able to stand in a state of knowledge and consciousness and pray."[2]

The text's emphasis on days *and* nights tells us that these were long stretches of time, inviting us to use our imaginations in a particularly rich way. One conjures images of a man distraught, trapped in the darkness of fish gut, breathing in the suffocating maritime smells one might find in the intestines of a leviathan. In children's books on Jonah, the prophet is sometimes pictured sitting crouched, holding his knees to his chest, encircled by the fish's ribs, much like a caged animal. Artist Annie Lucas, who often uses needlework and paint in her depictions of Bible stories, drew a primitive rendering of Jonah inside the fish across the wall of her Alabama house when she had a dream about it. Imagine a large black whale on top of the water and an arched cutout of a window on the side of the mammal displaying a white-haired prophet, as if riding on a bus. In American artist Chris White's illustration, Jonah sits at a desk floating on a wooden platform inside the fish's gut. He holds a quill pen and is busy at work, hardly aware of where he has landed. A door on the platform has a bell for guests to ring and a laundry line is drawn, with some of Jonah's clothes ironically drying even as his raft floats in the water inside the fish. There is a small bed, a wood stove, and dim lighting. The prophet gets an upgrade from contemporary artist Fred Jinkins in his "Jonah in His Whale Home." In a comic bubble we see Jonah leaning back in a chair watching television while his wife, in a skimpy outfit, offers him refreshments. A TV antenna is attached to the fish's surface and a sign that says "Jonah" sits between the fish's eyes. Lying on the floor next to Jonah is his dog and above the television, another sign says "Home Sweet Home," as if nothing could be more natural than this scene of domestic bliss – except for the curious detail that this takes place inside a whale. In perhaps the strangest image of an already bizarre story, British artist Fred Aris has Jonah stepping out of the fish's gaping jaws in a black pinstripe suit with cane and briefcase in hand, doffing his bowler hat in the direction of the whale, as if the fish has deposited the prophet on Wall Street, whence he walks to his office to begin the day's business. In this oil

---

2. Radak to Jonah 2:2, 8.

painting, the fish basically serves as Jonah's driver for three days and nights, until such a time when Jonah can finally reconcile himself to the job he was given earlier.

JONAH IN THE FISH: THE TEXT'S DESCRIPTION

Inside a fish, how could one think, let alone pray? And yet the text is very specific. Jonah did not pray until the three-day period had ended. He did not scream out as he was being swallowed or complain on day one of mistreatment. Later, when the prophet cried out because of a cold wind and a hot sun, his complaints seem to us trivial next to what he did not complain about: being in the fish. Day and night and again and again, he endured this trial without a word.

One wonders what Jonah was waiting for or why these specific events led him to introspection and expression. Three days is a long time and not a long time, interminable if you are unsure when you will be released – the blink of an eye when looked back upon retrospectively as a transformative moment in the course of a lifetime. In this short book, three days is a detail long on meaning because these three days created the necessary conditions for repentance and readiness. And yet, outside of Radak making a passing reference to this miracle, not one classic medieval commentator uses this expression as a linguistic opening or platform upon which to interpret, as if the duration of Jonah's stay in the fish had little significance. What earlier exegetes notice gets the attention of later exegetes, spurring powerful conversations across time and countries. But an equally fascinating question is what earlier interpreters neglect and why. Perhaps in this case, the time frame was not sufficiently of note to exegetes because it is a detail that appears as a background piece of information for the much more dramatic tale at the foreground. Jonah was alive. He prayed. He tried to reconcile himself to God and to his calling. That surely was enough. The details are only a distraction.

They are a distraction unless you are Erich Auerbach or any other student of literary readings of the Hebrew Bible who appreciates that details like time, interiors, currency, or clothing are only referenced in the Hebrew Bible if they contribute and support the fundamental meaning of the story. As Auerbach elegantly describes it:

The Liminality of Three Days and Three Nights

> The externalization of only so much of the phenomena as is necessary for the purpose of the narrative, all else left in obscurity; the decisive points of the narrative alone are emphasized, what lies between is nonexistent; time and place are undefined and call for interpretation; thoughts and feeling remain unexpressed, are only suggested by the silence and the fragmentary speeches; the whole, permeated with the most unrelieved suspense and directed toward a single goal (and to that extent far more of a unity), remains mysterious and "fraught with background."[3]

Auerbach, in his seminal essay, compares the loquaciousness of detail in *The Odyssey* and Homeric literature generally to the emotional starkness and neglect of details in the Binding of Isaac in Genesis 22 (which also involves a three-day journey to the mount). The Bible's narrative style spotlights the central drama, stripping the story of the taste and texture, the sensory pleasures of reading. This leaves a great deal open to interpretive exploration. Thus midrashim and commentators are eager to fill in the gaps and ellipses created by these absences. And yet the sparseness of the primary text remains. All else for Auerbach is background. This, he contends, is different from the Greek dramatic style which places great emphasis on a story's foreground – down to the scar on Odysseus' foot.

Homing in on the three-day period, Auerbach takes us into the tension of Abraham's unknowing for three days where he was to offer up his son as a sacrifice; the tension is achieved in large part by the story's many mysteries:

> Thus the journey is like a silent progress through the indeterminate and the contingent, a holding of the breath, a process which has no present, which is inserted, like a blank duration, between what has passed and what lies ahead, and which yet is measured: three days! Three such days positively demand the symbolic interpretation which they later received. They began "early in the morning." But at what time on the third day did Abraham lift up

---

3. Erich Auerbach, *Mimesis: The Representation of Reality in Western Literature*, trans. Willard R. Trask (Princeton: Princeton University Press, 2013), 9.

his eyes and see his goal? The text says nothing on the subject. Obviously not "late in the evening," for it seems that there was still time enough to climb the mountain and make the sacrifice. So "early in the morning" is given, not as an indication of time, but for the sake of its ethical significance; it is intended to express the resolution, the promptness, the punctual obedience of the sorely tried Abraham. Bitter to him is the early morning in which he saddles his ass, calls his serving-men and his son Isaac, and sets out; but he obeys, he walks on until the third day, then lifts up his eyes and sees the place.[4]

By not overstating detail, the text invites us to enter the moment with Abraham and Isaac. We walk slowly with them and in trepidation. We count the change of days and wonder when God will let our protagonists know that it is time to stop and begin the treacherous ascent. Had the story bogged us down in names and places or the physical and emotional topography of the moment, we would not be able to enter the narrative with our imaginations intact and active, much in the way that a movie provides visuality to a story that steals our own mental picture of activities. And in withholding critical details that situate us in a particular way, the narrative is also suggesting that such a trial of faith and self-sacrifice might take place at any time and in any location in the future.[5]

Using this lens to focus on the three days in Jonah, we find that the absence of detail accomplishes the same frustrating and compelling pull. What we do not know far exceeds what we do know as readers, prompting us to travel with Jonah in the fog of uncertainty.

---

4. Ibid., 8.
5. Shalom Spiegel, *The Last Trial: On the Legends and Lore of the Command of Abraham to Offer Isaac as a Sacrifice* (New York: Pantheon Books, 1967). Spiegel powerfully contrasts Genesis 22 to texts and fragments of poems and commentaries that use this story in contrast to the faith trials and martyrdom that other individuals and communities experienced throughout Jewish history, particularly during the Crusades. This comparison is particularly painful when the authors of these many fragments conclude that their suffering was far greater than Abraham's since he was able, at the last moment, to keep his child.

The Liminality of Three Days and Three Nights

BIBLICAL THREE-DAY PERIODS

Students of the Hebrew Bible almost instantly conjure other places where three days or three days and three nights are referenced. The interpretive weave is so strong among narratives that include this detail of duration that they force the reader to naturally make generative connections.

The first, as noted, is Abraham's emotionally long and weary journey to his son's binding: "On the third day Abraham looked up and saw the place from afar" (Gen. 22:4). In the Jacob narratives, Laban only heard of Jacob's leave-taking three days after it happened: "On the third day, Laban was told that Jacob had fled" (31:22). Later in Genesis, we have this period mentioned more obliquely when Joseph engaged in dream interpretation in prison. In fact, this time duration is mentioned often throughout the Joseph narratives:

> He asked Pharaoh's officials who were in custody with him in his master's house, "Why are your faces so sad today?" "We both had dreams," they answered, "but there is no one to interpret them." Then Joseph said to them, "Do not interpretations belong to God? Tell me your dreams." So the chief cupbearer told Joseph his dream. He said to him, "In my dream I saw a vine in front of me, and on the vine were three branches. As soon as it budded, it blossomed, and its clusters ripened into grapes. Pharaoh's cup was in my hand, and I took the grapes, squeezed them into Pharaoh's cup, and put the cup in his hand." "This is what it means," Joseph said to him. "The three branches are three days. Within three days Pharaoh will lift up your head and restore you to your position, and you will put Pharaoh's cup in his hand, just as you used to do when you were his cupbearer." (Gen. 40:7–13)

The number of branches for Joseph was correlated with time, not space. Note that in three days, fate would change the life of this man, the cupbearer – dramatically. He would return to his former position. Heartened by this hopeful prediction, the chief baker also requested dream interpretation:

> When the chief baker saw that Joseph had given a favorable interpretation, he said to Joseph, "I too had a dream: On my head were

> three baskets of bread. In the top basket were all kinds of baked goods for Pharaoh, but the birds were eating them out of the basket on my head." "This is what it means," Joseph said. "The three baskets are three days. Within three days Pharaoh will lift off your head and hang you on a tree. And the birds will eat away your flesh." (vv. 16–19)

Again, objects translated into time for Joseph but all three-day periods are not the same. For the cupbearer, three days would be the wait for salvation. For the baker it spelled doom. Sure enough, three days later at a birthday party held in his honor, Pharaoh did exactly as Joseph predicted. Perhaps learning from these experiences, Joseph came to appreciate just how much destiny can change in three days – thus he used this time frame to his advantage in negotiating with his brothers:

> Joseph said to them, "It is just as I told you: You are spies! And this is how you will be tested: As surely as Pharaoh lives, you will not leave this place unless your youngest brother comes here. Send one of your number to get your brother; the rest of you will be kept in prison, so that your words may be tested to see if you are telling the truth. If you are not, then as surely as Pharaoh lives, you are spies!" And he put them all in custody for three days. On the third day, Joseph said to them, "Do this and you will live, for I fear God: If you are honest men, let one of your brothers stay here in prison, while the rest of you go and take grain back for your starving households. But you must bring your youngest brother to me, so that your words may be verified and that you may not die." This they proceeded to do. (42:14–20)

We can imagine Joseph's brothers incarcerated for three days, totally unsure of the future, and then being told to bring back their youngest brother. Even prison was preferable to the disappointment and mortal fear of that demand. Here the fate of another lay in that awful wait.

Since three days signaled not only misery but a happy destiny, we turn to its appearance in the Exodus story. Moses was told to ask Pharaoh for a three-day reprieve so that the Israelites could worship their God in the wilderness: "Now, therefore, let us go a distance of three

The Liminality of Three Days and Three Nights

days into the wilderness to sacrifice to the Lord our God" (Ex. 3:18). And this they did later in Exodus (15:22) but instead of worshipping their God in the wilderness, three days turned into the realization that their freedom did not feel entirely free, burdened as they would soon become with the quest for food and water: "Then Moses caused Israel to set out from the Sea of Reeds. They went on into the wilderness of Shur; they traveled three days in the wilderness and found no water.... And the people grumbled against Moses, saying, 'What shall we drink?'" (vv. 22–24). Later, Moses told the Israelites to prepare for the giving of the Ten Commandments on Sinai for three days: "Let them be ready for the third day, for on the third day the Lord will come down in the sight of all the people, on Mount Sinai" (19:11). After the tight organization of the wilderness camp in Numbers, the Israelites set out on their journey behind the Ark of the Covenant: "They marched from the mountain of the Lord a distance of three days. The Ark of the Covenant of the Lord traveled in front of them on that three days' journey to seek out a resting place for them" (10:33). And yet, right after this three-day period, the Israelites again began to complain bitterly.

In the first chapter of Joshua, after Joshua was established as the new leader through a clarion call of encouragement – "be strong and of courage" (1:6) – he gave his first order to the leaders who served under him: "Go through the camp and charge the people thus: Get provisions ready, for in three days' time you are to cross the Jordan, in order to enter and possess the land that the Lord your God is giving you as a possession" (v. 11). In the very next chapter, Rahab warned the two spies who came to reconnoiter the land and report back on the Israelites' capacity for victory to hide for three days before going their way in order to throw their pursuers off the track (2:16). And again, one chapter later, Joshua led the people in this momentous transition: "They did not cross immediately, but spent the night there. Three days later, the officials went through the camp and charged the people" (3:1–2).

Not mentioned in chapter 1 of Joshua were the spiritual preparations necessary to ready the camp for this defining moment, which also involved a three-day period. The Ark of the Covenant, Joshua taught, would serve as their signal to move forward, much as it did in Numbers 10. Even though it provided the charge to advance, the Ark had to remain isolated; the people were warned to remain two thousand cubits' distance from it but also not to lose sight of it "so that you may know by which route to march, since it is a road you have not traveled before" (Josh. 3:4). This holy navigational system was not to be taken for granted: "Purify yourselves for tomorrow the Lord will perform wonders in your midst" (v. 5).

Later in the same book, the inhabitants of Gibeon had heard of Joshua's raging success and in fear they created a ruse. They took worn-out sacks and waterskins, put on threadbare clothes and patched sandals, and approached Joshua at his encampment in Gilgal to create a pact for their protection as a people from a distant land. Had Joshua realized they were residents of the area, he would have had to conquer them and make them subjects or worse. Joshua and the Israelites believed their deception. They had no reason to suspect the Gibeonites were lying. "But when three days had passed after they made this pact with them, they learned that they were neighbors, living among them" (9:16). The Israelites then set out for three days to their towns; however, despite the grumblings of their army's leaders, the Israelites did not touch the Gibeonites. Joshua had promised as much. Instead, the Gibeonites were relegated to the lowest status in the community, woodcutters and water drawers. When Joshua confronted them about their deceit, they told the truth. They were frightened that their lives were at peril in this new and sudden conquest. In this passage, a three-day cycle is mentioned twice: the time it took for the Israelites to realize their error and the time it took them to formulate a fair and just response.

Not long after, in the Book of Judges, Samson suffered his wedding party a riddle for three days, believing that they could never solve it (14:14). And later on, in a narrative told twice, King Rehoboam, Solomon's son, was approached by Jeroboam with a request that he be softer on his laborers than his demanding father, who had tens of thousands in his labor force to build his palace and God's Temple. Rehoboam needed three days to consider a response. In that short time, he approached both his father's counselors who advised him to be more lenient and his own peers, who told him to be harsher than ever in order to establish a strong and uncompromising reign. When three days had passed,

The Liminality of Three Days and Three Nights

Jeroboam returned to unhappy news. Rehoboam went with the advice of his friends, boosting his sense of authority and power. This strategy failed; the laborers sought their revenge by stoning to death their oppressive taskmaster (I Kings 12; II Chr. 10).

In David's many and varied adventures, the period of three days also emerges as a time when the warrior learned of his enemy's behavior. When the Philistines prevented him from joining their troops in battle (I Sam. 29:1–11), he returned to Ziklag and on the third day, when he finally reached Ziklag, he learned that Amalekites had raided the city, burned it down, and taken its women captive (30:2). Information takes time to travel.

When Esther decided after Mordechai's prodding to approach the king and request the salvation of her people, she fasted and prayed for three days and asked others to do the same: "Go, assemble all the Jews who live in Shushan and fast on my behalf; do not eat or drink for three days, night or day. I and my maidens will observe the same fast. Then I shall go to the king, though it is contrary to the law; and if I am to perish, I shall perish" (Est. 4:16). Esther understood that for such a brazen breach of royal policy – the king summoned his wives; they did not summon him – she could be killed. Ostensibly she knew what happened to Vashti and yet came to realize that her life was small next to the matter of the lives of every one of her people.

Three days appears to be both a short and long time in the ancient biblical world for news of enemy whereabouts or behavior to make itself manifest. This amount of time enables learning and the passage of information to become digestible and an initial reaction to have time to percolate and form; it also creates the space for physical and spiritual preparation to face a crisis ahead.

WHY THREE DAYS?

All of these three-day periods suggest the anxiety of waiting, the urgency or need for personal transformation, the state of readiness that must be created to usher in a moment of significance. All could be deemed as negative, small, and unnecessary acts of suffering. This, however, is not the view entertained by the sages in the following observation made in Genesis Rabba about three-day periods: "God does not allow the righteous to remain in a state of distress for more than three days."[6] The midrash continues...

> And he placed them in the prison for three days: Never does The Holy One, Blessed Be He, leave the righteous in dire straits for more than three days. So was it taught to Joseph, to Jonah, to Mordechai, and to David. And so is it stated: "He will revive us from the two days on the third day" (Hos. 6:2), "He will bring us up – and Joseph said to them on the third day."[7]

The suggestion here is that by the second day, fate is already looking upward and strange activities or bad decisions are about to be upended or suspended. What the midrash does not ask but its readers must is why the righteous need to suffer for three days at all. Being righteous should ideally be a state free of any suffering because of spiritual merit. What the sages who authored this midrash must mean is that three days is not only a legitimate time for a pious person to suffer, it is actually a desideratum.

In another talmudic passage, three days without something necessary creates deeper needs and fatigue. It stimulates desire because of want or absence. "Since the Jews traveled for three days without hearing any Torah, they became weary" (Bava Kamma 82a). As a result of this wilderness reality, the sages later instituted the practice of making sure the Torah was read on Shabbat, Monday, and Thursday so that three days would not elapse without the spiritual injection of Scripture: "that they would not tarry three days without hearing Torah."

In virtually every case of a biblical three-day wait listed above, three days were enough time to pause on the significance of the moment, prepare in haste to be worthy of it, and spend time understanding the consequences impending any particular decision or action. Waiting is a virtue. A three-day wait balances the virtue of waiting with the holy impatience of not waiting and, therefore, settling for something short of excellence. It also reminds us that liminality is not something to be

---

6. Genesis Rabba 91:7.
7. Ibid.

The Liminality of Three Days and Three Nights

feared but a time of indeterminacy and possibility that gives us the inner strength to face circumstances we may not have bargained for, as is evident in case after case. On day one we are thrown into crisis, a change that we confront or deny with irritation. On day two we cannot deny the inevitable. By day three, we will hopefully confront the change and prepare for it. The writer on epic heroism, Joseph Campbell, offers us this: "We must be willing to let go of the life we've planned, so as to have the life that is waiting for us."[8] The third day reminds us that it is not only the waiting that matters. It is also what we do when we are waiting to prepare for when the wait is over that counts.

Jonah needed three days to stop the madness of his escape, to turn and face it, lean into it, experience the shame of it and the joy of being saved, and redirect himself to a future that awaited him. Three days brought him to prayer, to the conversation he needed to have with God about who he must become. It seemed, at this juncture, worth the wait.

---

8. Joseph Campbell, *Reflections on the Art of Living: A Joseph Campbell Companion*, ed. Diane K. Osbon (New York: Harper Perennial, 1995), 18.

Chapter Six

Jonah's Prayer: Things Said and Unsaid

> In my trouble I called to the Lord,
> And He answered me;
> From the belly of Sheol I cried out,
> And You heard my voice.
> You cast me into the depths,
> Into the heart of the sea,
> The floods engulfed me;
> All Your breakers and billows
> Swept over me.
> I thought I was driven away
> Out of Your sight:
> Would I ever gaze again
> Upon Your holy Temple?
> (Jonah 2:3–5)

Many scholars have pondered the role and meaning of Jonah's prayer. Some have concluded from its similarity to particular fragments of existing psalms that the prayer was a later addition, one that softened the prophet's demeanor in the eyes of those who read the Bible and could not fathom the book's inclusion in the canon as a tale of a wayward prophet. Gaster, for example, suggests that when Jonah was swallowed by the great

Jonah Adrift

fish, the pause in the story's action created an opportunity for "audience participation" in the singing of a common hymn, namely, what we regard as Jonah's prayer.[1] We have evidence of this in a book cited early in these pages. In *Moby-Dick*, when Father Mapple offers his discourse on Jonah, he commences with a hymn that echoes Jonah's experience:

> The ribs and terrors in the whale,
> Arched over me a dismal gloom,
> While all God's sun-lit waves rolled by,
> And lift me deepening down to doom.
>
> I saw the opening maw of hell,
> With endless pains and sorrows there;
> Which none but they that feel can tell –
> Oh, I was plunging to despair.
>
> In black distress, I called my God,
> When I could scarce believe him mine,
> He bowed his ear to my complaints –
> No more the whale did me confine.
>
> With speed he flew to my relief,
> As on a radiant dolphin borne;
> Awful, yet bright, as lightning shone
> The face of my Deliverer God.
>
> My song for ever shall record
> That terrible, that joyful hour;
> I give the glory to my God,
> His all the mercy and the power.[2]

Medieval exegetes typically parse the words of the prayer and find linguistic parallels and referents without suggesting the prayer's overall

---

1. Gaster, *Myth, Legend and Custom in the Old Testament*, 655.
2. Melville, *Moby-Dick*, 81.

function. As it dominates one of only four chapters, the prayer is not an insignificant text, both in terms of its meaning and also as a transitional conceit that explains the extremes of Jonah's behavior from the escapee of chapter 1 to the highly influential prophet of chapter 3. Something must have happened to create this transformation. Something did. Prayer happened.

Jonah's prayer is important as an explanatory tool that offers us insight into his interiority and at the same time, the very act of prayer – minus any intimation of content – suggests a confrontation that needed to take place between the Creator and the created, between God and His prophet. But more must be said about the nature of prayer, biblical prayer, and this prayer before considering its actual words. It was an act of prayer that finally moved Jonah from a prophet adrift to a prophet with newfound direction, with a renewed commitment to become the leader God expected him to be. What happened to Jonah as he prayed?

JONAH'S REFUSAL TO PRAY

The theologian Henri Nouwen, in his book *Intimacy*, explains the language born of suffering that becomes the roots of prayer. "New life is born in the state of total vulnerability – this is the mystery of love. Power kills. Weakness creates. It creates autonomy, self-awareness and freedom. It creates openness to give and receive in mutuality."[3] Only once Jonah was emotionally flattened, at the sea's very bottom, when his whole life passed before him and he realized the sacrifice that death would elicit in terms of his relationship with God and the Temple, was he able to summon the words that would ultimately sweep him back into the waters of life, offering him the self-awareness and freedom to approach God with bowed head.[4] Rabbi Joseph Soloveitchik equates speech with redemption.

---

3. Henri Nouwen, *Intimacy* (New York: Harper One, 1969), 32.
4. R. Yoḥanan makes Jonah's connection to the Temple more explicit: "Jonah ben Amitai was among the pilgrims [those who came to the Temple to offer sacrifices on the three major holidays]. He entered the water libation festival [on the holiday of Sukkot], and the divine spirit rested upon him. This teaches us that the divine spirit rests only on one who is happy" (*Yalkut Shimoni*, II:550; *Tanḥuma, Vayikra* 8). How odd it is to use Jonah as a standard-bearer of happiness, particularly because he only expressed joy over the tree God gave him and then quickly took away. Jonah

Jonah Adrift

Prayer moves an individual from silence to speech and the emergence of speech is the beginning of a move from constraint to freedom. "When a people leaves a mute world and enters a world of sound, speech and song, it becomes a redeemed people – a free people. In other words, a mute life is identical with bondage; a speech-endowed life is a free life."[5] In the silence that marked his interactions with God, Jonah was trapped. In prayer, Jonah's understanding of God and the world unfolded.

Yet, as will later be discussed, Jonah's was a prayer of thanksgiving, not of atonement. Jonah approached God without the humility of a penitent and, when criticizing the idol worshippers he left and those he would soon approach, Jonah even included what resembled a touch of hubris at the close of his prayer.

Ideally, in this prayer, we would have found the germination of true feeling for God, the depth of love that comes with an act of reconciliation. Following Nouwen's understanding of intimacy, we hope that Jonah – in his state of vulnerability – would fully submit himself, not to the mission but to the relationship. With a healed bond to God, Jonah's reformation of Nineveh's would have been only one of many manifestations of this renewed communication and dedication:

> Love is based on the mutuality of the confession of our total self to each other. This makes us free to declare not only: "My strength is your strength" but also: "Your pain is my pain, your weakness is my weakness, your sin is my sin." It is in this intimate fellowship of the weak that love is born.[6]

What Jonah needed to do in this moment of self-reflection before and after action was to create a fellowship of the weak with God. God was

---

yearned to see the Temple again when he realized that a death at sea would take that future away from him – but this is a far cry from happiness at the Temple's existence. One wonders what prompted R. Yoḥanan, outside of the water images in the story and the reference to the Temple, to situate Jonah this way and in this particular emotional state of mind.

5. Rabbi Joseph Soloveitchik, "Redemption, Prayer and Talmud Torah," in *Confrontation and Other Essays* (Jerusalem: Maggid, 2015), 64–65.
6. Nouwen, *Intimacy*, 29.

Jonah's Prayer: Things Said and Unsaid

hardly weak in this story. God needed prophets to represent the divine word on this earth. If Jonah could only have used his prayer words to achieve submission, the book would likely have had another ending.

Instead, Jonah achieved what Anton Boisen, an American priest who developed hospital chaplaincy work, wrote of prayer: "I do believe in prayer. I believe that its chief function is – to find out what is wanted of us and to enable us to draw upon sources of strength which will make it possible for us to accomplish our task whatever it may be."[7] Jonah's prayer created the possibility of achieving a stated task rather than the platform for a different relationship with God. While this was not a small accomplishment for a prophet so damaged by his flight, it was ultimately not enough to help him even execute the task without backing down.

Jonah's prayer is not unlike those we find elsewhere in the Bible, particularly in Psalms. Biblical prayer comes in many forms and covers an emotional range from thanksgiving and the celebration of good tidings to supplication and a desperate call for aid. Prayer can be intercessory or highly personal – a call for intimacy, a desire to bridge the abyss between God and human beings through an act of vulnerability, or a confession of humility. Biblical scholar Moshe Greenberg, in *Biblical Prose Prayer*, observes that prayers and praying are mentioned in the Hebrew Bible approximately 140 times outside of the Book of Psalms. Within that number, there are ninety-seven actual texts of prayer. Thirty-eight of these prayers are articulated by laypeople and fifty-nine by kings, prophets, and other leaders.[8] With this panoply of spiritual offerings, Greenberg wonders why these prayers and their commonalities and contrasts have not been the subject of more scholarly inquiry. He arrives at the conclusion that because these prayers are embedded in narratives, they often go unstudied; they are not regarded as distinct from the storyline but part of it. But, in his opinion, "every text is part of a literary artifact. Even the mere report of an act of prayer represents a deliberate choice of the narrator, let alone the verbal formulation of a prayer embedded in a story."[9]

---

7. Anton Boisen, *Out of the Depths* (New York: Harper & Brothers, 1960), 111.
8. Moshe Greenberg, *Biblical Prose Prayer: As a Window to the Popular Religion of Ancient Israel* (Eugene, OR: Wipf & Stock, 1983), 7.
9. Ibid., 8.

Jonah's prayer is no different. It is not only part of the story; it also catalyzes the plot. As such, it would be easy to ignore the significance of the language and focus instead on the role prayer has as an act and as a motivator of future action. Prayer was the sailors' critical and elemental response to natural – or supernatural – disaster. The fact that Jonah did not pray was a cause for serious concern, so odd that it prompted the captain to leave his post of collective responsibility simply to single Jonah out for malfeasance. But the act of prayer alone should not distract the reader from the content of the prayers, when that content is revealed. In the first instance, we are unsure what the sailors said – the content of their heartfelt and urgent words – and part of this uncertainty rests in the cacophony of prayer. Everyone made a verbal offering to his respective god/s. The words and the languages likely differed greatly and may have reflected the full spectrum of the ancient Mediterranean. One can imagine a sort of chaotic prayer convocation, a blend of customs and petitions united by the universal response to suffering – the cry:

> But the Lord cast a mighty wind upon the sea, and such a great tempest came upon the sea that the ship was in danger of breaking up. In their fright, the sailors cried out, each to his own god; and they flung the ship's cargo overboard to make it lighter for them. Jonah, meanwhile, had gone down into the hold of the vessel where he lay down and fell asleep. The captain went over to him and cried out, "How can you be sleeping so soundly? Rise, call upon your god! Perhaps the god will be kind to us and we will not perish." (Jonah 1:4–6)

Jonah was an outlier whose behavior was not tolerated. Sleep was an inappropriate response – and not because the desired response to calamity was to throw ballast overboard, the sailors' second act. No, the captain was not looking for another hand on deck; he was looking for another heart. He was unsure what formula would be effective but was very sure that sleeping would not be efficacious at this moment of peril. Sleep was an insult. Prayer is an expectation, as Greenberg again demonstrates, "Telling evidence of the Scriptural assumption of the universal capacity for prayer and its unlimited efficacy is found in Jonah."[10] Prayer is not a Jewish reaction to pain; it is a human reaction. Here it was actually not the Jewish reaction. Jonah's regression to the bowels of the ship showed a lack of interest in basic self-preservation, the only explanation for his lack of supplication.

Striking in this scene is what happened after the captain confronted Jonah: nothing. Jonah did not pray – or, if he did, it is not recorded. Even when told vociferously that not praying was not an option, Jonah nevertheless ignored once again the voice of authority – human, this time – and kept silent until asked a question that was not rhetorical. The sailors went on to draw lots to identify the party responsible for the storm, a move that distracts the reader from asking the question: Did Jonah actually pray at this time and, if so, what did he ask for? What could this runaway, shame-faced prophet possibly ask for?

JONAH'S PRAYER: A CLOSER LOOK

The sailors' prayers and pledges are not articulated in the text with the words they actually used, in contrast to Jonah's prayer, which is included in full in chapter 2. The prayer is instructive both in what it says and in what it fails to say.

Jonah's prayer was one of thanksgiving; it was decidedly not one of atonement. In it, the prophet looked forward to what he must do. He did not look backward to confess responsibility for loudly ignoring God's calling. And it revealed something telling when it was uttered. Ostensibly, Jonah took a full three days to digest what had happened to him and to pledge to make good on his assignment. Add to this the fact that Jonah was trapped in a fish that could have swallowed him or spat him out depending on the choice he made, and Jonah's death wish underwent its final scrutiny. No, if given the choice, Jonah would now choose life. The fact that the fish spat Jonah out was not an obvious miracle, just as the fact that the fish swallowed him in the first place was never assumed by Jonah when he pleaded with the sailors to throw him over.

To engage this prayer, presented in full at the opening of this chapter, completely, we will break it up into thematic pieces. When read in the

---

10. Ibid., 15.

Jonah Adrift

Hebrew, a student of this text cannot but help notice the repetition of two Hebrew sounds: "*ee*" as in "me" or "I," and "*kha*," "you." In this case, the direct object is God. The playful intertwining of these sounds creates a rollicking of sudden intimacy between God and His once distant prophet. Where there was devastating silence, now there is compressed yearning, a desire for communication and reunion, captured in the "I" and the "You."

PHYSICAL DESCENT

When we segment Jonah's prayer, we begin to notice that Jonah traces his religious descent with his physical descent. He brings the reader into the spiral downward by referencing the terrible experience of falling.

> In my trouble I called to the Lord,
> And He answered me;
> From the belly of Sheol I cried out,
> And You heard my voice.
> You cast me into the depths,
> Into the heart of the sea,
> The floods engulfed me;
> All Your breakers and billows
> Swept over me. (vv. 3–4)

As we open up this prayer, we find similar descriptions of initial distress, using similar language, in Psalms, wrapped in a desire to connect with God and be saved by God:

> The cords of death entangled me; the torrents of destruction overwhelmed me. The cords of the grave coiled around me; the snares of death confronted me. In my distress I called to the Lord; I cried to my God for help. From His Temple He heard my voice; my cry came before Him, into His ears. The earth trembled and quaked, and the foundations of the mountains shook; they trembled because He was angry. (18:5–7)

Like Jonah, the subject of this psalm finds himself *afafuni*, "entangled," (*afafuni* appears in both texts as do *harim*, "mountains") and near death. Nature

Jonah's Prayer: Things Said and Unsaid

is threatening and provokes an outcry. And then there is the moment of salvation in this Psalm, similar to Jonah's redeeming sweep out of danger: "He reached down from on high and took hold of me; He drew me out of deep waters" (v. 16). Elsewhere in Psalms, we feel the same crisis of the sea:

> Save me, O God, for the waters have come up to my neck. I sink in the miry depths [*metzula*, which also appears in Jonah's prayer], where there is no foothold. I have come into the deep waters; the floods engulf me. I am worn out calling for help; my throat is parched. My eyes fail, looking for my God. (69:1–3)

God here is distant for the drowning man, who now needs Him more than ever:

> But I pray to You, O Lord, in the time of Your favor; in Your great love, O God, answer me with Your sure salvation. Rescue me from the mire, do not let me sink; deliver me from those who hate me, from the deep waters. Do not let the floodwaters engulf me or the depths [*metzula*] swallow me up or the pit close its mouth over me. (69:14–16)

There is no time to spare. The subject's enemies pay him no heed. God is his first and last hope. The psalmist helps us appreciate redemption by creating the strong visual pull of descending into perilous waters that necessitates urgent divine assistance.

> Answer me, O Lord, out of the goodness of Your love; in Your great mercy turn to me. Do not hide Your face from Your servant; answer me quickly, for I am in trouble. (69:17–18)

In the sea, this kind of falling is called drowning. There are many ways to die. Drowning as a choice is the suicidal equivalent of running away; it represents a desire to become invisible. The sea takes a few gulps of a flailing prophet and then it returns to its earlier, horizontal equilibrium. There is no trace that anyone was ever on the water's surface, so devastatingly final is drowning. The water is indifferent to human life.

In his classic work, *Suicide*, Émile Durkheim notes that in research on one thousand suicides conducted in multiple countries and using multiple methods, suicide by drowning was not, as expected, seasonal. One would anticipate that those wishing to commit suicide in this fashion would wait for warmer days. But temperature is evidently not a factor in those who choose this method. There is nothing convenient about it. Durkheim notes that certain settings – city versus countryside, for example – and particular professions lend themselves to perceptions of life-taking that are more noble or crass. Soldiers are most likely to take their lives with guns, sailors by drowning.

And yet, on the surface, the fact that Jonah was on a ship was accidental. He lived in Gath-hepher, not far from the port city of Jaffa. Sailing out of one's life may have seemed the most natural escape route to him. Drowning may have functioned in much the same way – unless one pays careful attention to another distinction Durkheim makes, between altruistic suicide and egoistic suicide. In altruistic suicide, "The individual kills himself at the command of his conscience; he submits to an imperative."[11] This person may be a martyr who dies for his faith, a man dogged by debt or scandal who wishes to spare his family additional disgrace, or a woman who gives up her life rather than submit consensually to a sexual crime. Durkheim contends that those who take their lives in this fashion have "serene conviction" and their deaths and the methods by which they take their lives are often characterized by passion or enhanced energy. In contrast, the egoistic suicide "is characterized by a general depression, in the form either of melancholic languor or Epicurean indifference."[12] The individual in question is often isolated from society and likely has "a high development of knowledge and reflective intelligence."[13] Yet such an individual may suffer intensely from anomie and a questioning of everything, leading to greater confusion, emptiness, and purposelessness:

---

11. Emile Durkheim, *Suicide* (New York: The Free Press, 1963), 283.
12. Ibid.
13. Ibid., 281.

Dreamy melancholy is replaced by skeptical, disillusioned matter-of-factness, which becomes especially prominent at the final hour. The sufferer deals himself the blow without hate or anger, but equally with none of the morbid satisfaction with which the intellectual relishes his suicide.... He is not surprised at the end to which he has come; he has foreseen it as a more or less impending event. He therefore makes no long preparations; in harmony with all his preceding existence, he only tries to minimize pain.[14]

Because Jonah realized that he had no possible escape from his destiny as prophet, he came to accept death as the only viable alternative. He stopped running and hiding and volunteered his submission to fate, a demise that was his construct alone. Even when Jonah was interrogated by the sailors, no response in the text even obliquely suggests this punishment crossed their minds. What makes Jonah's request fit into Durkheim's categorization is the passivity with which Jonah approached this defining hour. He essentially asked the sailors to murder him by throwing him over rather than by throwing himself over or taking his life by other means. So passive was he at the end that the prospect of death by drowning – not the initial plunge but the eventual return of calm – must have seemed to him as an ultimate and existential relief.

The final support for such a reading again contrasts Jonah to the sailors. Even after agreeing to Jonah's absurd request that they assumed was the will of Jonah's God, they resisted. Only having exhausted all possibilities, and themselves, did they pray not to be guilty of shedding innocent blood:

> They said to him, "What must we do to you to make the sea calm around us?" for the sea was growing more and more stormy. "Pick me up and throw me into the sea," he replied, "and it will become calm. I know that it is my fault that this great storm has come upon

---

14. Ibid., 282.

you." Nevertheless the men rowed hard to regain the shore, but they could not, for the sea was growing more and more stormy about them. (Jonah 1:11–13)

With zeal, the men aimed for the shore, which indicates that this event happened not long out to sea. The energy they put into rowing is characterized by the use of the Hebrew verb *vayaḥteru* which conveys a sense of "digging" into the sea. One exegete offers this linguistic parallel from the Book of Amos: "Though they dig down to the depths of the grave, from there My hand will take them" (9:2). The rowing appeared like digging, a collective and energetic effort to propel their mission forward. In the shadow of Amos, the digging also communicates mortality, a digging of the grave in the vast ocean. Had they been able to drop Jonah on the shore and return to the ship, they would have spared themselves both a storm and a guilty conscience. Their intensity is again a contrast to Jonah's lachrymose indifference to his own life. Yet no matter how hard they rowed, they could not do it. And here another exegete on the expression "they could not" compares it to a verse from Exodus, where Pharaoh's magicians were finally stymied by a plague they could not mimic: "The magicians did similarly with their spells to produce lice, *but they could not*" (8:14). This led them to a conclusion which they readily shared with Pharaoh: "This is the finger of God!" (v. 15). No doubt, the sailors arrived at the same conclusion. If they could not, using all of their professional might, get to shore, then God must have wanted them to act on the prophet's advice.

Jonah also realized the power he had over these men, who regarded him as a man of God and a conduit of God's wishes. Thus was he able, without much persuasion, to get them to do his atrocious bidding. When Jonah retorted that the sea would achieve calm once they threw him in as an ultimate sacrifice, was he not also admitting that he too would achieve calm with this end?

And just when Jonah was close to achieving the calm he sought in an ultimate repose in the sea, the shattering crash onto the waves, the shrill contact with sea water and its immersive power to engulf brought out another Jonah: a Jonah who wanted to live, who tells us why he wanted to live. Jonah, as mentioned, achieved this through the act and the content of his prayer, a prayer that did not emerge suddenly: "And Jonah was inside the fish three days and three nights. Jonah prayed to the Lord his God from the belly of the fish" (Jonah 2:1–2). The fish was his prison and his sanctuary. Of all the unlikely places to reach out to God, the stomach of a leviathan is one of the oddest – but it is clear that his location was not incidental to his intention: "He said, 'In my trouble I called to the Lord, and He answered me; from the belly of Sheol I cried out, and You heard my voice'" (v. 3).

Rashi, citing *Pirkei DeRabbi Eliezer*, believes that Jonah's prayer came later, perhaps once Jonah was expelled from the fish; Jonah could not possibly have sustained the concentration to pray in this torturous and frightening location. Yet this sentiment runs counter to the language, which explicitly states that Jonah's act of prayer took place there. God answered Jonah not in the fish's insides, Rashi contends; rather, God answered Jonah's prayer to remove him *from* the belly of the fish. Ibn Ezra observes that commentaries interpreted the *mem* in *mim'ai hadaga* as "from the fish" and not *bemei*, "in the fish," to suggest that Jonah had left the fish when he praised and thanked God. Ibn Ezra then marshals a number of verses and a common-sense reading to suggest that Jonah's prayer had to be inside the fish because he explicitly stated that he was in distress, in a low place of crisis and collapse. One might argue that this is a silly detail unworthy of attention, much the way that scholars discussed what type of fish might be able to swallow a human and keep a human alive for such a long time. Yet the text's author simply wanted the reader to know it was a large fish, as if to suggest that one not get distracted by the practical mysteries this story presents and focus, instead, on its deeper meanings. If the large bug that Gregor Samsa became in Kafka's *Metamorphosis* was a cockroach or a beetle, would it make a difference to its symbolism? It might, but it is unlikely. The phantasmagoric aspects of the story force a multivalent approach.

PUSHED AWAY FROM THE TEMPLE

Reading Jonah's prayer, we become voyeurs, watching a man who travels through the hell of descent and takes us with him, as we trace his perilous downward voyage into the sea. Far from being a superfluous detail or a later addition pulled as a pastiche of verses from Psalms, as some modern Bible scholars regard this chapter, Jonah's prayer was his statement of transformation. This change took place incrementally, if not quite quickly, as Jonah was sinking:

> The floods engulfed me;
> All Your breakers and billows
> Swept over me.
> I thought I was driven away
> Out of Your sight:
> Would I ever gaze again
> Upon Your holy Temple? (Jonah 2:4–5)

When Jonah first hit the sea and the waves began to toss him about, the water swept over him – and so did a realization. He would never again gaze upon God's holy Temple, the place of the Divine Presence. Seforno understands the waves that swept over him as a constant swirl of water, as if Jonah were saying, "I cannot hope to escape from wave to wave." One wave calmed as another rose, making Jonah feel hopeless and helpless against his circumstances. This sort of despair made him finally come to terms with what he was losing. He would never see the Temple in its glory. Lost would be pilgrimages and sacrifices, communal prayer and personal confessions. But the loss that would be greatest for this prophet was the intimate relationship he enjoyed with God, a relationship that collapsed when he ran away from his duty. This escape was finally, with Jonah's drowning, terminating – and with it any chance of redemption.

If we pause for a moment on the words of the prayer, we notice something strange. We might expect this realization from a priest or a Levite, whose sacred responsibilities all center around the Temple; death would put an end to all that. Yet the prayer, and arguably the entire Book of Jonah, centers on location: where he was supposed to be, where he ended up, and how he made his way back. Place determines plot. The water was a place of instability and vulnerability: "The waters closed in over me. The deep engulfed me" (2:6). The dry land was a place of stability, as indicated chiefly by the aftermath of Jonah's prayer: "The Lord commanded the fish, and it spewed Jonah out upon dry land" (2:11). A ship is a place in between. It provides temporal stability, providing a safe, dry place of refuge on the surface of moving waters: "He went down to Jaffa and found a ship going to Tarshish" (1:3). The Temple, in this framework, was the place of ultimate stability, where suddenly Jonah found himself in his imagination when he was at his greatest point of fragility, dreaming of a building made of heavy stone sitting atop a mountain, far from the sea. In this solid, looming structure, God lived. It was His house. Jonah suddenly found himself craving that house. Oh, to look upon it. Oh, to knock on its doors and revel in its chambers. Oh, to be home when Jonah was so far away. Even later, when he built his small booth, he was aware that it would never have the solidity of God's favored space.

Jonah was not mourning the loss of his responsibilities in the Temple, since he did not have any. Instead, he grieved the lost possibility of intimacy that would never be his again: "Would I ever gaze again upon Your holy Temple?" (2:5). We are reminded of the famous scene in the midsection of Song of Songs in which the beloved failed to rise and answer the door when her lover knocked. Her slow, ambling pace was regarded by her lover as absence – or worse, rejection. By the time she got to the door, her lover was gone: "I opened the door for my beloved, but my beloved had turned and gone...I sought, but found him not; I called, but he did not answer" (5:6). She then became crazed with seeking, realizing that she just may have lost him this time through her own neglect. Jonah too realized that he had sacrificed a relationship with God that likely would never heal with his demise. And yet, unlike the lover, Jonah expressed himself as if it were not his fault but God's. "I thought I was driven away, out of Your sight" (Jonah 2:5). But he drove himself out of God's sight; he was not driven. His passivity had reached such depths that he could not take responsibility for initiating his own escape.

> The waters closed in over me,
> The deep engulfed me
> Weeds twined around my head. (v. 6)

Jonah moved from the initial breakers at the water's crest to under the surface of the sea, his head surrounded by seaweed and the water's detritus.

> I sank to the base of the mountains;
> The bars of the earth closed upon me forever.
> Yet You brought my life up from the pit.
> O Lord my God!
> When my life was ebbing away,
> I called the Lord to mind;
> And my prayer came before You,
> Into Your holy Temple. (vv. 7–8)

Note here the total descent to the base of the mountains. There was nowhere left to go. Jonah had sunk to the very depths and could go no further. Only then, in total desperation, when there was no longer anywhere to escape to, did God bring Jonah back up to life, creating the trajectory to his personal redemption.

FOLLY AND KINDNESS

> They who cling to empty folly
> Forsake their own kindness. (Jonah 2:9)

This verse is perhaps the most curious line in Jonah's prayer. Instead of focusing on and reporting his own experience, as he had done in the words preceding these, Jonah suddenly and abruptly turned to unnamed others in criticism. There are people, Jonah contended, who are not as sincere in their prayers or offerings as he. As a result, they forfeit their kindness, "they who cling to empty folly." He implied that this group of people, whoever they were, did more than propagate false beliefs; they held on to them dearly. This usage is also found in Deuteronomy: "They made me jealous by what is no-god and angered me with their worthless idols. I will make them envious by those who are not a people; I will make them angry by a nation that has no understanding" (Deut. 32:21). Jonah suggested in his prayer that while idol worshippers may act the part of monotheists for a small window of time, they cleave to their false beliefs stubbornly and are unlikely to change their fundamental commitments.

The use of *ḥasdam*, "their kindness," is equally bewildering. What kindness could they be forfeiting through belief? Some are of the view

Jonah's Prayer: Things Said and Unsaid

that because these worshippers put their stock and trust in the promises of false gods, they forfeit the kindnesses that they would have otherwise received had they believed in the one true God.[15] Ibn Ezra takes the position that the worshippers believe that their very faith is a kindness but also takes another view reflected in a number of translations: the word "kindness" morphs into "welfare," implying that those of temporary piety put themselves in jeopardy.[16] They believe they are protecting themselves with their prayers and sacrifices, but spiritual opportunists will soon realize that their pagan promiscuity has negative repercussions. This unusual derogatory usage appears in Leviticus in reference to sexual shame: "If a man marries his sister, the daughter of either his father or his mother, so that he sees her nakedness and she sees his nakedness, it is *a disgrace (ḥesed)*; they shall be excommunicated in the sight of their kinsfolk" (20:17). In other words, whoever the subject of this verse is will be disgraced one day by his or her empty ways. Radak identifies, as do most medieval commentators, that these were the sailors who relied upon God's kindness for their salvation; once out of trouble, they would renege on their pledges and return to who they always were as if their miraculous redemption had not happened. Human nature returns to a default position of ingratitude.

Ostensibly, in this verse, Jonah was contrasting his own renewed commitment to God with what he regarded as the false and empty manner of the sailors, idol worshippers, and opportunists who believed in whatever promised them salvation; when deliverance passed so did their commitment. This sort of spiritual promiscuity would have been intolerable to a prophet like Jonah, who, in the eponymous book, appears to be an extremist. When he ran away, he made a passionate escape. When he returned to God, he did so with equal force. Those who cling to this empty folly, the verse implies, hold on to these notions, protecting and nurturing them, making a foundational attribution error. They hold on to false beliefs with tenacity. The sailors may have appeared to be good on the surface, but scratch even lightly, Jonah claimed, and the veneer of piety would peel away as they moved on to the next god, the new focus of their limited attentions.

---

15. See Rashi and *Daat Mikra* to Jonah 2:9.
16. See, for example, the Jewish Publication Society translation of Jonah 2:9 in the *JPS Hebrew-English Tanakh* (Philadelphia: Jewish Publication Society, 2003).

The people referred to could also be the citizens of Nineveh, a future rather than a past group. This would explain why Jonah finally decided to advance God's plan. He believed that God would soon see the falsity of Nineveh's ways, their superficiality would become apparent, and Jonah would be spared the humiliation of his task. This also explains why Jonah felt intense anger at the fate of Nineveh in chapter 4. He had expected God to see through the transparency of Nineveh's repentance; instead God regarded their *teshuva* as sincere and acceptable. "God saw what they did and how they turned from their evil ways" (3:10). Jonah saw and God saw, but what they each saw was vastly different. Jonah saw their past and their future. He saw their ways and believed they would never change. God, however, saw them at that moment. God's naiveté, if you will, was infuriating for the prophet; it was theologically unacceptable, untenable to Jonah's view of truth with a capital "T." This understanding is reflected in the rabbinic interpretation of a clause in Jonah 3:8: "Let everyone turn back from his evil ways and from the injustice that is in his hands." The sages regarded the expression "in his hands" literally. R. Yoḥanan famously said that they returned what was in their hands – what could be seen – but not what could not be seen. "Shmuel said: If they had built a stolen beam as the main support of their house, they dismantled their house to return the beam to its original owner" (Taanit 16a).

Shmuel's interpretation is more charitable and demonstrates an excessive zeal on the part of the Ninevites to get it right, to repent in a way that demonstrated utter commitment to change. According to Shmuel, they repented from their evil ways to the extent that they demolished buildings using stolen wood to return that wood to their owners, at significant inconvenience and expense. R. Yoḥanan is not as generous. They returned what they had easily at hand but hid what was not visible in drawers and closets. This criticism, however, does not cohere with Jewish law. In Jewish law, a thief is not expected to return the very beams he stole and used but rather must make equivalent financial restitution for the beams.[17] Punishing the

---

17. See Gittin 55a: "The rabbis taught: If a man stole a beam and built it into a palace," Beit Shammai say that he must demolish the whole palace and restore the beam to its owner. Beit Hillel, however, say that the latter can claim only the monetary value of the beam, so as not to place obstacles in the way of penitents. In principle, the

penitent thief to the degree that he had to collect everything he ever stole and return it would discourage the thief from ever repenting.

But it was this very extreme that Jonah – in his exacting and rigid understanding of principled behavior – expected. Anything short of this would demonstrate that Nineveh had, indeed, not changed. For Jonah, the process of change was not instantaneous, at least not in the way he judged his enemies. Although his transformation took three days, as did theirs, he felt that his was genuine. Theirs was insincere and temporary. This interpretation fed into Jonah's closing:

> But I, with loud thanksgiving,
> Will sacrifice to You;
> What I have vowed I will perform.
> Deliverance is the Lord's. (Jonah 2:10)

By closing with God's deliverance, Jonah suggested that only God could know the sincerity behind the actions, and that God would behave accordingly. The sailors may have sacrificed to God in their moment of thanksgiving, but they could not possibly have meant what Jonah meant with his offerings. Jonah believed that only his transformation was valid when ironically, his prayer lacked the commitment to transformation; instead, it contained only thanksgiving.

THANKSGIVING

We are not surprised, then, that Jonah left Nineveh so quickly. Although he fell to the depths of the water, his change was more superficial than that of those he criticized in his prayer. What offering was promised here? Jonah himself was "the sacrifice." He had finally pledged to devote himself to God's mission, and he did so with a loud voice of avowal. Such articulated commitment made others witness to Jonah's transformation – although one wonders who could possibly have heard this prophet at sea, where words get swallowed by the

---

building should be taken apart, but in practice, this would prove so onerous that a person contemplating repentance would change his mind. The law, as it usually does, follows the school of Beit Hillel.

crash of waves and all human sounds are but a whisper relative to the bellows of nature.

Rashi contends that in Jonah's renewed commitment, he pledged to bring a thanksgiving offering, as implied by the expression "I, with loud thanksgiving, will sacrifice to You." A super-commentary on Rashi adds that Jonah was referring quite specifically to the obligation to bring such a sacrifice accompanied by the blessing of *hagomel*. This blessing devolves upon four types of individuals, according to the Talmud: one who crosses the desert, one who is healed from sickness, one who is freed from prison, and one who completes a sea voyage.[18] What is striking is not that Jonah wished to vow and to sacrifice to God – much like the sailors and the citizens of Nineveh – and to do what he was destined to do in chapter 1. It is that Jonah offered a thanksgiving sacrifice rather than one of atonement and expiation.

Why a sacrifice of thanksgiving? Surely, Jonah must have realized that his behavior was inappropriate and that thanksgiving was not sufficient in addressing God. Jonah had to make amends for his great wrong, not simply offer a gift and move ahead. And yet, following Rashi's interpretation, this moment of contrition never took place, and this explains so much of what happened to Jonah in the ensuing chapters. Without deep reflection on his actions and their consequences, Jonah could not properly serve God or Nineveh with a full heart and mind.

Gratitude can only deliver limited human responsibility and agency. It is a temporal inspiration. It wears thin. Jonah condemned the sailors for not sustaining their belief beyond the time when it served them, but Jonah was unable to acknowledge the same thin commitment in himself. Without negotiating acceptable terms for his mission and wrestling with the demons that led to his escape, Jonah's prayer was urgent but not lasting. Greenberg writes that "every human being is capable of formulating a petitionary prayer according to his need."[19] Jonah indeed did this but his need and the need of the hour were not the same.

The Seforno, on the words "Jonah prayed" (Jonah 2:2), explains that when he was expelled from the belly of the fish Jonah said this prayer,

---

18. See the Mahari Kra to Jonah 2:10; Berakhot 54b based on Psalms 107:4–5, 26.
19. Greenberg, *Biblical Prose Prayer*, 17.

Jonah's Prayer: Things Said and Unsaid

confessed, and returned to God in repentance. Yet his prayer had little to do with repentance. Jonah never once expressed contrition. If he was sorry, these words do not appear in the book. If he felt he wronged God or the people of Nineveh, he made no such admission. Many regard this as a thanksgiving prayer, particularly since those very words are used toward the prayer's culmination: "But, I, with loud thanksgiving, will sacrifice to You" (2:10). Yet this word of thanks was literally that: one word. Jonah's prayer, if it fits anywhere in a canon of biblical supplications, uses the Bible's familiar language of personal crisis. Naturally, thanksgiving is a consequence of this articulation of pain and redemption but the prayer was, in reality, mostly a recognition of past despair that had been eclipsed because God heard the prayer of the desperate: "In my distress I called upon the Lord, and cried to my God: He heard my voice out of His Temple, and my cry came before Him, even into His ears" (Ps. 18:6). The cry's reverberations extended to the Temple, and God heard this petitioner. But even without the Temple, the voice of human beings in pain is enough to stir God's response: "In my distress I cried unto the Lord, and He heard me" (120:1). This is not only a generic trope; it appears in the narratives in the Book of Samuel when David prayed to God, who had spared him from his enemies and the punishing hand of Saul: "In my distress I called to the Lord; I called out to my God. From His Temple He heard my voice; my cry came to His ears" (22:7).

DELIVERANCE

The last verse of the chapter neatly presents the reader with a happy postscript. As if on cue, with Jonah's words, "Deliverance is the Lord's," the fish expelled Jonah. "The Lord commanded the fish, and it spewed Jonah out upon dry land" (Jonah 2:10–11). God, convinced that Jonah was ready, did not make him endure the strange salvation/torture of being inside the great fish any longer. As mentioned earlier, if dry land is a place of stability and water a place of chaos and turmoil, the fish – like Noah's ark – was a place of liminality in the narrative. It was dry land *within* water. Providing temporary respite even as it served as its own punishment, the fish as a conduit of God's will was forced to spit out the prophet. Since one expects that such a watery beast would consume Jonah, the act of release became yet another miracle in this strange story.

But just as the earlier drowning was violent and difficult, so, too, is the image offered here. Unlike artists who depict Jonah stepping out of the fish, using the fish's tongue as an off-ramp to freedom, the text uses language very intentionally. Vomiting out a prophet is hardly a gentle push in the right direction. It is immediately reminiscent of the verse in Leviticus that explicitly states that the land of Canaan will vomit out the Israelites should they not be morally worthy of living there. "And if you defile the land, it will vomit you out as it vomited out the nations that were before you" (18:28). Should the inhabitants of Canaan commit an array of sexual offenses detailed in the chapter, the land will not be able to tolerate their presence. This was not only true for the Israelites, the future inhabitants of the Land of Israel, but also true of those who were cast out to make room for them: "Do not defile yourselves in any of those ways, for it is by such that the nations that I am casting out before you defiled themselves. Thus the land became defiled, and I called it to account for its iniquity, and the land spewed out its inhabitants" (18:24–25). Vomiting out its inhabitants is a recurring behavior, a clear signal to the incoming Israelites that what happened before will likely happen again if they are not vigilant in their observance of God's command. Baruch Levine in his commentary on this verse suggests the reasoning behind this intense causal behavior:

> The interdependence of the people and the land is a prominent theme in prophetic teaching. Those who violate the code of family life commit an outrage that defiles the land – which, in turn, will spew them out.... It is as though the land, personified, is angered by its defilement at man's hand. Exile is punishment for an abhorrent way of life, not only as regards Israel, but also for all other nations.[20]

The sort of heaving and retching that vomiting implies accomplishes the ejection of negative matter but only by way of force and violence. Poison hurts – and so does the ejection of the same offending poison. But it must be spewed out of the system to be sure that nothing damaging remains. Rashi explains the language by virtue of a parable: "This is

---

20. Baruch Levine, *The JPS Torah Commentary/Leviticus* (Philadelphia: Jewish Publication Society, 1989), 124–125.

Jonah's Prayer: Things Said and Unsaid

comparable to the case of a prince to whom one gives a repulsive item to eat which he cannot keep down but vomits it out; thus, the Land of Israel cannot tolerate sinners on its land."[21] The *Targum* translates it as "to empty out"; the land will empty itself out of them (ad loc.). The prince is someone royal, special, a person we assume is of superior traits and upbringing and who we assume would not be involved in behavior so repulsive. Yet it happens. Nahmanides (1194–1270) puzzles over this verse precisely because "the transgressions of the body are not dependent on [connected to] the land."[22]

One naturally assumes that the behavior of those on the land is disconnected from the land – it has nothing to do with the land. And yet, from the Garden of Eden onward, the relationship of human beings to land is integral to the proper functioning of both. Man and woman were born in a garden, blessed with the tasks of working and protecting it, then cursed to work it because of disobedience involving plant life, then further cursed in Cain's day to work it without a guaranteed yield. Just as the primordial couple was expelled from the garden, so will Israel – the ultimate garden – throw out inhabitants that cannot abide by the rules that create its distinctiveness.

Excessive transgression pushes people away, much in the way the term *vomit* is used in Proverbs to describe over-indulgence: "If you find honey, eat only what you need, lest surfeiting yourself, you throw it up" (25:16). Even that which is sweet and pleasant can become a torment when not eaten in measured amounts. Zopher, one of Job's supposed companions, chastised Job by insinuating that he took pleasure in evil and this explained his downfall: "His food in his bowels turns into asp's venom within him. The riches he swallows he vomits; God empties it out of his stomach" (Job 20:14).

And yet, there is another characteristic of vomit: the immediate and sudden release expels the danger and leaves the sufferer feeling lighter, better, clearer. Whatever the past was that got dredged up and surfaced has spilled out and let its victim free.

---

21. Rashi to Lev. 18:28.
22. Nahmanides to Lev. 18:25.

The vomiting out of the prophet is perhaps emblematic of the excretion of a former self that needed to happen to allow the new prophet to emerge. Vomiting out is not as kind and loving an image as birthing, which also requires physical force through a narrow space and whose aftermath achieves release and relief. The prophet here was not born again; he was not a new creation but a pre-existing one who banished himself and then was expelled from the place that entrapped him. We have an inkling of what this last difficult act is in the words of Jean-Paul Sartre in *Nausea*: "People. You must love people. Men are admirable. I want to vomit – and suddenly, there it is: the Nausea."[23] The confusion caused by nausea matches the confusion Jonah would eventually feel when he was unable to make peace with his mission. This violent end to his stay in the belly of the fish parallels the violent swallowing suggested by the Hebrew infinitive *livlo'a*. The word has a generally negative connotation in the Hebrew Bible suggesting "brute force," as in Aaron's staff swallowing the rods of Egyptian magicians or the earth swallowing Korah and his followers.[24] It also suggests that if Jonah was comfortable in the salvation and solitude offered by the fish, God made sure that the relationship was sharply severed by forcibly pushing him out to pursue his original mission.

Jonah, of course, prayed one more time. This time it was not a prayer of gratitude but a prayer that God take his life: "Please, Lord, take my life, for I would rather die than live" (Jonah 4:3). This prayer grew in intensity when Jonah found post-Nineveh life less and less palatable. "He begged for death, saying, 'I would rather die than live'" (v. 8). God was so incredulous that He questioned Jonah twice about his death wish: "Then God said to Jonah, 'Are you so deeply grieved about the plant?' 'Yes,' he replied, 'so deeply that I want to die'" (v. 9). Arguably, Jonah had been dying since his very first appearance, with his suicidal mission to flee from God, to descend into the bowels of a ship in the midst of capsizing and then, finally, with his request for the sailors to throw him overboard. The fish's ambush, as it turns out, was only a brief hiatus in

---

23. Jean-Paul Sartre, *Nausea*, trans. Lloyd Alexander (New York: New Directions, 1964), 122.
24. Examples of this include Ex. 7:12; Num. 16:30, 34; Jer. 51:34; Ps. 124:3; Job 7:19; 20:15, 18.

Jonah's dreamscape of leaving a world he could barely tolerate. When he captured this sentiment in prayer, however, something had intensified about his plea. This is more evident in the Hebrew than in the English translation: *Tov moti meḥayai*, "my death is good, better than life."

This conclusion should be morally repugnant to the reader, who recognizes in these words that Jonah would never prophesy again. When prayer can be changed from a vehicle of spiritual intimacy to a murderous impulse, the prophet has lost his capacity for revelation. Zornberg uses this inversion of prayer's purpose and content to question Jonah's very identity:

> The core of his prayer constitutes an inversion of the public norms of prayer: death is his desire and it is associated with goodness (*tov*). He has already inverted the consensual uses of the Thirteen Divine Attributes, which classically celebrate God's mercy.... Jonah alone speaks in a tone of aggrieved despair.... The God who is classically celebrated as "renouncing evil" has acted true to form; and Jonah is mortally sick because of it. Who, then, is this Jonah, who unsettles the associations of words, demonically repudiating love while desiring death and calling it good?[25]

Ironically, although God spoke to Jonah in chapter 4, God did not speak to Jonah after he prayed in chapter 2. He merely commanded the fish to spew Jonah out onto dry land. Jonah was not yet ready for a dialogue with God. Embraced by God's salvific powers, Jonah was not at the point where he could confront God about his deep theological misgivings or perhaps listen to God's response. God was not yet able to teach Jonah how wrong he was about the world. For now, the prayer was an expression of simple thanksgiving that set Jonah on a temporary path back to his mission. And for now, at least, this seemed to be enough.

---

25. Zornberg, "Jonah: A Fantasy of Flight," 80.

Part Three
Radical Transformation

Chapter Seven

Nineveh: That "Great" City

Nineveh was an enormously large city, a three days' walk across. Jonah began by going a day's journey into the city, proclaiming, "Forty days more and Nineveh will be overturned." The Ninevites believed God. A fast was proclaimed, and all of them, from the greatest to the least, put on sackcloth. When Jonah's warning reached the king of Nineveh, he rose from his throne, took off his royal robes, covered himself with sackcloth, and sat down in the dust. This is the proclamation he issued in Nineveh: "By the decree of the king and his nobles: Do not let people or animals, herds or flocks, taste anything; do not let them eat or drink. But let people and animals be covered with sackcloth. Let everyone call urgently on God. Let everyone turn back from his evil ways and from the injustice that is in his hands. Who knows but that God may turn and relent? He may turn back from His wrath so that we do not perish." When God saw what they did and how they turned from their evil ways, He relented and did not bring on them the destruction He had threatened. (Jonah 3:3–10)

In Rembrandt's ink drawing, "The Prophet Jonah beside the Walls of Nineveh,"[1] the prophet lies beneath what could be a gourd or a bush

---

1. This small drawing (8.5 by 6.8 inches) is located in Vienna's Albertina Museum and was likely done in 1651.

outside the walls of a fortress. His hands are clasped together. He seems weak and defeated. We are unsure if this is a depiction of the moments before Jonah entered the city in chapter 3 or if it is from chapter 4, when Jonah left the city and sought refuge by constructing a small booth; the text implies that Jonah went far from the city to observe it from a distance. His mood in chapter 4 is anger and outrage, not sadness and anguish. If it is our prophet before encountering Nineveh, Jonah could have been exhausted from leaving the fish and arriving at his task, no longer with the same zeal he had earlier. Facing the daunting and impenetrable stronghold of Nineveh by retreating into himself, the man as portrayed by Rembrandt is an Israelite humbled by Assyrian might. In Jonah's despairing face, we see the prophet wondering if he can penetrate the hearts of these foreigners if he was not even able to penetrate the city's walls. In either interpretation, the city of Nineveh proves too much for one man. The prophet, still fresh out of his fish habitat, lacks the endurance and strength of will to stay true to his new commitment.

It is this singular sense of a city's lone savior, however, that encapsulates Jonah's mission and makes readers wonder: What was it about the city of Nineveh that engendered God's attention and concern, so much so that God sent only one of His prophets to reform the entire place? When Nineveh is mentioned early in Genesis, the very same adjective, "great," is used, just as it appears in the Book of Jonah: "From that land Asshur went forth and built Nineveh, Rehoboth-ir, Calah, and Resen between Nineveh and Calah, that is the *great city*" (Gen. 10:11–12). The city, built by Nimrod, was great in size, seemingly from its very earliest days. The only difference in description is one word attached to the city's description the third time it is mentioned in the Book of Jonah: "Nineveh was an *enormously* large city, a three days' walk across" (Jonah 3:3). Its size is modified by a description of how long it took to traverse. Yet the word for enhanced greatness in Hebrew here is *leElohim*, which has been translated in a variety of ways. Huge, enormous, or very large are common translations. The Jewish Publication Society notes an ambiguity, however: "Meaning of Heb. uncertain." But its meaning is important – perhaps critical – to understanding the entire enterprise God sought in deputizing Jonah to go to Nineveh in the first place.

Nineveh: That "Great" City

The uncertainty around the word *Elohim* can be traced to its frequent and often inconsistent meaning in the Hebrew Bible. It appears 2,602 times – yet can still confound the Bible reader. It can refer to the true or majestic God or Judge,[2] false gods,[3] human leaders,[4] or angels and other supernatural beings[5] – all terms that connote power or authority. Rather than translate *leElohim* as a description of its size, something that has already been mentioned twice in the Book of Jonah, perhaps its intended meaning is that this is a city great to God. God cared greatly about this city, as we can see by the book's closing line: "And should I not care about Nineveh, *that great city*, in which there are more than 120,000 persons who do not yet know their right hand from their left, and many beasts as well?" (4:11). If this is the case, what we have to unearth is why God cared specifically for this city when, no doubt, there were other ancient locations of sin and corruption that could have benefited from God's guiding hand.

Nineveh was a large Mesopotamian city located on the eastern bank of the Tigris River in what would today be part of Iraq, likely Mosul. It covered a vast physical territory – the Book of Jonah mentions that it took a three-day journey to cross it. It was located on a hill dotted with palaces and temples, which may explain the lengthy physical exertion needed to cross it. Nineveh served as the capital of the Assyrian empire from the time of Sennacherib (705–681 BCE). Sennacherib waged war against the Babylonians, the Egyptians, and the much smaller Judah. Isaiah warned Hezekiah not to join an uprising against the Assyrian king but, as so often happened in Israelite history, the king paid the prophet no heed. Sennacherib later destroyed Judean cities, including placing a siege on Jerusalem, and exacted heavy tribute from Hezekiah.

At the height of its power, Nineveh was one of the most significant cities in antiquity and a place of territorial importance for every warring nation in the ancient world. In cuneiform, it is symbolized by a

---

2. Examples of this include Gen. 1:1; 14:18; Ex. 20:2–3; Deut. 10:17; Ps. 136:2.
3. Examples of this include I Sam. 5:7; I Kings 11:5, 33; 18:24.
4. Examples of this include Ex. 4:16; 7:1; 21:6; 22:7–8, 27.
5. See Ps. 8:6; 97:7; 138:1.

fish in a house, giving an indication of its significance as a port city and a place rich in aquatic life. Naturally, it was important as a water highway for merchants and sailors. Sennacherib built a very large palace in Nineveh and named it "the palace which has no equal."[6] Reliefs have been found which depict the luxury of the palace that seemingly had no equal. Sennacherib's grandson Ashurbanipal (668–627 BCE) built an additional palace in Nineveh and a large royal library. A relief from his palace shows the monarch alone, in his palace high on a hill surrounded by trees in every direction.[7]

Nineveh is mentioned in II Kings as a place of refuge for Sennacherib when he later failed to capture Jerusalem.[8] This decision proved deadly:

> He [Sennacherib] shall not enter this city, he shall not shoot an arrow at it. Or advance upon it with a shield, or pile up a wage mound against it. He shall go back by the way he came; he shall not enter this city, declares the Lord. I will protect and save this city for My sake, and for the sake of My servant David. That night an angel of the Lord went and struck down 185,000 in the Assyrian camp, and the following morning they were all dead corpses. While he was worshipping in the temple of his god Nisroch, his

---

6. See Yuval Kamrot, *Encyclopedia Judaica* (1972), s.v. "Nineveh."
7. See an illustration of the relief by A. M. Appa, based on a drawing of S. Dalley, "Ancient Mesopotamian Gardens," *Garden History* 21 (1993): 10, fig. 2, as seen in Philip J. King and Lawrence E. Stager, *Life in Biblical Israel* (Louisville, KY: Westminster John Knox Press, 2001), 221.
8. For a description of what likely happened and how Judah defended itself against this powerful Assyrian king through its fortresses, see Chaim Herzog and Mordechai Gichon, *Battles of the Bible* (London: Greenhill Books, 2001), 210–212. Herzog and Gichon describe Judah's security as dependent on the balance of power between Egypt, Assyria, and Babylon: "As long as these three cancelled out much of each other's surplus aggression, there was a good chance of more than mere survival for the smaller states" (256). Hezekiah and then Josiah after him, keenly aware of the way Judah stood as a geographic center to these three warring empires, took advantage of Assyria's weakening power due to internecine struggles, "Assyria had been torn by internal rivalries, Babylonia and Media having combined to deprive her of most of her eastern possessions including Nineveh, the capital" (ibid.).

sons Adrammelech and Sarezer struck him down with the sword. They fled to the land of Ararat, and his son Esarhaddon succeeded him as king. (19:32–36)

Nineveh, the city, was decimated in 612 BCE after the great Battle of Nineveh, a transitional and critical victory in the twenty-six-year war between the Byzantines and the Sassanids. The city was captured and plundered and "became a desolate heap."[9] The Byzantine victory changed the political landscape of the ancient Near East, giving the Persian Empire greater power and influence over the region. Nineveh in the ancient world functioned as a seat of important political power. No doubt, any influence on Nineveh – as God desired in Jonah – would spill over into the entire Assyrian Empire. If God wanted to impart a message to Jonah about His attitude toward the world at large and not just the Israelites (as we will see in further depth in the next chapter), Nineveh was an apt choice.

NINEVITE CRIMES AND REPENTANCE

The great crimes of Nineveh are not articulated in the biblical text, but in the rabbinic imagination the crime is identified as thievery. This and sexual immorality were among the chief sins of the Ninevites, as we see in an interpretation of the verse "Let everyone turn back from his *evil ways* and from the *injustice* that is in his hands" (Jonah 3:8). *Darko haraa* is "sexual deviance" and *hehamas asher bekhapeihem* is "stealing" (literally: the corruption that is in their hands). We find resonances of this same latter crime in the generation of Noah that was destroyed by water:

> The earth became corrupt before God; the earth was filled with lawlessness. When God saw how *corrupt* [*hamas*] the earth was, for all flesh had *corrupted* its *ways* [*darko*] on earth, God said to Noah, "I have decided to put an end to all flesh, for the earth is filled with lawlessness because of them: I am about to destroy them with the earth." (Gen. 6:11–13)

---

9. Ibid.

Radical Transformation

As we saw earlier, the sages debate how far-reaching Ninevite repentance was, discussing whether they would dismantle an entire house in order to return a stolen beam.[10] This signals just how penetrating was Nineveh's immersion into the universe of atonement, but also makes us wonder if this was a common pattern in Nineveh – to quickly muster dramatic change to distract or appease God or their gods. The chapter describes it as almost commonplace that an entire city and its animals should wear sackcloth and fast. It does not even sound odd to those who experienced it. It is just odd to those of us reading it.

This city of sin had so reformed itself, according to one opinion, that its citizens went beyond the call of law in paying the price for their waywardness. Thus, another mishnaic passage makes perfect sense in light of this transformation:

> What is the order of the fast days? The Ark containing the scrolls of the law is to be brought to the public square ... the elder is to address [the people] in ways that inspire them to repent: "My brothers, consider that it is not written in respect to the citizens of Nineveh that God gave heed to their sackcloth and their fasting but that 'God saw what they did and how they turned from their evil ways' (Jonah 3:10) and this is also what the prophets said, 'Rip apart your hearts and not your garments' (Joel 2:13)." (Mishna Taanit 2:2)

The Ninevites modeled *teshuva* at its best. They both engaged in the outer signs of repentance by wearing sackcloth and fasting and, more importantly, understood that clothing is only a layer above the skin. For atonement to be complete, it must reach the innermost parts of the penitent.

The fact that Nineveh's residents were exemplars of positive change seems a mere continuation of a theme generated by the non-Jews in chapter 1, and the text begs a comparison. The sailors prayed characteristically before and once again after Jonah was identified as the culprit and requested to be thrown overboard. Their prayer was not the urgent call for salvation from men on a ship about to collapse. It was

---

10. See Mishna Gittin 5:5; Gittin 55a; Taanit 16a; as well as our discussion in the previous chapter.

a prayer to be judged as innocents for the action they were about to undertake, namely, throwing a Hebrew prophet off their ship and into the sea. While they could not know for certain if they had caused the storm, they knew without question that taking a person's life, let alone that of a prophet of the ancient Hebrews, was a grave and punishable offense. Suddenly their prayer was uniform and of one voice:

> Then they cried out to the Lord, "Please, Lord, do not let us die for taking this man's life. Do not hold us accountable for killing an innocent man, for You, Lord, have done as You pleased." They took Jonah and threw him overboard, and the raging sea grew calm. (Jonah 1:14–15)

In tossing him out to sea, the sailors knew that perhaps Jonah would die and they too would die, putting an end to the possibility that the storm was their only problem. Yet they framed their action not as Jonah's request but as God's very desire: "for You, Lord, have done as You pleased" (v. 14). When the storm calmed, they understood that they had executed God's wishes and for this, they surely would not be punished. As Greenberg describes it:

> The heathen sailors, momentarily converted to acknowledge Israel's God, pray in the familiar pattern of address, petition, motivation. As previously noted, their prayer climaxes their service to the story as a spiritually sensitive foil to the unresponsive, finally lethargic, prophet.[11]

Greenberg claims that the sailors' prayer acknowledged God's sense of fairness, which "even the heathens recognize as divine, as in God's interest to confirm."[12]

By the end of chapter 1, the sailors have undergone a religious transformation from random supplications to myriad gods to a fully focused reverence for one God. The last verses in the chapter offer two different perspectives, on deck and beneath the deck – way beneath:

---

11. Greenberg, *Biblical Prose Prayer*, 16.
12. Ibid., 17.

Radical Transformation

"and the raging sea grew calm. At this the men greatly feared the Lord, and they offered a sacrifice to the Lord and made vows to Him. But the Lord provided a huge fish to swallow Jonah, and Jonah was inside the fish three days and three nights" (Jonah 1:15–2:1). The sailors had no idea, nor would they ever find out, that they had not killed Jonah. In fact, the text jumps to the end of chapter 2 in revealing to the reader the duration of Jonah's stay inside the belly of the fish. From the sailors' perspective, Jonah was gone, as was the storm. In its place, what they received was a new God, not one of many but a God of the sea *and* the dry land.

One does not have such a transformational experience without repercussions. Although they each made separate vows in the plural, the sacrifice they offered was in the singular. This event brought together a disparate group who formed a community of prayer. It is no wonder that some exegetes, Rashi chief among them, regard the pledges and sacrifice to Jonah's God as an act of conversion. Rabbi Joseph Kara (the "Mahari Kra," 1065–1135), a contemporary and possibly a student of Rashi in Troyes, uses four Hebrew words to Rashi's one: "They converted themselves in the name of God." Radak regards these pledges as gifts of charity to the poor as opposed to an actual animal offering, since such an offering would be inappropriate outside Temple precincts. This may also explain why the *Metzudat David* (Rabbi David ben Solomon ibn Abi Zimra, 1479–1573) adds that the pledges they made were to sacrifice to God in the actual Temple. Ibn Ezra adds that they could only offer the sacrifice when they left the ship, for obvious reasons. We are unsure of the journey's duration, but if Ibn Ezra's re-creation of the scene is accurate, these sailors did not forget the goodness bestowed upon them days, weeks, or possibly months after the events of their sea voyage. The overpowering trauma of the storm, the audacity of the prophet in running away from his God, and the aftermath of being found was enough, no doubt, to inspire awe and fear in these innocents. At the moment of the sea's instant transformation they learned that what they had long suspected was true: one cannot run from God. The natural outgrowth of this conclusion, now borne out experientially and not only in principle, led them – as it led the people of Nineveh – to prayer and to commitment.[13]

---

13. Such stories of conversion as a result of experiencing the power of the Hebrews' God were more common in the Talmud than in the Bible, where individuals of note rather

Nineveh: That "Great" City

The sailors and the Ninevites were twinned in their sincerity and zeal. According to Radak, this parallel was actually causal: "The men of the ship were in the city and bore witness concerning him [Jonah], that they threw him into the sea. 'All of our testimony is precisely what happened.' Therefore, they believed his prophecy completely."[14] The sailors did not drop out of the Jonah narrative. Their ship, in this reading, anchored in Nineveh where they once again encountered the prophet and told the city's residents to take his message seriously, prompting the residents to repent.

CONVERSIONS IN BIBLICAL BOOKS

Though this reading of Jonah is dependent on midrashic interpretation, the Bible does have a number of similar accounts in which a foreign group converted en masse, information which is almost always offered in passing and not detailed in the text. This transformation takes place for a variety of reasons, often because Jewish fortune changed for the good, and outsiders of an opportunistic bent sought to change their own destinies by attaching themselves to the Jewish people. When Abraham journeyed to Canaan with his wife and nephew, the verse specifies ambiguously that they were joined by an unnamed group who were clearly influenced by Abraham. He left with "all the possessions and those they had acquired

---

than unnamed commoners converted. Gittin alone offers the conversion of Nero Caesar and Nebuzaradan, identified as the captain of the guard for Nebuchadnezzar, because of a miraculous experience of God and the Israelites. In Nero Caesar's case, the simple testing of an arrow's fall indicated to him that the verse of Ezekiel 24:14 ("And I will lay My vengeance upon Edom by the hand of My people Israel") would come true, which led Nero to the conclusion that "the Holy One, Blessed Be He, wishes to destroy His Temple, and He wishes to wipe His hands with that man (himself)." The Talmud concludes that "he fled and became a convert" (Gittin 56a), not wishing to be the person who was God's agent in bringing about destruction. Nebuzaradan, a vicious murderer, feared his punishment at God's hand and "fled, sent his house a document with the details of his estate, and converted" (Gittin 57b). This victory for the Jews – that their sworn enemies would convert to their faith as the ultimate validation of their often scorned existence – seems to be more a product of rabbinic fantasy than actuality, although one understands its potency, especially in times of siege and oppression.

14. Radak to Jonah 3:5.

Radical Transformation

in Haran" (Gen. 12:5). Thus, Abraham, future builder of a nation, arrived in the Land of Israel with family and new adherents. The Israelite Exodus out of slavery also seduced some outsiders to leave Egypt with them: "The Israelites journeyed on foot from Raamses to Succoth, approximately 600,000.... A mixed multitude also left with them" (Ex. 12:37).

In the Book of Esther, when the Jews finally asserted their dominance as a previously oppressed minority, there were those who wanted to join in their faith commitment: "In every province and in every city to which the edict of the king came, there was joy and gladness among the Jews, with feasting and celebrating. And many people of other nationalities became Jews because the fear of the Jews had seized them" (8:17). We do not know if these individuals who joined stayed within the fold or not. We have no idea how and if they integrated into this minority community or if they represented the lowest in status who basically led lives of quiet desperation and saw, as a last chance, Jewish success as a way to climb out of poverty or despair.

One biblical narrative in which God's clear love of the Israelites impressed but did not inspire conversion remains a mystery in light of these other stories: Yitro. Moses' father-in-law was regarded as a wise gentile who offered his son-in-law important advice to grow his leadership as a mentor and guide. A *parasha* of the Pentateuch is named after him and it opens with Yitro's visit to Moses early on in the wilderness sojourn: "Yitro, priest of Midian, Moses' father-in-law, heard all that God had done for Moses and for Israel His people, how the Lord had brought Israel out from Egypt" (Ex. 18:1). This news occasioned a family visit. When Moses and Yitro entered Moses' tent, Moses regaled his father-in-law with "everything that the Lord had done to Pharaoh and to the Egyptians for Israel's sake, all the hardships that had befallen them on the way, and how the Lord had delivered them" (v. 8). Yitro's response was not neutral:

> And Yitro rejoiced over all the kindness that the Lord had shown Israel when He delivered them from the Egyptians. "Blessed be the Lord," Yitro said, "who delivered you from the Egyptians and from Pharaoh, and who delivered the people from under the hand of the Egyptians. Now I know that the Lord is greater than all gods, yes, by the result of their very schemes against [the

people]." And Yitro, Moses' father-in-law, brought a burnt offering and sacrifices for God. (vv. 10–12)

Out of all the stories in which God's might is made apparent to a gentile in a way that moves that individual or group profoundly, none expresses Yitro's depth of understanding and acknowledgment that the Israelite God was the one true God. And yet, although like the sailors Yitro offered sacrifices, he decidedly did *not* convert. This is affirmed in a later story that involves either Yitro or his son, Hobab, when Moses lacked a guide in the wilderness and turned to Hobab for assistance:

> Moses said to Hobab son of Reuel the Midianite, Moses' father-in-law, "We are setting out for the place of which the Lord has said, 'I will give it to you.' Come with us and we will be generous with you; for the Lord has promised to be generous to Israel." "I will not go," he replied to him, "but will return to my native land." (Num. 10:29–30)

There was no need to recount the miracles God wrought on behalf of the Israelites here. Moses needed a set of eyes, literally, and knew that as inhabitants of the desert, Yitro's house would be able to navigate the terrain better than he could. Moses was willing to share Israel's good fortune, but this was not incentive enough. Hobab, like Yitro, was happy to be instrumental but was not sufficiently inspired or motivated to join.

Another biblical instance in which a group joined the Israelites but conversion did not take place – despite an acknowledgment of God's might – is found in the curious and disturbing story of the Gibeonites in the Book of Joshua. As we saw earlier,[15] after news spread about Israelite victories and instilled fear in Canaan's residents, the Gibeonites disguised themselves in order to secure a vow of protection. In fact, they used the language familiar to us from accounts like Yitro's: "Your servants have come from a very distant country, because of the fame of the Lord your God. For we heard the report of Him: of all that He did in Egypt, and

---

15. See chapter 5.

of all that He did to the two Amorite kings on the other side of the Jordan" (Josh. 9:9–10). It was only three days later that the Israelites realized that these were not a distant tribe; they were permitted to remain but punished with the low status of woodchoppers and water drawers.

Just as in these other cases, with the exception of the Gibeonites, the sailors' powerful confrontation with the God of the Hebrews necessitated a reassessment of personal belief. In the Book of Jonah, this first took place when Jonah ostensibly drowned and the moment of danger passed. The sailors experienced a shattering and altering shift that forced them to redirect their prayers and offerings. Far beyond the gifts they gave, the sailors had to evaluate anew their very notion of worship. After all, the God of Jonah, according to the prophet, was the God of sea and dry land, an all-encompassing God who traveled with them in the two domains sailors straddled in their work. This God was an everywhere God, where previously they had worshipped gods of different domains and varying natural forces. There was an ease in their lack of rigidity and willingness to take the truth whence it came, a feature present in the Ninevites as well.

Both the Ninevites and the sailors serve as foils for Jonah's recalcitrance and inflexibility. And yet, the shifts they experienced must have forced an uncomfortable re-evaluation of personal and collective belief. How could they not when the ship carrying them was about to capsize and imperil all their lives and instead they received an instant reprieve? Their response – to embrace fully this epistemological transformation – tugged at Jonah's reticence and his unwillingness to change, even when shown evidence that his inherent assumption was incorrect. He could not run away from God. He even admitted as much when the storm came and he was confronted by the sailors to explain the odd climate changes, for "I know that it is my fault that this great storm has come upon you" (1:12). He claimed to know that this was God's doing, but instead of reforming and accepting the fact that he could not escape a destiny assigned to him, Jonah further escaped into the sea. Could not the God who pursued the prophet on the surface of the sea find him underwater? The sailors allowed their newfound knowledge of this God to change them. Jonah did not. However, the sailors and the residents of Nineveh, including its king, did not have to convert to receive God's mercy or His praise.

AN ALLUSION TO AN EARLIER ERA

Nineveh became a symbol in God's moral arsenal. It pointed to an earlier, pre-Israelite time, a time when there were only universal man and woman, primordial beings that God created before He created the first Jews. It is as if God wanted both the prophet and the Bible reader to be reminded of this earlier iteration of the universe – with its expansive nature and with God's sweeping and wide-ranging concern for all of creation, even those who were once enemies to His favored child. This interest and mercy did not stop when the Israelites were called God's firstborn – a theme deeply entrenched in the Exodus story, beginning with Moses' words to Pharaoh: "Thus says the Lord, 'Israel is My firstborn son. Let My son go that he may worship Me'" (Ex. 4:22–23).[16] Jeremiah was told to proclaim to Jerusalem: "Israel is holy to the Lord, the first fruits of His harvest" (Jer. 2:3). Externally and internally, the Bible rings with a message of the unique and special status that God enjoyed with this people, His people. But a special status does not imply an exclusive relationship. Parents may have particular affection for firstborns because those are the children that made them into parents. That will always be exceptional. But love, if it is true, is expansive and generative. Even expectant parents who cannot imagine loving other children as much as firstborns learn quickly with the birth of another just how much affection and adoration they can dispense – it is boundless because love, unlike so many other "commodities" and emotional currencies, has no artificial boundaries. It cannot be contained. There is no scarcity that contracts love. As the word *gedola* implies, it is "large." It is enormous. It is immense.

The use of the same terminology for Nineveh in the Book of Jonah as in chapter 10 of Genesis takes the reader back to this formative time. When Noah and his sons were charged with rebuilding a post-diluvian world, they spread out across the ancient map. This etiological record in Genesis 10 offers an account of the multiplicity of languages and cultures in this new universe, so different from the one that emerged from the first five chapters of Genesis:

---

16. For more on this special firstborn relationship and its implications for the Exodus story and Passover, see David Fohrman, *The Exodus You Almost Passed Over* (New York: Alpha-Beta Press, 2016).

> The sons of Ham: Cush, Egypt, Put, and Canaan. The sons of Cush: Seba, Havilah, Sabtah, Raamah, and Sabteca. The sons of Raamah: Sheba and Dedan. Cush was the father of Nimrod, who became a mighty warrior on the earth. He was a mighty hunter before the Lord; that is why it is said, "Like Nimrod, a mighty hunter before the Lord." The first centers of his kingdom were Babylon, Erech, Accad, and Calneh, in Shinar. From that land he went to Assyria, where he built Nineveh, Rehoboth-ir, Calah, and Resen, which is between *Nineveh and Calah, which is the great city.*" (10:6–12)

This constellation of places, the geographic arteries of the descendants of Ham, constituted a group that would provide, in the aggregate, no end of oppression to the Israelites, who did not, at this point in Genesis, even exist.

The connection between Ham and Egypt appears here and elsewhere in the Bible, specifically in Psalms and Chronicles. This connection will be important in understanding the significance of Nineveh in the Book of Jonah. In a thoughtful synopsis of the Egypt story, we read of this early connection:

> Then Israel entered Egypt; Jacob resided as a foreigner in the land of Ham. The Lord made His people very fruitful; He made them too numerous for their foes, whose hearts He turned to hate His people, to conspire against His servants. He sent Moses His servant, and Aaron, whom He had chosen. They performed His signs among them, His wonders in the land of Ham. (Ps. 105:23–27)

Ham is also identified with Egypt in I Chronicles (1:8): "The sons of Ham: Cush, Egypt, Put, and Canaan" and once again in Psalms (106:21–22): "They forgot the God who saved them, who had done great things in Egypt, miracles in the land of Ham and awesome deeds by the Reed Sea." Josephus claims that Ethiopians descended from Cush the son of Ham: "For of the four sons of Ham, time has not at all hurt the name of Cush; for the Ethiopians, over whom he reigned, are even at this day, both by themselves and by all men in Asia, called Cushites."[17] It would seem that Ham's children dominated the northeast regions of Africa.

One might claim that the identification of Ham with Egypt was merely geographical. But it seems as if a richer interpretation awaits.[18] Ham was one of Noah's three sons who left the ark. In Genesis 9, Ham saw his father Noah naked and drunk in his tent and went out to belittle Noah to his brothers. Noah awoke, startled at what his youngest son had done, and cursed Ham's son. He wanted Ham to feel that the consequence of dishonoring a parent was that Ham would, subsequently, be dishonored by *his* children. Noah's curse was targeted: "The lowest of slaves shall he be to his brothers" (Gen. 9:25). Noah's other sons were quick to cover up their father and turn their gaze away from him. As their reward, they would be situated higher in the human hierarchy; they would lead while Canaan's descendants would serve them: "Blessed be the Lord, the God of Shem; let Canaan be a slave to them. May God enlarge Japheth, and let him dwell in the tents of Shem; and let Canaan be a slave to them" (Gen. 9:26–27).

In this narrative, Noah was making an observation about his family and about humanity, the new world he was consigned to repopulate. In this new world there would continue to be evil – immorality, enmity, envy, and small-mindedness – represented by one of his sons. There would be children who could be saved by a parent and still ridicule a parent. But in this new world, this behavior would be overshadowed by goodness, by children who honored and obeyed. Those who were little in spirit would become little in stature. Instead of being leaders, they would be slaves to pettiness and thoughtlessness.

In the vast epic narrative that is our origin story, Ham's children, including Egypt and Assyria, would forever be associated with war and slavery; their homelands would be places that reduced people to suffering. As a result, they themselves would eventually become humbled. The Israelites, a small, oppressed people, rose above their situation when

---

17. Josephus, *Antiquities*, 1.6.
18. Some of these ideas are excerpted or paraphrased from a blog post called "Egypt, A Synopsis," on my site, "Weekly Jewish Wisdom," April 7, 2016 (http://www.ericabrown.com/new-blog-1/2016/4/7/exodus-a-synopsis).

leaving Egypt and were commanded to bring others out of suffering as a result. Thus, the story of Genesis was replayed on a national scale in the story of Exodus in the Pentateuch as a crucible that formed the Israelites, and then later represented by Nineveh and Assyria generally as a bullying force for evil and belligerence.

It is for this reason that God had to remind the Israelites that all creatures are God's creatures. He did this by hearkening back to a time before battle, a time of newness and innocence – an innocence that Nineveh tried to recapture with its transformation. God Himself also changed, as will be described in greater detail in a later chapter. The God who was quick to regret His creation of humanity in Genesis experienced a shift in His teleology, so to speak, and tried to bring Jonah – a representative of God's firstborn – into a world in which there was enough concern and compassion from a Father for every child. Locked as we are into a portrait of the prophet or the city to which he ministered, we forget that the book tells us much more about the evolving identity of God.

In addition, the connection in this passage among Egypt, Assyria, and Babylon, oppressor nations that so often fought each other, is not coincidental for the spread of monotheism. Abraham was the first monotheist. The Jews germinated an idea that was iconoclastic and revolutionary, but it was not an idea that was meant to influence the Israelites alone. To have the influence that, in hindsight, swept the world, God had to ensure that the major voices of the ancient Near Eastern world were touched in some important way by the power of the Hebrew God. In the Exodus narratives, this is abundantly clear:

> And Egypt will know that I am the Lord. (Ex. 7:5)
> And the Egyptians shall know I am the Lord. (14:4)
> And the Egyptians shall know I am the Lord. (14:18)[19]

---

19. Several other verses indicate that the purpose of the plagues was to know God, but these three verses exclusively refer to the Egyptians, as opposed to the Israelites re-acquainting themselves with the God of their forefathers. For knowledge of God in a general sense throughout the Exodus story, see Ex. 8:6, 18; 9:14, 29; 10:2; 11:7. See also Neḥama Leibowitz, "The Purpose of the Plagues" in *Studies in Exodus*

The plagues were designed as a faith curriculum for a foreign nation as well as an affirmation to the Israelites that the risk to them was warranted to secure their freedom and cement a covenant with the God of their forefathers.

Pharaoh, however, proved to be uneducable. His stubbornness and antagonism to Moses, Aaron, and the God of these brothers prevented this educational project from ever making deep indentations in the psyche of this leader, his magicians, and his courtiers. But unquestionably the impact of the plagues let the Egyptians as a nation understand the power and precision of the Hebrew God in contrast to the pantheon of their gods. We never return to Egypt following the Splitting of the Sea to see how the Egyptians fared after their reigning Pharaoh and his army were killed. This must have been, in their collective psyche, the final act that helped them understand how ultimately powerless their own king/god was in confrontation with the Israelite God. Yet this knowledge of God in the Exodus narrative, influential as it was, was inherently negative. People suffered at the hands of this God because of their recalcitrant ruler.

In contrast, the Jonah story offers us a narrative antipode as an alternate possibility. When the king of a powerful foreign nation was moved to change because of his fear and awe of God and encouraged his people to do so as well, God too changed and accepted the repentance of this otherwise hostile nation. Nineveh was *ir gedola leElohim*, "important to God," precisely because it represented a subversion of the Egypt narrative. One can know a powerful God not through might but through the Deity's compassion. The plotline of Jonah offers a platform to tell this alternative narrative and to demonstrate the words of Isaiah:

> Let not the foreigner say, who has attached himself to the Lord, "The Lord will keep me apart from His people...." As for the foreigners who attach themselves to the Lord, to minister to Him,

---

(Jerusalem: Haomanim Press, 1986), 170–177 for her discussion of these verses and David Fohrman, "The Case for Monotheism" as it relates to the Exodus story in *The Exodus You Almost Passed Over*, 79–82.

and to love the name of the Lord, to be His servants – all who keep the Sabbath and do not profane it, and who hold fast to My covenant – I will bring them to My sacred mount and let them rejoice in My house of prayer. Their burnt offerings and sacrifices shall be welcome on My altar, for My house shall be called a house of prayer for all peoples. (Is. 56:3, 6–7)

God was convinced that Nineveh, the great city, was worth saving; for that, He was willing to change, accepting its residents' repentance. Jonah, God's reluctant prophet, was sure that the city was not worth saving; he was, therefore, ultimately unwilling to change. One need look no further than the one-day travel into a city that takes three days to cross to realize that Jonah was better off in the sea than on land.

Chapter Eight

Two Watery Tales of God's Sudden Compassion

> "The word of the Lord came to Jonah, son of Amitai. Rise, go to Nineveh, that great city, and proclaim judgment upon it; for their wickedness has come before Me." (Jonah 1:1–2)

The parallels between the Jonah story and the Noah story are too similar to ignore. Scholars and exegetes who compare and contrast the two often focus on the water imagery or the forty-day period that appears in both narratives. While these technical details do signal a need to compare the two stories, few observe the far more profound and striking similarities that underlie the narratives, many easily noticed by a simple glance at the opening of the Noah story:

> The earth became corrupt before God; the earth was filled with lawlessness. When God saw how corrupt the earth was, for all flesh had corrupted its ways on earth, God said to Noah, "I have decided to put an end to all flesh, for the earth is filled with lawlessness because of them: I am about to destroy them with the earth. Make yourself an ark of gopher wood; make it an ark with compartments, and cover it inside and out with pitch. This is how you shall make it." (Gen. 6:11–15)

Corruption not only existed in both narratives; it caught God's attention. It came before God and precipitated a response: one human representative needed to address the decadence and immorality, either through a blunt and dire prediction or by the slow and incremental building of an ark that would become enough of a curiosity to stimulate questioning by those who saw it being carefully constructed.

Outside of the text, other similarities abound, namely, the treatment of both narratives in art. Many artistic depictions of the Noah and Jonah stories focus on friendly animal images: an ark teeming with God's creations as animals proceed up a wooden ramp to salvation two by two; a smiling whale with a prophet inside it. It is an illustrator's happy moment – that is, an illustrator who has not read beyond the first lines of either story. But for those who immerse themselves in the text, a different canvas emerges.

In the late nineteenth century, painter William Scott Bell captured the chaos of the Genesis scene: the sea rises while sheets of grey-blue rain hit hard on Noah's generation, the people who ignored his frivolous ark-building until they realized that he was the only one prepared for the apocalypse. The painter Francis Darby, in the mid-eighteenth century, shows a small scrim of land, the last remaining earth of the world God originally created, as waves pound its cliff-sides and a few scattered people hold on to tree trunks. Only when we look through the darkness of the scene do we realize that the top of these last rocks is not covered with loose vegetation but human beings, clamoring to live. The small winged angel on the right side of the canvas bathed in light shares his radiance with only one person: Noah. The survivor guilt alone could kill a man.

Jonah too appears in his fair share of thoughtful renderings. Gustave Doré etches Jonah as a typical Hebrew prophet, robed in a flowing tunic with hands outstretched in front of an impressive stone pillar, trying to beseech the people of Nineveh to change. Some look up at him with interest, some have their heads bowed in contrition, one man lies prostrate on the ground weeping. In the distant background, people mill about the bold edifices of the city, unaware of the moral wave that will soon sweep through. This depiction, one of Doré's last two of the Hebrew Bible, is not a particularly unusual or gruesome scene. It could be of any prophet addressing an audience in public. Yet a different engraving, that of Jonah being cast forth by the great fish, is mesmerizing in its abject terror. The fish, with large pointed dorsal fins and two flowing water spouts, is turned away from Jonah and making its way back to the heart of the sea. Jonah holds on tightly in the bleak darkness to the rocky shore looking back, not forward. His mission is unclear, his fear is palpable, and any nostalgic look at the fish leaving reminds us that Jonah's only safety and security lay ironically in the inside of that leviathan.

But Jonah and Noah are not always alike. While Jonah, through his prayer, takes us through the process of losing himself in the sea, it was his heartfelt wish to end his life this way, as we saw earlier. Noah, on the other hand, was to be on the other side of this suffering. He stood on the ship listening to the decimation of humanity, helpless to prevent a drowning he understood was God's will. He also carried the unbelievable burden of recreating a world better than the one he left when the rain stopped and the ground dried. What was worse for Noah, we wonder, the rain that seemed to last forever or the thought of how he was to make every tomorrow different from all the terrible yesterdays? Both seemed impossible.

NOAH AND JONAH: GOD AS UNIVERSALISTIC AND PARTICULARISTIC

The greatest common denominator in both narratives is the water. "Ocean: A body of water occupying about two-thirds of a world made for man – who has no gills," observed American satirist Ambrose Bierce.[1] Water is everywhere. Water involves great risk; the sea is unpredictable and indifferent to human life. It is vast. It is calming. It is treacherous. Its surface can betray its depths and its dangers. Jonah and Noah are both watery tales, and their maritime flavor forces a natural comparison between these two protagonists and the landscape that shaped them: one was almost lost to water and another redeemed through it. Jonah put others at peril when he boarded a ship. Noah preserved the remnants of a lost world when he boarded his. Both stories involve animals: those that save and those that are saved. Both involve a background of nameless human beings: those who are inexpressibly good and those who are irredeemably wicked. And the comparisons continue.

---

1. Ambrose Bierce, *The Devil's Dictionary* (New York: Dover, 1993), 87.

These narrative similarities can seem obvious on the surface, and can cleverly disguise the way that the Noah story upends the Jonah story theologically or serves, as we will see, as the beginning of a divine evolution in God's relationship with humanity. As noted, both are stories with water as their backdrop – and, at times, their foreground – providing a ready escape for both protagonists. The Flood lasted forty days, the same time frame given to Nineveh for repentance. The dove in one story shared the name of the prophet in the second. Other animals were also critical in the shaping of the stories, as were winds and wood: the planks, the olive branch, the unusual gourd, the waves, the bottom of the mountains. Noah saved the animals in Genesis. Jonah was saved by the animals. Noah was tasked with protecting them, in line with the role of steward to animate life that Adam and Eve were given in the first chapters of Genesis. Jonah had no interest in a steward role and bemoaned the tree that died merely because it had serviced him.

In both stories, animals also behaved out of character for their genus. In the Noah story, animals mated outside of their species, according to medieval readings of the expression "all flesh had corrupted its ways on earth" (Gen. 6:12). Animals were sinners in this story, an illustration of how rotten the universe that God wished to destroy and rebuild had become. In the Jonah story, a big fish did not kill a vulnerable man, cattle wore sackcloth, and a small worm destroyed large ambitions. We are used to human beings acting against their better natures, but when animals do this, we pay a different kind of attention to the small details of the narrative.

Beyond the obvious similarities, both are stories of second chances. Noah and his sons were given the same blessing as Adam to be fruitful and multiply and engage in the universal experiment again. Jonah was given the same mission when he headed for Nineveh that he had been given when he was in Gath-hepher before he ran away. The use of the same language in Genesis 1 and 9, and the same language in Jonah 1 and 3, signals a total acceptance of the protagonists' repentance. Both were called to expel immorality from their midst and from "before God," yet neither seemed to be committed to the population around them and its challenges. As Sheila Tuller Keiter points out, "There is no mention of the Noah story in any of the classic commentaries on the Book of

Jonah, nor is there any mention of Jonah in the commentaries to the Noah narrative."[2] The connections made today among literary scholars of the Bible were not as apparent to ancient scholars.

One contemporary essayist on the comparison, Noah Greenfield, observes that these two narratives are "most noted for their universalism." This too provides material for comparison:

> Noah is considered the father of all nations (Gen. 10); and Jonah is the only prophet sent on a mission to a gentile – indeed, an enemy – nation. They are the two stories in the Bible most concerned with animals: Noah's ark is a floating zoo of endangered species; Jonah is the only biblical book in which animals are made to fast, don sackcloth and pray. Its last words are: "Should I [God] not care about...many beasts!" (Jonah 4:11).[3]

Greenfield posits that these two narratives in relation with each other do not merely share language and themes. "Jonah is a literary-theological response to the Flood story of Noah." Their intertextuality revisits the destruction in Noah's generation and presents an evolved Divinity, one whose mercy now exceeds His commitment to destruction. These two stories are comparable on a larger scale: both examine the nature of God's relationship with all living things, far beyond the particularism of God's relationship with the Israelites.

It is this "first," more expansive world into which Abraham made an appearance eleven chapters into Genesis. God's initial failed experiments with universalism ended with Abraham, as God realized that a particularistic approach would best serve the moral ends He sought for the whole created world. The strategy of investing in the growth of a small people into a nation who then would become a beacon to other nations, as touted throughout prophetic literature, replaced the original

---

2. Sheila Tuller Keiter, "Noah and the Dove: The Integral Connection between Noah and Jonah," *Jewish Bible Quarterly* 40, no. 4 (2012): 261. Available online at http://jbqnew.jewishbible.org/assets/Uploads/404/jbq_404_noahdove.pdf.
3. Noah Greenfield, "Jonah's Ark and Noah's Flood: Reading the Book of Jonah after the Flood," *Annual of the Japanese Biblical Institute* 33 (2007). I am grateful to Stu Halperin for alerting me to Greenfield's helpful essay.

universalistic narratives we have when Genesis opens. An early midrash on Genesis contends that "God created worlds and destroyed them, created worlds and destroyed them."[4] Like an artist making adjustments or starting again, God worked the world into His handiwork and yet...

The new world, in its various iterations, failed miserably. Terms like ḥamas, "corruption," appear in both narratives. Corruption is not merely a concept that makes a cameo appearance in both stories; it is the catalyst that drives both stories. God needed to do something dramatic because the moral fiber of humankind was at risk. In the first story, God was inflamed by His creations to the point of destruction.

> The earth became *corrupt* before God; the earth was filled with *lawlessness.* When God saw how corrupt the earth was, for all flesh had corrupted its ways on earth. God said to Noah, "I have decided to put an end to all flesh because the earth is filled with *lawlessness* because of them: I am about to destroy them with the earth." (Gen. 6:11–13)

God did not combat the corruption and lawlessness with heightened structures to enhance and amplify the observance of the law. If indeed there was any notion of law communicated then, we as readers are unfamiliar with it since no laws had yet been explicitly rendered in Genesis. One could even argue that Cain's punishment was unfair; no one told him that murder was prohibited. Yet the lack of evident strictures did not prevent God from declaring His divine handiwork amiss, as if His lack of control over His creatures mounted until it became an intolerable morass. Here, we find a God in deliberation: "I have *decided* to put an end to all flesh" (v. 12). God resolved with a strident and indignant sense of certainty that the path forward should be through destruction rather than rehabilitation. As Jack Miles observes in *God: A Biography,* "The destruction is not a means, it is an end, an expressive not an instrumental act."[5]

In the Book of Jonah, however, the threat of destruction does appear as an instrument or incentive for rehabilitation. God's interest was

---

4. Genesis Rabba 3:7.
5. Jack Miles, *God: A Biography* (New York: Knopf, 1995), 43.

Two Watery Tales of God's Sudden Compassion

clearly not in Nineveh's demise but in its transformation. "The word of the Lord came to Jonah, son of Amitai: 'Rise, go to Nineveh, that great city, and proclaim judgment upon it; for their wickedness has come before Me'" (Jonah 1:1–2). Notification of their wickedness did not prompt God's alarm or disgust but God's evident concern and then delight – or, at the very least, satisfaction – when the Ninevites took agency, banking on the assumption that this was a changed God from the God of Genesis. This God desired atonement, not destruction. The people of Nineveh must have believed this was a possibility or else they would not have undertaken such a dramatic enterprise as reforming the entire city.

> Let everyone turn back from his evil ways and from the injustice that is in his hands. Who knows but that God may turn and relent? He may turn back from His wrath so that we do not perish. (3:8–9)

It was Jonah, not God, who could not tolerate salvation. One could imagine that such a question would not have been asked of our prophet: "Who knows but that Jonah may turn and relent? He may turn back from His wrath so that we do not perish." Jonah's surety about Nineveh's waywardness and the obvious need for their punishment was much more certain than God's. God Himself seemed to have repented, and instead of condemning Nineveh to ruin, He patiently created the conditions for their change and prodded Jonah to his. Successful with Nineveh, God struck out with Jonah, who seemed angry on account of Nineveh's success.

Greenfield takes this reading a step further and contends that Jonah, in the appositional story to Noah, was not merely disappointed with Nineveh's repentance. He actually wanted to turn back time; he desired a flood-like response to Nineveh's corruption, rejecting God's soft tactics. In contrast with His conversation with Noah, God did not tell Jonah of any explicit destruction on the horizon. Thus Jonah fabricated one in his imagination and perhaps physically backed out of Nineveh in chapter 4 on the assumption that something explosive would likely happen when their repentance was short-lived:

> Jonah is *only* told to give a warning. But God does not indicate any actual plan of destruction, and He certainly doesn't tell Jonah

to build an Ark. Ironically enough, when Jonah eventually gives his warning, it is not a warning at all – it is a declaration of doom that suggests a flood: "Forty days more, and Nineveh shall be overthrown." It seems, then, that although God only tells Jonah to warn Nineveh, Jonah hears only the doom and destruction of the sort that God announced to Noah. Furthermore, Jonah takes another cue from Noah's prophetic mission: he acquires for himself a boat – "and he paid its price." By stubbornly re-interpreting God's command – to merely warn Nineveh – into a veritable flood prophecy resembling that of Noah, Jonah expresses his dissatisfaction with God's recent dry spell and makes clear his wish for a reintroduction of floods into the world. Jonah is adamant that floods be brought back into God's punitive repertoire – a natural development of his rejection of God's post-diluvian commitment to the contrary.[6]

Greenfield contends that Jonah boarded a ship in anticipation of a flood, and then, when unsure if God would opt for this form of punishment or any punishment at all, upped the ante by doing all that he could to enrage God and, if you like, precipitate the precipitation. When this failed because the sailors tried too hard to isolate the storm on account of one man, Jonah retreated and resigned himself to death at the hands of the very sailors whom he imperiled.

This contemporary reading has a midrash-like quality to it, and one can imagine it on the pages of *Pirkei DeRabbi Eliezer*, where many of the more fanciful midrashim on Jonah are anthologized. Jonah was, no doubt, familiar with the story of Noah and God's ire there; this Flood narrative was recorded among the earliest stories in the Pentateuch and in other ancient oral and written traditions, universes away in time and

---

6. Greenfield, "Jonah's Ark and Noah's Flood," 13. Greenfield bases this reading on a passage from Nedarim 38a: R. Yoḥanan said, "*Vayiten sekhara*: Jonah purchased the entire ship." Jonah paid for the ship and everyone's passage which would, presumably, limit his accountability. Ibn Ezra rejects this reading, suggesting that Jonah paid for only his own share. R. Yoḥanan may have offered this interpretation because a transportation fare is an odd and unusual detail in a biblical text that must have some additional meaning if it was included.

in conception from Jonah's life in the Land of Israel.[7] The fact that God had promised post-Flood never to repeat it was deeply embedded in the prophetic mindset of all who followed. We also lack any indicator that the sailors were sinners who turned into saints, as Greenfield suggests, who would have perhaps been "worthy" of this kind of extreme punishment. The fact that the sailors were a consistent model of responsibility and decency throughout should have been proof to Jonah that negative assumptions he made about gentiles, indeed pagans, were not descriptive in this instance.

Nahum Sarna suggests that the Flood story makes its closest reappearance in the indictment of Sodom, also in the early pages of Genesis, and is aligned with the outcry in the Book of Jonah. "Then the Lord said, 'The outrage of Sodom and Gomorrah is so great, and their sins so grave! I will go down to see whether they have acted according to the outcry that has come to Me'" (Gen. 18:20–21). Sarna defines this outcry as "heinous moral and social corruption, an arrogant disregard of elementary human rights, a cynical insensitivity to the sufferings of others."[8] For Sarna, what outraged God was not a lack of fealty or worship to the monotheistic God but a total lack of regard for the fabric of community:

> It is not the neglect of sacrificial gifts, the disregard of an oracular utterance, or the making of a false oath that arouses the ire of the Deity. The sins are entirely on a moral plane, and of idolatry there is not so much as a whisper. As with the Flood, the Sodom and Gomorrah narrative is predicated upon the existence of a moral law of universal application for the infraction of which God holds all men answerable. *The idea that there is an intimate, in fact, inextricable connection between the socio-moral condition of*

---

7. For more on the Flood as a shared ancient Mesopotamian event, see Norman Cohn, *Noah's Flood: The Genesis Story in Western Thought*, particularly chapter 1: "Mesopotamian Origins" (New Haven: Yale University Press, 1996), 1–10, and Nahum Sarna, *Understanding Genesis: The Heritage of Biblical Israel* (New York: Schocken, 1970), 37–56.
8. Sarna, *Understanding Genesis*, 145. In support, he marshals Exodus 2:23; 22:21–23; Isaiah 5:7; and Ezekiel 16:49–50 and could have used many other biblical verses with the terms *tze'aka/ze'aka* in them to suggest this kind of moral corruption.

Radical Transformation

> *a people and its ultimate fate is one of the main pillars upon which stands the entire biblical interpretation of history.* The theme is central to the Flood story, basic to the Sodom and Gomorrah narrative and fundamental to the understanding of the Book of Jonah.[9]

OBEDIENCE AND DISOBEDIENCE IN THE NOAH AND JONAH NARRATIVES

And here another contrast between Noah and Jonah emerges, not one found in the minor similarities of words or images but rather the larger issue of authority. Noah was overly obedient. Jonah was overly disobedient. Noah's obedience is evident as much in what he failed to say as in what he failed to do. When God singled out Noah, He explained His strategy and motivation. The earth was corrupt and lawless. Every creature God had created was a source of great moral disappointment. Besides Noah and his family, there was no one worth saving, so God decided upon a plan that would position the earth that God had so tenderly created and gifted in the form of a majestic Garden – one that humans were supposed to steward – to act as His agent of destruction. As a *leitwort*, the word "earth" or *haaretz* appears in several forms in the first chapter of Genesis thirteen times, almost as if the earth itself birthed humans and cradled primordial man and woman. But now the very earth that nourished and nurtured humans would seek its revenge on those who were supposed to be its caretakers. This is a reversal of what happened in the Book of Jonah, where the land and nature were generally instruments of salvation. The blanket indifference of nature to humanity in the Noah story – a theme found not only in the deluge narratives but also in the famines of Genesis and the wilderness trek that ensnared the Israelites in thirst, hunger, and frustration – was seemingly reversed by the extreme concern for a single human being, demonstrating that nature has the capacity to partner with human life in the task of redemption.

The adversarial relationship of land against humans is heightened in the Noah narrative because Noah, the one human being who may have had the ability to change God's oppositional strategy, seemed to care little about those he was about to leave forever. Noah was given his

---

9. Sarna, *Understanding Genesis*, 145–146; italics in the original.

Two Watery Tales of God's Sudden Compassion

name by his father Lamech to bring redemption to the land: "When Lamech had lived 182 years, he begot a son. And he named him Noah, saying, 'This one will provide us relief from our work and from the toil of our hands, out of the very soil which the Lord placed under a curse'" (Gen. 5:28–29). Adam and each subsequent generation had amplified a curse through the land. Adam was punished for his disobedience by having to work the land by the sweat of his brow. Cain, after he committed fratricide, was told that the blood of his brother cried out from the ground; he was punished by being made a wanderer on the land, having to work the land without a guarantee of its yield. If Adam worked, he could eat. Not so with Cain; effort and outcome were no longer aligned in this brave, new, and frightening world. Noah, whose name means "to rest," was to bring an end to this land curse. In him lay the potential to put a stop to it.[10] Ironically, the land had no rest in Noah's generation. Noah was not the emissary of a more blessed future because he did not lead the people around him. He built a boat. He sailed away.

If we pay careful attention to the lengthy passage in which Noah received his assignment, we find God moving in subject and focus from the state of the universe to the practical instructions for Noah's ark. Consider the sharp change from death to life in these literary switchbacks:

> God said to Noah, "I have decided to put an end to all flesh, for the earth is filled with lawlessness because of them: I am about to destroy them with the earth. *Make yourself an ark of gopher wood; make it an ark with compartments, and cover it inside and out with pitch. This is how you shall make it: the length of the ark shall be three hundred cubits, its width fifty cubits, and its height thirty cubits. Make an opening for daylight in the ark, and terminate it within a cubit of the top. Put the entrance to the ark in its side, make it with bottom, second, and third decks.* For My part I am about to bring the

---

10. One midrash supports this reading by suggesting that Noah "introduced plows, sickles, axes, and all kinds of tools to his contemporaries, thus freeing them from doing everything with their hands" (*Tanḥuma, Noah* 11). Noah's blessing came from his practical assistance to the mechanics of farming. Thus his inventions made working the land easier and more efficient.

Flood – water upon the earth – to destroy all flesh under the sky in which there is breath of life; everything on earth shall perish. *But I will establish My covenant with you, and you shall enter the ark, with your sons, your wife, and your sons' wives. And of all that lives, of all flesh, you shall take two of each into the ark to keep alive with you: they shall be male and female. From birds of every kind, cattle of every kind, every kind of creeping thing on earth, two of each shall come to you to stay alive. For your part, take of everything that is eaten and store it away, to serve as food for you and for them."* Noah did so; just as God commanded him, so he did. (6:13–22)

Bookending the passage and punctuating its mid-section, God's moral imperative to destroy the world is interrupted by the strange and detailed directions God gave Noah to build the ark. Yet we might read this in the opposite way as well. Was God interrupting this tirade against humans to give Noah building directions, almost as an aside? Or was God's primary task to give Noah specific instructions, the width and depth of cubits, during which God's anger seeped out as an explanation for this curious ark project? The difference lies in what it was that God wanted Noah to do as his primary responsibility: Did He want him to build an ark to escape humanity? Or did He hope Noah would advocate for humanity, for all those who would not have a boat with which to flee their desperation and destruction? One midrash suggests that because of the intricacy and time-consuming nature of this enterprise, people would ask Noah questions about the ark, giving him the opportunity to explain and gently guide them back to the true and correct path. Another midrash in defense of Noah suggests that wherever the Bible uses the term "righteous" in reference to a person – as we find in the story of Noah (v. 9) – "it is a reference to one who forewarns others."[11] And yet no such understanding is apparent from a literal reading of this narrative. In a certain way, Noah and Jonah become almost mirror images of each other, those who can lead but choose to save themselves instead – one by listening to God and the other by defying Him.

In explaining the odd expression "Noah was blameless in his generation" (v. 9), one well-known midrash picks up on Noah's

---

11. Genesis Rabba 30:7.

Two Watery Tales of God's Sudden Compassion

fidelity to one set of God's words and his virtual dismissal of the other words that came with no directions. Noah's greatness was relative to those around him, but not in the scheme of biblical history, where the greatness of Abraham and Moses was measured by their fierce protectiveness of humanity, or specifically the Israelites, against the very God who willed them into existence (Sanhedrin 108a). Philo wonders why the biblical text says, "Noah found grace in the eyes of the Lord" (Gen. 6:8), "when previously, as far as our information goes, he had done nothing good?"[12] In other words, we have no indication in the text to illustrate Noah's goodness; whatever we do have does not seem to support this supposition. Noah failed to advocate for humanity, failed to save others, and even failed when he left the ark and drank himself into a stupor. In *City of God*, Augustine contends that Noah was "perfect, not as the citizens in the City of God are made to be perfect in the immortal condition in which they will become equal to the angels of God, but as they can be perfect during their pilgrimage on earth."[13]

The contrasting reading is that Noah was great in his generation and would have been that much greater had he been born into a generation that was more worthy of God's compassion.[14] And yet we cannot let Noah off lightly. The ark in the rabbinic imagination was to serve as an outreach tool, bringing the two thematic strains in the passage together. Noah spent decades in its construction (fifty-two years, according to *Pirkei DeRabbi Eliezer*); his neighbors must have questioned the project, providing Noah with an opportunity to engage them in conversation and possibly save them.[15] But this is not what Noah did. Midrashim stress that Noah built the ark for himself and that he became an object of ridicule; over time, he cared even less about those around him.[16] Noah was so obedient to God's

---

12. Philo, *Legum Allegorarium* 3:77.
13. Augustine, *City of God*, trans. Henry Bettenson (New York: Penguin, 2004), 643.
14. See Sanhedrin 108a; Genesis Rabba 30:10.
15. See *Tanḥuma, Noaḥ* 5, which suggests that Noah delayed construction to encourage repentance. In Josephus, *Antiquities*, 1.74, we find a similar reading of Noah's advocacy for his generation.
16. See Sanhedrin 108a; *Pirkei DeRabbi Eliezer* 22; Genesis Rabba 30:7; Leviticus Rabba 27:5.

word alone that even once he had built the ark, in one midrashic reading, he did not step into it until God commanded him.[17]

Noah was commanded by God to build an ark and bring his family to safety in it because he, alone, was worthy: "Then the Lord said to Noah, 'Go into the ark, with all your household, for you alone have I found righteous before Me in this generation" (7:1). Jonah, in boarding a ship to run away from God, used the ship to avoid God's command. Moreover, Jonah had no family in his story, other than the passing mention of his father, Amitai, an insertion that proves more of a taunt to the prophet's warped sense of truth over mercy.

CONTRASTS IN JONAH AND NOAH

Jonah had an indication that events were stirring because a storm started with him as its center and target. Oddly, Noah – who was given such explicit instructions before the Flood – was told nothing about its conclusion. He was never told directly by God when His storm would pass and it would be safe and desirable for him and his family to leave the ark, situate the animals, and begin the rough task of repopulating a desolate world. Jonah's world was never lonely except when he put himself in isolation in the bottom of the ship and then later in his booth. Noah was to exit the noisy boat for an apocalyptic landscape, perhaps what we imagine the surface of the moon to look like from a distance.

But first Noah sent forth a *yona*, "a dove." The use of the term "*yona*" in Noah's story adds even greater cohesion between the two stories of destruction and construction. Noah sent out a raven at the end of forty days to examine the land and test its readiness for human habitation (Gen. 8:7). The raven flew back and forth; it returned quickly, circling, according to Rashi, without any definite role. Tuller Keiter, in her contrast of these two birds, mentions that Noah would no doubt have known that a raven is an omnivore that would have left the ark in search of carrion. If it did not find anything, it would return.[18] If Noah wanted

---

17. Genesis Rabba 34:4.
18. The Talmud presents an interesting story that also involves both the raven and the dove. R. Ilish was taken captive and dwelled beside a man who knew the language of birds. A raven came to R. Ilish and called him. The bird whisperer translated the

to know if the ground was dry enough to settle the ark, he could simply have looked outside. Tuller Keiter believes that the reason Noah sent out this bird initially was, in her words, more chilling than the practical reason mentioned above:

> He did not send the raven to make sure that the earth was dry enough to leave the ark. Noah feared that the ground was dry but strewn with corpses. After the Flood, *the ark came to rest… on the mountains of Ararat* (Gen. 8:4). From that perch, Noah could probably see below and determine whether the land was still inundated, but he would not have been able to discern its condition in any greater detail. He, therefore, dispatched a scavenging bird capable of eating carrion to see if his fears were real. Since the raven did not find food of any kind, Noah (with a sense of relief perhaps) had the answer to his question.[19]

It is almost impossible to imagine the extent of Noah's existential suffering over the many weeks in the ark. He had the immense distraction of managing the practical responsibilities of animal care in a confined space with rain pounding on his roof, but then, in limited quiet moments, there were probably haunting images of screaming, of drowning, of human and animal loss outside his protective walls.

Ackerman, in contrast, offers this understanding of why Jonah's name means "dove, son of truth:"

---

raven's message: "Ilish, escape, Ilish, escape." But the scholar was unmoved, "It is a lying raven, and I will not rely on it." Then a dove appeared and R. Ilish asked the bird expert to explain what the dove meant with its coos. This bird too offered the same message: "Ilish, escape, Ilish, escape." R. Ilish took this message to heart. "The congregation of Israel is compared to a dove. I conclude from this that a miracle will happen to me. I will go" (Gittin 45a). The raven in this story has a reputation for not telling the truth; perhaps because it is dark and a bird of prey, it was associated with shadowy opportunism. Yet significantly, both birds conveyed the same message to this sage. Had the dove not come, R. Ilish would have stayed a captive, missing the message because of his distrust of the messenger. In the Noah story, both birds were also used as messengers but it was only the dove that brought back the olive branch.

19. Tuller Keiter, "Noah and the Dove," 262.

> The dove has two major characteristics in the Hebrew Bible: it is easily put to flight and seeks secure refuge in the mountains (Ezek. 7:16; Ps. 55:6–8), and it moans and laments when in distress (Nahum 2:7; Is. 38:14; 59:11). Will these characteristics, we wonder, also apply to our hero?[20]

The dove brings these two narratives together again. Why, then, does the raven also appear? This switch of birds sounds intentional but confusing. Why not just send the dove first or stick with one bird? Unlike the raven, whose presence would have portended the brutality of death, the dove is the harbinger of life. It seeks and returns to its original location and can fly great distances in this pursuit. Perhaps more than a temporary dry place to situate the ark, Noah sought something more elusive and important: home.

> Then he sent out the dove to see whether the waters had decreased from the surface of the ground. But the dove could not find a resting place for its feet, and returned to him to the ark, for there was water over all the earth. So putting out his hand, he took it into the ark with him. He waited another seven days, and again sent out the dove from the ark. The dove came back to him toward evening, and there in its bill was a plucked off olive leaf! Then Noah knew that the waters had decreased on the earth. He waited still another seven days and sent the dove forth; and it did not return to him any more. (Gen. 8:8–12)

Noah's *yona*, his "dove," left the confines of the ship to find a place to rest. Jonah the prophet entered a ship to find rest and fell into a deep sleep there. The bird became an advisor to Noah; nature behaved as it should to indicate whether the conditions were sufficiently promising to return human beings to dry land. The dove flew back and then a week later, Noah sent it out once again. When it brought back an olive branch, it was a sign that Noah and his family could leave the ark; a week later, the dove was returned to the freedom it had once enjoyed. In the Jonah story, animals behaved against convention and against time. Noah incrementally

---

20. Ackerman, "Jonah," in *The Literary Guide to the Bible*, 234.

tested the natural world. In Jonah, trees grew and died in a day. Animals swallowed human beings and transported them. Both the bird and the prophet traveled and returned, but the bird did so as faithful messenger, set free only upon completing its mission. Jonah left and returned of his own volition. Even when we reach the story's culminating verse we do not know if the prophet completed his mission or fled it once again.

As mentioned earlier and most obviously, water in both stories surrounded our protagonists, forcing them to find appropriate shelter. Jonah spent three days and nights under the protective sheltering membrane of a fish. Noah, protected by the ark he built – for which he was wholly responsible – was protected for forty days and nights. Not only did Jonah not take any responsibility for the ship he boarded, he placed the others on the ship in danger by virtue of his presence and then in falling asleep signaled that he cared nothing for human life – least of all his own.

The pace of time in Jonah's narrative seems to be accelerated such that events take place *too* quickly, whereas in the Noah story, time seems to stand still, demanding patience and silence. It only took Jonah three days and nights to return to his mission. Jonah was only one day into his three-day trek through Nineveh when the city buzzed with enthusiasm to atone. We can imagine Jonah dragging his feet and uttering the prophetic words he was given with hesitation, perhaps more softly than necessary, to induce repentance and change – the mark of one begrudgingly discharging a responsibility not of his own making. But no matter, Jonah's brevity carried great weight with his new followers:

> Nineveh was an enormously large city, a three days' walk across. Jonah began by going a day's journey into the city, proclaiming, "Forty days more and Nineveh will be overturned." The Ninevites believed God. A fast was proclaimed, and all of them, from the greatest to the least, put on sackcloth. When Jonah's warning reached the king of Nineveh, he rose from his throne, took off his royal robes, covered himself with sackcloth, and sat down in the dust. (Jonah 3:3–6)

In just one day, Jonah's words burned with the intensity and speed with which fire travels; his words swept the city and reached the king's palace, where they had immediate resonance. The same forty days that it would take for Noah's storm to blow over and clear would mark the end of Nineveh. Forty days would begin the rebirth of Noah's generation – one destroyed for immorality – and the same forty days would signal the pending destruction of an immoral city.

Finally, we end chapter 1 of Jonah and Noah's stay in the ark with sacrifices. Noah was told to bring into the ark two of each animal and then a number of "pure" animals ostensibly to be used for sacrifices later as the storm gave way to dry land and Noah's family was able to leave. Perhaps Noah intuited that if the old world was destroyed because of thievery and immorality, a new world must be built on giving; thus the sacrifice he offered immediately upon leaving the ark: "Then Noah built an altar to the Lord and, taking of every clean animal and of every clean bird, he offered burnt offerings on the altar" (Gen. 8:20). This pleased God immensely and seems to have stimulated God's generous response: "The Lord smelled the pleasing aroma and said in His heart: 'Never again will I curse the ground because of humans'" (v. 21). One wonders what God's reaction would have been had Noah failed to offer sacrifices.

In Jonah, sacrifices are a more muted affair, the culminating act of reverence and gratitude from sailors on an overly dramatic voyage who felt God's presence and salvific powers: "At this the men greatly feared the Lord, and they offered a sacrifice to the Lord and made vows to Him" (Jonah 1:16). Where we have no reason to assume that God rejected the sailors' vows, we have ample support for Jonah's rejection of their sacrifices in the odd line he emitted in his prayer, a possibly oblique reference to the sailors: "They who cling to empty folly forsake their own kindness. But, I, with loud thanksgiving, will sacrifice to You" (2:9–10). Jonah was sure that his vow would be paid; he was unsure of the worth of others who vowed and offered sacrifices – others whom he deemed less worthy.[21] Again, Jonah assumed a God-like role as chief judge and

---

21. This rejection may have been based on a general dismissal of any pagans worshipping the God of the Hebrews or on the fact that their sacrifice, like Noah's, was made immediately upon the completion of their task and might not, in Jonah's skeptical mind, endure beyond one incident. For more on the nature and difficulty of biblical sacrifice, see Moshe Halbertal, *On Sacrifice* (Princeton: Princeton University, 2015).

Two Watery Tales of God's Sudden Compassion

prosecutor when all those around him, including God, had less rigidity and were more open to possibility.

GOD'S REGRET: THE EMERGENCE OF A NEW APPROACH

In *Subversive Sequels in the Bible*, Judy Klitsner, after drawing the parallels between the narratives, pulls our attention to some of the glaring differences in the stories, with the second story – that of Jonah – as a subversion of the first:

> In general, Noah's story reverses that of Jonah in its approach to destruction. In the Noah narrative, humanity's annihilation was neither negotiable nor avoidable; God and His prophet were united in viewing death as inevitable. The inverted details of the Book of Jonah will lead us away from destruction as a narrative necessity. They will point instead toward a more generous view of humanity adopted by God and by humanity itself.[22]

Klitsner provides support for this thesis by using words like N-Ḥ-M, to regret, which appears in the Noah story as an indication of God's regret for ever creating humans – with their penchant for evildoing – and then later in the Jonah story when God regretted or backtracked on the decision to destroy Nineveh. The ambivalence created by the word N-Ḥ-M worked against humanity in the early chapters of Genesis but a more forgiving, merciful God emerged later in prophetic texts. This word will be discussed in greater detail in the next chapter, but for now, it suggests a change of heart in this specific situation. Here, it reflects a larger understanding that if human beings and God are to live in any covenantal bond, God will have to have less exacting standards and allow for the flawed to express their pain and remorse. In chapter 3 of Jonah, the king demanded the transformation of his people on the supposition that God may change His mind, something Jonah could not fathom or tolerate. Indeed, God did this very thing. "God saw what they did, and how they turned from their evil

---

22. Judy Klitsner, *Subversive Sequels in the Bible: How Biblical Stories Mine and Undermine Each Other* (Jerusalem: Maggid Books, 2011), 10.

ways. He relented and did not bring on them the destruction He had threatened" (v. 10). It is an astonishing reversal of pity. "The Book of Jonah will revisit humanity's ability to assume responsibility for its own future. As opposed to the story of Noah, this time the doomed population is able to conceive of and carry out a reversal of its behavior and consequently to overturn its fate."[23]

This change in God may take the spotlight away from the humans in these stories. Noah was regarded as righteous in his generation. His, then, is the story of one pious man in contrast with an entire generation. In Jonah, we find one impious man in contrast with communities of other men – the sailors and the Ninevites – who were far more likely to garner God's favor through their piety than was the prophet, the obvious but disappointing choice. God had shown a change of heart after Noah left the ark and offered his sacrifice.

In comparing Jonah and Noah, what emerges most significantly is that neither individual is the real focus of either narrative, although lessons about obedience and disobedience prove intriguing as we study the contrasts. God was the main character in each story, and God, in these watery tales, demanded to be revisited from one story to the next. Upended in this story is God's relationship with the world. God's experiment shifted from universalism to particularism after the Flood, a particularism that would lead, if successful, to a greater universalism. Instead of creating a world of countless souls pock-marked by human disobedience, the Flood and the Tower of Babel indicated that a new model was essential in God's Genesis experiment. Abraham, who appeared at the close of the post-diluvian narratives, would be, in essence, the new Adam, but totally and wholly faithful, unlike his ancestor Adam. He answered God's call with his very being, unlike Adam, who hid in the garden and needed to be brought out in whispers of shame. Building a nation and then a more authentic universe from one struggling epic hero would prove to be a better formula than the one used in Genesis's first chapter. And because of Abraham and all the subsequent generations after him, God's blessing at the end of the Flood enabled the existence of the God of Jonah.

---

23. Ibid., 11.

> "I now establish My covenant with you and with your descendants after you and with every living creature that was with you – the birds, the livestock, and all the wild animals, all those that came out of the ark with you – every living creature on earth. I establish My covenant with you: Never again will all life be destroyed by the waters of a flood; never again will there be a flood to destroy the earth." And God said, "This is the sign of the covenant I am making between Me and you and every living creature with you, a covenant for all generations to come: I have set My rainbow in the clouds, and it will be the sign of the covenant between Me and the earth. Whenever I bring clouds over the earth and the rainbow appears in the clouds, I will remember My covenant between Me and you and all living creatures of every kind. Never again will the waters become a flood to destroy all life." (Gen. 9:9–15)

The Book of Jonah hearkens back to this covenantal agreement in the form of God's question at the book's end. God needed to have compassion on a city born immediately after the Flood because God had promised it long before. And not only was the city of Nineveh in God's purview, but also every living creature, moral and immoral, every sentient being, creatures of every kind, would find relief in the covenant God bellowed through an empty universe. Jonah may have heard this announcement in his familiarity with all that happened to his people, but perhaps he never internalized it or took it seriously. The fragrant aroma of repentance that wafted to God's nose and caused God great delight had little impact on the doubting prophet's perception of wrongdoing. "Never again will I doom the earth because of man since the devisings of man's mind are evil (*ra*) from his youth, nor will I ever destroy every living being as I have done" (Gen. 8:21). God acknowledged the evil of youth but assumed, post-Flood, that humans could grow out of the adolescent self-absorption that drives sin. In contrast, Jonah found repentance so problematic, so unnerving, that it created a state of evil for him: "But Jonah was greatly displeased (*vayera el Yona ra'a gedola*) and became angry" (Jonah 4:1). To God, repentance overshadowed and diminished evil. To Jonah, repentance was itself an evil.

Where the God of Abraham represented particularism after the failed experiment of universalism, in the Book of Jonah universalism was God's antidote to a Jewish world that had become overly particularistic. The world needed, in the guise of a stubborn prophet, a lesson in outreach and diversity from the very God who modeled these qualities to His prophet. Without particularism, there is no context in which to build a model nation. Without universalism, there is no reason to live outside the boundaries of the self. It was this message that God hoped to impart to Jonah.

Chapter Nine

Destruction or Redemption?

> "Let everyone call urgently on God. Let everyone turn back from his evil ways and from the injustice that is in his hands. Who knows but that God may turn and relent? He may turn back from His wrath so that we do not perish." When God saw what they did and how they turned from their evil ways, He relented and did not bring on them the destruction He had threatened. (Jonah 3:8–10)

There came a point, far into the biblical future from Jonah's strange narrative, when Nineveh lay in ruins. The prophet Nahum captured the harrowing experience, beginning his eponymous book with the words: "A pronouncement on Nineveh" (1:1). The book was likely written a few years after the fall of Assyria in 612 BCE. The author was the minor prophet who recorded the significance of the fall as a testament to God's abiding power and the relief the descent presented for ancient Israel. The prophet gloats:

> Desolation, devastation, and destruction! Spirits sink, knees buckle. All loins tremble. All faces turn ashen. What has become of that lions' den, that pasture of great beasts, where lion and lion's breed walked and lion's cub – with none to disturb them? (2:11–12)

Radical Transformation

Nineveh was the lion of the ancient Near East.[1] Bothered by no one, it plundered and killed and destroyed and yet then, suddenly, it met its rightful and just end. There was shock on the part of the observers who were once victims, and validation and renewed awe for God because justice had ultimately won out over the forces of evil. Nahum offers a remarkable description of this city, filled with onomatopoeic resonances:

> Ah, city of crimes, utterly treacherous, full of violence, where killing never stops. Crack of whip and rattle of wheel, galloping steed and bounding chariot! Charging horsemen, flashing swords, and glittering spears! Hosts of slain and heaps of corpses, dead bodies without number – they stumble over bodies. Because of the countless harlotries of the harlot, the winsome mystery of sorcery. Who ensnare nations with her harlotries and peoples with her sorcery, I am going to deal with you, declares the Lord of Hosts. (3:1–5)

Nahum takes us to the killing fields where we hear the power and mercilessness of the Ninevites: the crack of the whip and the chronic rattle of a chariot's wheel. We imagine the heaps of corpses that the Ninevites casually and callously stepped over and smell the stench of death that filled the darkened sky. We can feel the internal satisfaction of Nineveh's enemies when the prophet bellowed over their demise: "I will throw loathsome things over you and disfigure you and make a spectacle of you. All who see you will recoil from you and will say, 'Nineveh has been ravaged'" (vv. 6–7). The prophet uses language reminiscent of the Book of Lamentations, the grieving of Israel over the loss of Jerusalem and its

---

1. The lion-king in Nahum's prophecy was not only a reference to the current king of Assyria in Nahum's day but also to Demetrius II, the king of Syria six hundred years after Nahum's prophecy. See Kugel's observations on this in *How to Read the Bible*, 15, 658. Kugel uses this as an illustration of one of his four assumptions that readers typically make about the Bible, namely that it is relevant only for its historical context. Ancient interpreters, he writes, never assumed this. Rather the stories and law "were understood as being intended for people to obey in the interpreters' own time, even though they had been promulgated in a very different society many centuries earlier."

Temple, but does so with the full force of irony: "Who will console her? Where shall I look for anyone to comfort you?" (3:7). The answer is no one. No one will comfort Nineveh. And then the prophet concludes with the final silencing of this enemy:

> Your shepherds are slumbering, O king of Assyria; your sheep masters are lying inert. Your people are scattered over the hills, and there is none to gather them. There is no healing for your injury; your wound is grievous. All who hear the news about you clap their hands over you. For who has not suffered from your constant malice? (3:18–19)

On the note of malice, the book ends. It is the end that Jonah perhaps wished for Nineveh, what he reckoned was true justice for a people who took pleasure in aggression and victimized so many. Nahum's words capture one possible reading of Jonah's prophecy. After all, the fate of Nineveh pivoted on the five Hebrew words of one prophet. *"Forty days more and Nineveh will be overturned"* (Jonah 3:4).

It is because of Nahum's harsh and ringing prophecy that we understand the weight of Jonah's task. In forty days Nineveh would be destroyed, laid waste, utterly decimated.

OVERTURNED OR TRANSFORMED?

Readers can regard Jonah's words as a statement of fact, but this may not be the way that ancients heard this prophecy. Classic commentaries focus on the ambiguity of the word "overturned," *nehepakhet*, which can comfortably imply that the city would be ruined or that its fate would be reversed. Rashi states that this verb is used specifically

> because it can be understood in two different ways: bad and good. If they do not repent then Nineveh will be overturned. And if they do repent then that which was decreed about the residents of Nineveh will be overturned since they turned from bad to good and repented.[2]

---

2. Rashi to Jonah 3:4.

Radical Transformation

The message: Do right and fate will privilege you. Do wrong and you will be destroyed. This is much along the lines of an early message about free will that Cain received from God after God rejected both him and his sacrifice: "Surely, if you do right, there is uplift. But if you do not do right, sin crouches at the door. Its urge is toward you, yet you can be its master" (Gen. 4:7). This lesson preempted Cain's murderous act, but the raging brother gave it no heed.

Yet a similar message articulated as a prediction seemed to accommodate the way that the Ninevites, led by their king, understood Jonah. Jonah was not predicting doom, as did Nahum. He was presenting an opportunity for redemption. The *Targum* on Jonah 3:9 translates the verse with this meaning: "Who knows if there is here evidence [of *teshuva*] and this will be resolved and mercy will come to them from God?" This was not uncommon to the way that the ancients understood oracles in general. The predictions made by oracles were regarded as conditional statements, as Bickerman points out:

> Strange as it may appear to us, all peoples of antiquity firmly believed that signs or inspired men could foretell the future. The soothsayer was consulted on every important occasion. The usual objection to prophecy advanced by skeptic philosophers of Greece was that the believer in divination pretends to modify the foreordained causality which he postulates by his inquiry.... Foretelling...can help avoid pitfalls on the road into the future.[3]

This opens up a world of understanding when it comes to the reaction of the Ninevites and their king to Jonah's outcry. They did not believe they were doomed, only that they *would be* doomed if they did not heed the prophet/oracle. Thus, Jonah's prophecy was not a statement of fact as much as a conditional prediction. But, Bickerman contends, Jonah had a problem: If a prophet speaks the truth and yet the prophecy is understood differently than it was meant, the prophet would be called a false prophet. Jonah could have become an Israelite object of mockery

---

3. Bickerman, *Four Strange Books of the Bible*, 30.

or worse. He could have been killed, a view popularized by a number of classic medieval exegetes:

> Viewed in this light, Jonah had been placed in a great quandary. Jerome formulates the prophet's problem: he could say that God is merciful, but then the Ninevites would not have repented; or he could say that God is implacable. He said the latter, and thus predicted falsely, and was indignant that God made him a liar.[4]

This view is also reflected in a midrash about Jonah's mission:

> He [Jonah] was sent to Jerusalem to prophesy destruction; when they repented, God had mercy and repented of the evil and did not destroy it, and they called him a false prophet. The third time [Jonah was called], he was sent to Nineveh to cry its destruction. Jonah thought to himself: I know that the gentiles are near repentance and they will indeed repent… and not only will Israel call me a false prophet, but even pagan worshippers will call me a false prophet. I will flee to a place where God's glory is not present.[5]

Terence Fretheim, a scholar mentioned earlier,[6] argues compellingly that Jonah was not afraid of being labeled a false prophet – or if he was it was not his chief concern nor the underlying problem in the book. The Book of Jonah hardly focuses on the nature of prophecy at all. In chapter 4 when Jonah first confronted God verbally, he did not mention any specific criticism regarding the content of the prophecy or the fear of being labeled a false prophet. This would have been the case only if a prophet's word were contingent on the way people responded to the prophet's call and not the direct implication of his message. This is evidenced in verses like these from Jeremiah, which directly posit that conditional predictions were part and parcel of the prophet's educational repertoire and God's desire:

---

4. Ibid., 34.
5. Tanḥuma, Vayikra 8.
6. See chapter 4, note 13.

> At one moment I may decree that a nation or a kingdom shall be uprooted and pulled down and destroyed; but if that nation against which I made the decree turns back from its wickedness, I change My mind concerning the punishment I planned to bring on it. At another moment I may decree that a nation or a kingdom shall be built and planted; but if it does what is displeasing to Me and does not obey Me, then I change My mind concerning the good I planned to bestow upon it. And now, say to the men of Judah and the inhabitants of Jerusalem: This said the Lord: "I am devising disaster for you and laying plans against you. Turn back, each of you, from your wicked ways, and mend your ways and your actions!" But they will say, "It is no use. We will keep on following our plans; each of us will act in the willfulness of his evil heart." (Jer. 18:7–12)

If the people exhibited no remorse or commitment to change – much like those of Judah and Jerusalem – then God would execute His plans for their punishment or exile. But if they did regret their actions, then God would accept their repentance because God *did* change His mind.

The decree is better translated or understood as a threat or advance warning than an inevitable outcome. If not, what would be the purpose of repentance, a seminal value in the Bible and later rabbinic texts? "'Do I take any pleasure in the death of the wicked?' declares the sovereign Lord. 'Rather, am I not pleased when they turn from their ways and live?'" (Ezek. 18:23). The goal is not punishment or death but atonement and life. The very last biblical book adds emphasis to this message: "If My people who are called by My name humble themselves, and pray and seek My face and turn from their wicked ways, then I will hear from heaven and will forgive their sin and heal their land" (II Chr. 7:14).

God awaited contrition. And God did so no less for Jonah than for Nineveh. Jonah's prophetic assignment seemed unambiguous from the very second verse of the book. The city of Nineveh was wicked. Jonah was to "proclaim judgment upon it" (Jonah 1:2) but, as mentioned earlier, he was not yet given any words, the language, to execute his task. This alone may have terrified the prophet, the son of a prophet, who was perhaps familiar with the way in which God deposited words in the quiver of the prophet so that he could serve as a divine conduit.

Destruction or Redemption?

Lacking revelation in its every detail made a difficult job that much harder. The notion of going to Nineveh, a sworn enemy of the Israelites, and moralizing to them was bad enough. The idea that Jonah was to proclaim his own judgment made the responsibility that much more overwhelming. When Jonah revisited his mission in chapter 3, God told him to rush to Nineveh – no more possibility of wasting time in hesitation and escape – and "proclaim to it what I tell you" (v. 2). Finally, the words he awaited arrived. The message was brief and ominous: "Forty days more and Nineveh will be overturned" (v. 4).

How did the Ninevites come to understand Jonah's prophecy as an invitation to change instead of a calamitous declaration on their nonexistent future? Phyllis Trible, in *Rhetorical Criticism: Context, Method, and the Book of Jonah*, is puzzled by how the Ninevites could have arrived at their bold atonement initiative:

> Though he [Jonah] never exegetes his words, they appear to declare irreversible disaster. They make no call for repentance and propose no conditions for change. But the Ninevites hear in the words what Jonah may not have intended: the possibility of deliverance. The verb H-P-K (overturn) contains the irony of reversal. Through acts of penance and repentance Nineveh overturns, as Jonah predicted but not as he intended. Paradoxically his prophecy is both true and false.[7]

There was no Ninevite hesitation. It is almost as if they were poised and ready for change all along. One sentence was provocation enough. Note: they first believed in God. Without belief in the One who was determining their fate, there would be little point in changing their actions. But what familiarity could they have had with this God that would demonstrate such an easy faith change or at least acceptance?

Radak solves this puzzle with a far-fetched suggestion referenced earlier. The sailors on the ship docked and were in the city, and since they had experienced this Hebrew God's power at sea, they shared their

---

7. Phyllis Trible, *Rhetorical Criticism: Context, Method, and the Book of Jonah* (Minneapolis: Fortress Press, 1994), 190.

Radical Transformation

experience, thus stirring faith and repentance both. *Metzudat David* does not go as far as to say that they believed in God but he does say that they believed in the word of God; they were not adding this God to their panoply of gods but merely adhering to the prophecy. The *Baal HaTurim* (Jacob ben Asher, 1269–1343) travels further back in time, citing a rabbinic text that the king of Nineveh was none other than Pharaoh who had experienced God's miracles firsthand during the Exodus and, no doubt, shuddered to learn that the Israelite God had now found him elsewhere.[8] (Perhaps the real miracle of this reading is resurrection from the dead, since Pharaoh had drowned with his horsemen in the sea in Exodus 14.) The connection from this story to Exodus is not outlandish because there too the words "they believed in God" appear (v. 28). There it was the Israelites who finally overcame their many doubts but only when salvation seemed complete.

The ambiguity of the language has yielded a great deal of interpretation. A number of medieval exegetes preempt Trible's linguistic observation, Rashi among them. He defines *nehepakhet*, "overturned," unambiguously as *neherevet*, "destroyed." If the Ninevites did not change then they would suffer destruction, but since *nehepakhet* can have two meanings, "good or bad," should they repent, their fate would change from bad to good. Ibn Ezra cites and disagrees with Rashi's reading that *nehepakhet* signals transformation in either direction.[9] This homiletic reading, he contends, "is not correct." He instead directs us to the Book of Jeremiah, making the interpretation less linguistic and more theological:

> At one moment I may decree that a nation of a kingdom shall be uprooted and pulled down and destroyed; but if that nation against which I made the decree turns back from its wickedness, I change My mind concerning the punishment I planned to bring on it. At another moment I may decree that a nation or a kingdom shall be built and planted; but if it does what is displeasing to Me

---

8. *Pirkei DeRabbi Eliezer* 43.
9. Ibn Ezra to Jonah 3:4.

and does not obey Me, then I change My mind concerning the good I planned to bestow upon it. (Jer. 18:7–10)[10]

Here, God stands in judgment, weighing options, deciding on the best course and nimble enough to change course at any point. Trible observes:

> Perspective and interpretation make the difference. From the Ninevites' perspective the prophecy offers hope, though not the guarantee, of repentance human and divine. From God's perspective their repentance overturns divine evil to bring deliverance. From Jonah's perspective, the divine deliverance overturns his prophecy to discredit it. The reversal makes him angry and so leads to a confrontation with God in the next chapter.[11]

Bickerman argues that it was the brevity and directness of the message that made Jonah's prophecy unique from a biblical perspective and much less appealing to a prophet who already had enough hesitations. The potency of the message matched the pace of urgency set by God and the prophet. But, unlike Jonah's three-day introspection in the fish's belly, the city of Nineveh was given forty days to transform. When we read the words, "Forty days more and Nineveh will be overturned," we tend to focus on one word, *nehepakhet*, as we have done thus far. Yet there are two words that get far less exegetical attention that help us understand what "overturned" may denote as it leaves Jonah's mouth: forty days. God attached a deadline.

FORTY DAYS: A TEST OF THE HUMAN SPIRIT

Forty is not an uncommon number in the Hebrew Bible. The number forty in biblical tradition is used frequently – 146 times to be exact – as a measure of trial, testing, or transformation or as a symbol of a generation across the lifespan of a human being. The Flood covered the known world for forty days, forty are the years the Israelites wandered in the wilderness, forty are the days Moses spent on Mount Sinai on two separate occasions (Ex. 24:18; 34:1–28) and the period of time Moses sent

---

10. Rashi to Jonah 3:4.
11. Trible, *Rhetorical Criticism*, 190.

out scouts to Canaan to reconnoiter the land (Num. 13:25; 14:34). It is the cycle of time in which the Israelites were subjugated by punishing foreign rule in the Book of Judges (or other multiples of twenty, 3:11; 4:3; 5:31; 8:28; 13:1; 15:20; 16:31). Ezekiel lay on his right side for forty days to embody Judah's sins (Ezek. 4:6) and Elijah went for forty days, like Moses, without food or drink at Mount Horeb (I Kings 19:8).

Novelist Olga Grushin, in her novel *Forty Rooms*, has the protagonist, a mother, toward the book's end, contemplate life with her adult daughter:

> "It's always forty," her mother replied, snipping, smiling. "Forty is God's number for testing the human spirit. It's the limit of man's endurance, beyond which you are supposed to learn something true. Oh, you know what I mean – Noah's forty days and nights of rain. Moses' forty years in the desert, Jesus' forty days of fasting and temptation. Forty of anything is long enough to be a trial, but it's man-size, too. In the Bible, forty years make a span of one generation. Forty weeks makes a baby."[12]

Olga, the adult child, reflects to herself that life actually consists of forty rooms:

> So perhaps – yes, wasn't there something about the average person inhabiting forty rooms in his lifetime? And didn't someone close to God, some saint or prophet, say that the soul has many rooms? So perhaps that is the desert through which I am destined to wander – forty rooms, each a test for my soul, a pocket-size passion play, a small yet vital choice, a minute step toward becoming fully awake, fully human; and by the time I have crossed my own wilderness of forty rooms, I too will be able to see the world as it really is.[13]

There is an assumption in these words and in the biblical tradition that inspired them that such change requires time, but if too much time elapses

---

12. Olga Grushin, *Forty Rooms* (New York: Marion Wood, 2016), 300–301.
13. Ibid., 305.

without change then it is unlikely to ever happen. Within a period of slightly over a month, an individual – and here an entire community – can digest the implications and consequences of behavior, commit to change, and experiment with it to develop long-lasting habits. Forty days will not change anyone completely but can put someone on the trajectory to a different future.

And yet, when we turn to the Ninevites, it appears as if they did not even require forty days to change. The deadline was motivation enough to start an immediate process of cleansing and atonement. Their response was just as quick and to the chase as was the prophecy – immediate, so immediate that it seems almost ridiculous: "The Ninevites believed God. A fast was proclaimed, and all of them, from the greatest to the least, put on sackcloth. When Jonah's warning reached the king of Nineveh, he rose from his throne, took off his royal robes, covered himself with sackcloth, and sat down in the dust" (Jonah 3:5–6). The people believed in a God they knew not moments earlier, and their new fervor traveled in a rush to the palace, where the king not only absorbed the prophet's message, but was also quick to deputize others to wear sackcloth and ashes and join in the citywide fast.

The move to change preceded the king, which has important implications for the organic moral and spiritual growth of the city; the grassroots nature created a momentum that the king was able to leverage and affirm with his decrees. More than this, the king demanded an instant change of character on the assumption that the intensified and sudden piety of Nineveh would impress God and enable a change of the divine mind: "Let everyone turn back from his evil ways and from the injustice that is in his hands. Who knows but that God may turn and relent? He may turn back from His wrath so that we do not perish" (3:8–9).

UNFULFILLED PROPHECIES

The Hebrew Bible contains many fulfilled prophecies, which is important to note because we often have the false impression that predictions did not always materialize in reality. To illustrate with two well-known prophecies that came true, we turn first to Abraham at the Covenant between the Pieces. There God told Abraham what the future would bestow on his very small family: "Know well that your offspring shall be strangers in a land not theirs, and they shall be enslaved and oppressed four hundred

Radical Transformation

years; but I will execute judgment on the nation they shall serve, and in the end they shall go free with great wealth" (Gen. 15:13). Outside the debatable timeframe, God synopsized Israel's future to its first leader.

Jeremiah predicted that Babylon would rule over Judah for seventy years and then Babylon itself would be punished.

> "This whole country will become a desolate wasteland, and these nations will serve the king of Babylon seventy years. But when the seventy years are fulfilled, I will punish the king of Babylon and his nation, the land of the Babylonians, for their guilt," declares the Lord, "and will make it desolate forever." (Jer. 25:11–12)

True to Jeremiah's word, Babylon captured Assyria's last king – who held power over Judah at the time – in 609 BCE. The Temple was destroyed in 586 BCE, and the Jews were exiled to Babylon where they stayed for seventy years. In 516 BCE, the Jews returned to Jerusalem and restored the Temple.[14]

Although Nineveh's unnamed king was uncertain that God would relent, he took a righteous gamble and was correct: "When God saw what they did and how they turned from their evil ways, He relented and did not bring on them the destruction He had threatened" (Jonah 3:10). We can hardly blame Jonah for his skepticism since the repentance of the Ninevites could seem shallow and disingenuous because of its speed alone.[15]

---

14. Other examples include Isaiah's prediction that Babylon would be permanently overturned (Is. 13:19) and reduced to swampland (14:23). Nineveh would be destroyed by fire according to Nahum 3:15, and Tyre would be attacked by several warring nations according to Ezekiel 6:3. The Israelites would defeat the Edomites according to Ezekiel 25:14. Most of these prophecies took decades to be fulfilled; one might argue that with such long intervening periods, they were likely to be fulfilled without any prediction as part of the natural cycle of success and defeat in the war of nations and in political battles.
15. We cannot help but wonder why the king of Nineveh needed to command his followers to fast and wear sackcloth if they were already engaged in these behaviors. One might argue that the king's decree ensured total compliance and yet the verses above suggest that no such enforcement was necessary. One could argue that by making repentance a decree, like a parent who tells a child to say sorry, one saps

DIVINE TRANSFORMATION

It was not only that the residents of Nineveh changed. God changed. This change disturbed Jonah most. What happened to Nineveh was just a minor refraction of the much more pressing theological dilemma Jonah faced. How could he follow a God who changed His course and direction – His mind, if you will? "When God saw what they did and how they turned from their evil ways, He relented and did not bring on them the destruction He had threatened" (Jonah 3:10). The troubling word here is *vayinaḥem*, translated here as "renounced." This translation does not communicate the full range of meaning. Other translations render this word as "He regretted" or "He repented" or "He changed."

God changed in the Hebrew Bible. Had Jonah been a reader of the book in which he appears, he would have recognized this behavior from the earliest chapters of Genesis and would have been less surprised and less disappointed in his Creator. In the second chapter of Genesis God observed that Adam was alone and that this was not good. Adam never suggested this; it was an idea born of the world's Creator reflecting on the created. Where God's evaluation of the universe in chapter 1 was largely good and then cumulatively very good, God adjusted this view when seeing man without proper companionship.

The philosopher's God is perfect and makes only perfect creations with a master plan shielded from human view. The God of the Hebrew Bible is not the philosopher's God. Genesis Rabba confirms God as artist and experimenter: "God created worlds and destroyed them, created worlds and destroyed them until He arrived at this world."[16]

Yet these are not examples of regret, only of experimentation, innovation, and change. God added rather than subtracted from the world He originally conceived. The story of Noah in Genesis 6, which

---

the contrition and authenticity of the act, diminishing its potency and meaning. However, before the king made his decree, he himself fasted and wore sackcloth and sat in ashes. This is similar to the moment in the Book of Esther when the young and beautiful queen declared a personal fast for herself and then extended it to her maidens and her people. The collective bargaining chip created by inviting all to participate demonstrates the seriousness of the moment and bolsters each royal's influence and impact.

16. Genesis Rabba 3:9.

Radical Transformation

we saw earlier, however, yields a different, profoundly difficult approach to the created. God wished to destroy virtually all His creations because of their immorality and lawlessness, sparing only Noah and his family and a limited number of animals:

> The Lord saw how great was man's wickedness on earth, and how every plan devised by his mind was nothing but evil all the time. And the Lord regretted (*vayiNaḤeM*) that He had made man on earth and His heart was saddened. The Lord said, "I will blot out from the earth the man whom I created – men together with beasts, creeping things, and birds of the sky for I regret (*NiḤaMti*) that I made them." (6:5–7)

In strikingly anthropomorphic terms, God experienced sadness and regret and then acted on it with a kind of indignant rage that had obliterating force. Twice, the term regret is used, almost as if we are experiencing the thought process of the Deity, the One who stood back and observed what had happened to those He created and imbued with autonomy. Given the capacity to be self-determining, human beings decided on a course of action that compromised God's other creatures and His very notion of what this experiment should have yielded. But God did not destroy with the intent to forget the project. God's plan of destruction had a built-in clause for re-creation. God was committed to the idea of the universe, but not His original version that had so quickly soured. The God of the midrash who created worlds and destroyed them and thought that the last iteration was complete thought again.

In Noah's story, as in God's attitude to the Ninevites at Jonah's beginning, we open with destruction but close with God's reconciliation and a moment of genuine tenderness between Creator and created:

> Then Noah built an altar to the Lord and, taking of every clean animal and of every clean bird, he offered burnt offerings on the altar. The Lord smelled the pleasing aroma and said in His heart: "Never again will I curse the ground because of humans, even though every inclination of the human heart is evil from childhood. And never again will I destroy all living creatures, as I have done.

Destruction or Redemption?

As long as the earth endures, seedtime and harvest, cold and heat, summer and winter, day and night will never cease." (Gen. 8:20-22)

Noah left the ark, perhaps wondering what he could do to reverse the sentiments that had set God on a path of destruction; he arrived at the notion of sacrifice. He was commanded to put sets of sacrifice-ready animals on the ship, understanding that most of these pairs were there for purposes of reproduction but perhaps not all. Maybe a world destroyed because of stealing – the rabbinic understanding of *ḥamas* or immorality – would benefit from an act of excessive giving, a sacrifice, as the first act in the new world. We can imagine God "smiling" as He smelled the aroma of change that Noah's thoughtfulness created, prompting an unexpected long-term protection of this fragile universe. God would never again destroy the world. Miles, in *God: A Biography*, reads the sacrifice differently but arrives at a similar conclusion about the prospects for the new world:

> The Lord has to be seduced out of a recurrence of His rage by the scent of Noah's offering. God, by contrast, requires no offering from Noah. It is, rather, the other way around: God gives Noah a sign, the rainbow, that "never again shall flesh be cut off by the waters of a flood" (Gen. 9:11). And the covenant is not just with Noah but with all his descendants – that is, with the whole human race, since all will now be descended from him – and, beyond the human race, as always when God is speaking, the covenant is with all physical reality. The Lord, as before, does not bless. God blesses copiously, exhorting Noah and "your offspring to come" with a warmth greater than we heard at the first creation: "Be fertile, then, and increase; abound on earth and increase on it" (v. 7).[17]

God's regret appears later in the Book of Exodus in a different context that pits variations of the word N-Ḥ-M against each other. In order for the people not to regret their decision to leave Egypt, God did not "lead" them in an obvious direction. The play on words, which in translation

---

17. Miles, *God: A Biography* (New York: Knopf, 1995), 44.

communicates no correlation between "lead" and "regret," demonstrates how the term's elasticity implies a fluidity of direction.

> Now when Pharaoh let the people go, God did not lead them (*lo NaHaM*) by way of the land of the Philistines, although it was nearer; for God said, "The people may have a change of heart (*pen yiNaHeM*) when they see war and return to Egypt." So God led the people roundabout, by way of the wilderness at the Sea of Reeds. (13:17–18)

Later in Exodus, a more standard appearance of N-H-M appears in relation to forgiveness. After the sin of the Golden Calf, when God was prepared to dispense with the Israelites altogether but was assuaged by Moses' heartfelt plea, the text offers up this fluidity once more: "Then the Lord relented (*vayiNaHeM*) and did not bring on His people the disaster He had threatened" (32:14). Rather than destroy out of displeasure, God changed outcomes fundamentally by accepting that humans changed or had the capacity to transform themselves.

God's regret also surfaces later in the Book of Samuel over God's decision to make King Saul king over Israel. Saul had the opportunity to kill King Agag, chief of the Amalekites, but spared him. Samuel had to finish the job, putting Agag to death in Gilgal and effectively ending the relationship of king and prophet. "Until the day Samuel died, he did not go to see Saul again, though Samuel mourned for him. And the Lord regretted (*NiHaM*) that he had made Saul king over Israel" (15:35). Suddenly we move from God's regret over enormous global or communal issues to divine regret over one man's leadership.

This contrasts with an unambiguous message in the Book of Numbers that suggests that God, unlike humans, is not fickle or subject to error and change: "God is not a man, that He should lie, nor a son of man, that He should change (*NeHaM*) His mind. Does He speak and then not act? Does He promise and not fulfill?" (23:19). The verse is straightforward and denies the very anthropomorphism identified early in Genesis, where God was very much like man – almost too much. Later in Numbers, this is uttered by Balaam, the non-Jewish prophet who was forced to bless the Israelites rather than curse them, despite his personal proclivity to do the opposite. When he found himself unable to work his usual magic and in a position to report to King Balak, he had to explain the oddity of this God who did not shift and change in the polymorphous way of idols or behave like humans who changed suddenly and often. We find a similar sentiment in Isaiah, "Declaring the end from the beginning, and from the past things which were not done, saying, My purpose shall stand, and I will do all My pleasure.... What I have said, that will I bring about; what I have planned, that will I do" (46:10–11). Here too the reader senses that a praise of God is that commitments and promises hold and that carefully made divine plans reach a satisfactory and consistent execution. The last prophetic book, Malachi, also emphasizes that God does not change His mind: "Malachi declares, 'I, the Lord, do not change. So you, O descendants of Jacob, are not destroyed'" (3:6). Here because God did not change His mind, the people were saved rather than destroyed, although this verse runs counter to all of the other biblical examples thus far of unexpected mass destruction or salvation.

The thread throughout is that God does not change. Humans change. If this is so, then explaining the term regret or change to define N-Ḥ-M is particularly challenging unless one understands that change can have connotations both positive and negative, meaning both intentional transformation and fickleness. God often employs the former but never the latter.

Why all of this change vexes Jonah is an enigma. Traditional interpretations have Jonah worried that if a gentile nation repents, it will become the source of Israel's downfall. God could use this nation to bring unspeakable tragedy to Jonah's people. Jonah was not prepared to pay this price. He would rather sacrifice his own life and die in ignominy than be canonized as the prophet who catalyzed the decimation of the Jews by reforming their enemies. Many read Jonah's explanation in chapter 4 in precisely this fashion:

> But Jonah was greatly displeased [that God saved the Ninevites] and became angry. He prayed to the Lord, "O Lord, is this not what I said when I was still at home? That is why I was so quick to flee to Tarshish. For I know that You are a compassionate and

gracious God, slow to anger, abounding in kindness, renouncing punishment. Please, Lord, take my life, for I would rather die than live." (vv. 1–3)

Independent analysis of this passage will be offered later. In this context, we can say that Jonah was suggesting that the way this story would play out was all evident to him earlier, familiar as he was with God's changing behavior as recorded in earlier biblical narratives. Knowing this, he felt justified in asking God to take his life. Jonah was not able to facilitate his own death since, by this time, he was painfully aware that he could not escape God's destiny for him. Perhaps he too could change God's mind – not about the fate of Nineveh but regarding his own life.

A THEOLOGICAL OBJECTION

There is one significant problem with such an interpretation. When Jonah articulated his anger to God, he did not discuss the particulars of Nineveh's situation and the fact that the city would soon be responsible for Israel's eventual doom; instead, he spoke of the more global understanding he had of God's very nature. His problem was not practical; it was theological. Had Nineveh itself been the focus of his ire, he could have told God exactly that: "Isn't this what I said, Lord, when I was still at home? That is what I tried to forestall by fleeing to Tarshish. I knew that You would accept Nineveh's repentance, and one day You will use them to destroy the Jews and this will all be my fault for being complicit in Your demand." Instead, Jonah left the city. He built a booth, but such a makeshift structure could never afford him the protection he really needed because what he sought to shield himself from was not an external threat but an internal one.

Nineveh was prepared to change. God was prepared to change. Jonah was not prepared to change. Landes suggests that although Jonah had walked only one day's journey into the city's three-day radius when his message spread rapidly, Jonah must have experienced the entirety of Nineveh's change. In chapter 4, he is found east of the city,

> implying in the light of 3:3 that he must have spent at least three days within the city. This suggests not only a fascinating

parallelism with his three-day and three-night sojourn within the fish but also that he was within Nineveh long enough to have witnessed the penitent response of the Ninevites to his prophecy. This could mean that there actually is a textual clue that Jonah's departure from Nineveh was not immediately after he delivered his prophecy but sometime later.[18]

In other words, Jonah's vexation was not impulsive or rash but a simmering anger that developed when he was an observer of the scene. Jonah, witnessing the city's lightning-quick transformation when he expected its obliteration, understanding that God Himself had evolved, was enraged. The enigma of the prophet's approach to Nineveh is not answered but amplified in chapter 3. We must wait until chapter 4 to comprehend what Jonah was thinking on his short and lonely walk in and out of Nineveh.

---

18. Landes, "Textual 'Information Gaps,'" 286–287.

Part Four
The Final Word

Chapter Ten

Job, Jonah, and the Power of God's Justice

> But Jonah was greatly displeased and became angry. He prayed to the Lord, "O Lord, is this not what I said when I was still at home? That is why I was so quick to flee to Tarshish. For I know that You are a compassionate and gracious God, slow to anger, abounding in kindness, renouncing punishment. Please, Lord, take my life, for I would rather die than live." The Lord replied, "Are you that deeply grieved?" (Jonah 4:1–4)

We open chapter 4 with a dejected prophet. God had planned to destroy Nineveh, but He "did not bring on them the destruction He had threatened" (Jonah 3:10). The very notion that God could change was completely unacceptable to Jonah. It infuriated him and filled him with righteous indignation. What kind of perfect God changes His decree? Never mind that God did; according to the prophet, He could not. God's actions, in Jonah's limited mind, were divine and, therefore, immutable.

With this close to chapter 3, we turn away from the large city and its changing behaviors to focus the spotlight on God's change of heart, so to speak, and on Jonah's reaction to it. Jonah was crestfallen by the new and improved Nineveh. He effectively disappeared from chapter 3 with his quick announcement; the reader focuses his or her attention solely on Nineveh – its people, king, and cattle. Jonah slinked out of the city in despair. It is not what we expect – or is it?

Jonah was devastated by Nineveh's fast and thorough citywide transformation. But was it the speed, the outcome, or the process which troubled him so? His vexation caused him to pray and admit something that we as readers did not know. When he was given this task of preaching to Nineveh, Jonah was concerned that his message would be heeded. What he thought would happen actually did happen; God forgave the Ninevites. Usually people are pleased when what they believe will transpire occurs – unless, of course, they have premonitions of evil and find that they come true. So it was for Jonah. Nineveh's repentance could bring only evil in Jonah's worldview.

"For I know that You are a compassionate and gracious God, slow to anger, abounding in kindness, renouncing punishment. Please, Lord, take my life, for I would rather die than live" (4:2–3). This is an odd complaint. Jonah accused God of being too compassionate, of extending an undeserving and generous application of grace to the residents of Nineveh. Jonah, it seems, intentionally warped the formula Moses famously used in petitioning God for communal forgiveness after the sin of the Golden Calf, where mercy was to outstrip justice if the covenant was to be upheld. That verse ends with the resounding word *emet*; the God of Exodus 34:6 is not only "merciful" but also "faithful" or "truthful."[1] In omitting the word "truth," Jonah described a God too full of pity for humanity to ever exact a justice that is true. Jonah, son of Amitai – son of truth – could not tolerate this inexactitude, especially at God's hand. Like Billy Budd in Melville's eponymous novella or Inspector Javert in Hugo's *Les Misérables*, Jonah was prepared – indeed preferred – to die, rather than to live with the indefinite reality that things were not as they should be, that fate could change, that people could change.

RESPONSES TO GOD: JOB AND ABRAHAM

In response to Jonah's plea, we can imagine God turning to Jonah with the same quizzical look He must have given Job when asking him these questions:

---

1. See other places where variations of this formula appear: Ps. 86:15; 103:8; 145:8.

> Where were you when I laid the foundations of the universe? Speak if you have understanding. Do you know who fixed its dimensions or who measured it with a line? Onto what were its bases sunk? Who set its cornerstone when the morning stars sang together and all the divine beings shouted for joy? Who closed the sea behind doors, when it gushed forth out of the womb, when I clothed it in clouds, swaddled it in dense clouds. When I made breakers, My limits for it, and set up its bars and doors, and said, "You may come so far and no further; here your surging waves will stop?" (Job 38:4–11)

God, turning to Job, wants to know to what degree a human being can understand what it means to set the entire world in motion, to transcend time and place, to determine the boundaries of space. Here the image of God's power over the sea and the setting of its tides resonates with Jonah's experience of the sea compassing him about, showing him that he was powerless in the face of the usually indifferent natural forces that were then harnessed for his reformation. The surging waves did not stop until they delivered Jonah to a distant shore to make peace with God's booming voice of destiny, sounded out through water and sun, fish and worm. "Have you ever commanded the day to break," God continues in Job, "assigned the dawn its place?" (v. 12). God's work spans the entire universe, a truth so much more vast than the limits of human knowledge that human beings have to be put in their place when the arrogance of a refined intelligence leads them to assume too much.

In the above passage, God explained to Job that not only did he not understand the world and the way it operates in delicate balance and confluence, he failed to understand that the Creator's job is also as Sustainer. God sets the world in motion as its chief operator, day after day after day. God must sustain it and care for it – as God reminded Jonah with His last, enduring question. Jonah's rigid certainty about his four cubits was neither very certain nor very vast, as God tried to demonstrate with repeated rhetorical questions. Unlike Jonah, in Job's case there was eventual movement and remorse. This, however, did not take place before God continued His strategic line of interrogation, maintaining the stirring, stinging, and lengthy series of rhetorical questions in Job's path to demonstrate how little any human being can fathom the mysteries of God's universe:

> Have you ever given orders to the morning, or shown the dawn its place, that it might take the earth by the edges and shake the wicked out of it? The earth takes shape like clay under a seal; its features stand out like those of a garment. The wicked are denied their light, and their upraised arm is broken. Have you journeyed to the springs of the sea or walked in the recesses of the deep? Have the gates of death been shown to you? Have you seen the gates of the deepest darkness? Have you comprehended the vast expanses of the earth? Tell me, if you know all this. (vv. 12–19)

This is not a theological diatribe divorced from the listener. Unlike Jonah who retreated into silence, Job expended every ounce of his emotion and his intellect plumbing the nature of God's justice. Jonah fled. Job stepped into the pain. He listened to his supposed friends lecture him on causality and evil. He cried out to God, reviewing his own piety and wondering where the fault lines lay in his assumptions of self and universe. Until finally, finally God burst forward to explain that Job would never understand His master plan. There was no context in which Job could ever comprehend the scope of God's activities: Where were you when I laid the earth's foundations? God asked Job. With an almost biting sarcasm, God prodded Job to know the source of his self-confidence or even his trifling assumption that he could gain any understanding. Surely you know, God jabbed in words that appear in the text: "Tell me, if you know all this," (38:19) demanded God.

Job's task, then, was not to comprehend the workings of God's world but to act with his free will to conquer himself and leave the outcomes in God's surer hand. After several chapters of God's questions, God asked Job to respond. What we assumed to be rhetorical was actually an invitation to enter God's world and react to God's litany: "The Lord said to Job: 'Will the one who contends with the Almighty correct Him? Let him who accuses God answer Him!'" (40:1). Job had piety. He had wealth. He had a family and many blessings. But he lacked true faith and he lacked humility – and that had to be recalibrated for Job's story to end with the blessings with which it began.

Job, Jonah, and the Power of God's Justice

In chapter 1, Job brought sacrifices in case his children erred through their festivities; he used the word we analyzed earlier, *ulai*.[2] Perhaps his sacrifices on their behalf could serve as a corrective for their possible wrongdoings: "Perhaps my children have sinned and blasphemed God in their thoughts" (v. 5). Job believed he could change God's mind through a gift rather than through the true remorse and atonement that had to belong to someone else to be authentic and sincere. God needed to disabuse Job of his faulty thinking. His error was not only in his understanding of how the universe operates. God also needed Job to understand repentance – just as God tried to teach Jonah the same lesson.

Job and Jonah both needed to understand the way that God interacts with those imbued with free will. Specifically, they had to learn why God extends the power of forgiveness to those who make choices to sin or rebel. God is a God of vastness; the long-term perspective eludes humans and obstructs their understanding of the possible evolution of self over time. Jonah saw only crime and concomitant punishment. What he did not understand was a more compelling theological formula: sin, atonement, and then forgiveness. Forgiveness can vitiate or mitigate punishment. Even when punishment is meted out for the sake of justice, forgiveness keeps a relationship intact despite an act that challenges it. Finally, near the end of the Book of Job, the suffering man understood atonement:

> Then Job answered the Lord: "I am unworthy – how can I reply to You? I put my hand over my mouth. I spoke once, but I have no answer – twice, but I will say no more." Then the Lord spoke to Job out of the storm: "Brace yourself like a man; I will question you, and you shall answer Me. Would you discredit My justice? Would you condemn Me to justify yourself? Do you have an arm like God's, and can your voice thunder like His? Then adorn yourself with glory and splendor, and clothe yourself in honor and majesty. Unleash the fury of your wrath, look at all who are proud and bring them low, look at all who are proud and humble them, crush the wicked where they stand. Bury them all in the

---

2. See chapter 3.

dust together; shroud their faces in the grave. Then I Myself will admit to you that your own right hand can save you." (40:1–14)

The expression, "brace yourself like a man" also appeared earlier in the text, when God began the questioning period. Job was merely a man, and such a limitation made it impossible for Job to dress in the glory and splendor of God, whose creations reflect beauty and honor. But more than that, God made a claim for justice: Unless you know who is truly wicked and who is truly wonderful, you can never be divine, God reminded Job. Humans lack the penetrating scope and context in which to make accurate judgments about mercy.

> Then Job replied to the Lord: "I know that You can do all things; no purpose of Yours can be thwarted. You asked, 'Who is this that obscures My plans without knowledge?' Surely I spoke of things I did not understand, things too wonderful for me to know. You said, 'Listen now, and I will speak; I will question you, and you shall answer Me.' My ears had heard of You but now my eyes have seen You. Therefore I despise myself and repent in dust and ashes." (42:1–6)

After God's disquisition, Job had a glimmer of insight. He felt humbled and lowered in contrition. This was not the same lowering of the first chapter of Job, where he sat on the floor in sackcloth and ashes for seven days surrounded by "friends" in utter silence: "No one said a word to him because they saw how great his suffering was" (2:13). This was Job lowered by the weight of God's might. It was exactly the kind of humility God had waited for in His servant, and it yielded an unexpected consequence:

> The Lord blessed the latter part of Job's life more than the former part. He had fourteen thousand sheep, six thousand camels, a thousand yoke of oxen, and a thousand donkeys. And he also had seven sons and three daughters. The first daughter he named Jemimah, the second Keziah, and the third Keren-happuch. Nowhere in all the land were there found women as beautiful as Job's daughters, and their father granted them an inheritance along with their

brothers. After this, Job lived a hundred and forty years; he saw his children and their children to the fourth generation. And so Job died, an old man and full of years. (42:12–17)

When Job was able to submit himself fully to God's will and stop defending his goodness to God, God too softened. By the time Job died, he had amassed more wealth than he had before his trial. The writer assumes that the reader will contrast the first verses of Job with its last and realize that Job's property ultimately doubled. Where he had seven thousand sheep and three thousand camels, he was now the proud owner of twice that number. God, however, did not give Job more than ten children but the exact breakdown that he enjoyed before, perhaps because children can neither be easily replaced nor superseded – an issue that lingers for any reader of the last chapter of Job. Even if one reads into Job's behavior in the first chapter – his offerings after his children feasted – an explicit criticism of his children and his sense that they never lived up to his standard of piety, this is no reason not to mourn their loss. Nor would we find fault in a Job who stumbled in confusion with each of these life enhancements. Yet part of Job's new understanding of God's ways must surely have included the silencing of any impulse to protest or ask for explanations. For this, he was rewarded magnificently. He was able to give his daughters an inheritance, a subtle hint that he was able to compensate for legal injustices that would compromise the fiscal security of his offspring, and he was able to see generational continuity through the fourth generation, exceeding in years the optimal biblical age of death, 120, as measured by Moses' death.

Jonah, on the other hand, never underwent Job's softening, humbling process – as far as we see – thus no eventual rewards were prepared for him.

Abraham, who struggled mightily to resolve the conundrum of infertility with the promise of an heir to his nation, had, like Job, a sudden bump in his later senior years. He took another wife, Ketura, who bore him six children; Abraham's descendants from this marriage are also listed, as is the inheritance he provided for his children – just like Job. Both people, thrown into emotional chaos by a God inexplicable, end their lives nobly with loose ends tied.

Most importantly, Job ended his life with a good death, characteristic of Abraham himself: "And Abraham breathed his last, dying at a good ripe age, old and contented; and he was gathered to his kin" (Gen. 25:8). Dying of old age was regarded as a blessing in the ancient world, a reward for those who deserved it. These two figures, Job and Abraham, both suffered trials of faith at the hand of a God who seemingly asked the unreasonable, yet both rose in triumph. These trials involved the loss or potential loss of children and served as a demonstration of commitment and fealty to the one God, resulting in more children, more wealth, and more years of life for each protagonist. In *Subversive Sequels in the Bible*, Klitsner argues that "the Book of Job begins where the story of the *Akeda* [the Binding of Isaac] ended."[3] In Genesis 22, God challenged Abraham to sacrifice his son, threatening to topple God's covenant with Abraham lest he refuse. But the "happy" ending assures the reader that God would never have gone through with His plan, that this God was unlike other pagan gods who demand the gift of dead children to prove one's loyalty.[4]

The Book of Job takes up these questions by placing its hero in circumstances that are similar to those of Abraham, but exacerbated. As we have seen, both stories feature the suffering of righteous men as their children are imperiled by God. But the story quickly spins in a radically new direction when, in the Book of

---

3. Klitsner, *Subversive Sequels in the Bible*, xxi.
4. For the history of this controversial approach, see Jon D. Levenson, "Abusing Abraham: Traditions, Religious Histories and Modern Misinterpretations," *Judaism* 47 (Summer 1998): 259–277. Immanuel Kant's position is influential in this discussion, believing that this narrative represents the "euthanasia of Judaism" and is a text that lays bare the question of God's very nature. He believes Abraham should have replied: "That I ought not to kill my good son is quite certain. But that you, this apparition are God – of that I am not certain, and never can be, not even if this voice rings down to me from heaven." See *Conflict of the Faculties*, trans. Mary J. Gregor (New York: Abaris Books, 1979), 115. For reflections on the complexity of teaching this narrative see Erica Brown, "Religious Language and Modern Sensibilities: Teaching the *Akeidah* to Adults," *Wisdom from All My Teachers: Challenges and Initiatives in Contemporary Torah Education*, ed. Jeffrey Saks and Susan Handelman (Urim: Jerusalem, 2003), 213–228.

Job, God actually allows the blameless children to die. Moreover, ratcheting up the injustice, the hero loses not one, but ten children. These differences lead to the most striking point of contrast between the two stories, which is Abraham's silent compliance with God's plan to kill the innocent as opposed to Job's outspoken objections to God's injustice.[5]

Klitsner further demonstrates that God did not take Job to task for his questioning: "While God congratulates Abraham for his unquestioning acceptance of the divine will, He commends Job for his insistent challenging of God's actions."[6] This would show the Book of Job to be an appropriately subversive sequel to the Abraham narrative for a trial they both shared.

And yet some of the similarities in these two stories break down. Job was believed to be a mythical character because of the strange geographic locations, character names (or lack of names), and exaggeration of details. Job's plotline is thin, and the action in the story is covered mostly by the events of chapter 1 and the summation at the book's end. Everything else sandwiched in between constitutes expressive and emotional reflections on the nature of suffering and the role of God and humans in the world. The action is a mere conceit or holding platform for the prose, which is our main concern. It is as if the writer created a simple plot to provide the stimulus for the theology of the book.

Contrast this to the silence of the Abraham and Jonah texts where speech is desperately missing and silence overtakes the space of explanation. If there is anything subversive, it is not so much in the message or the challenge of Job; it is the speech versus the silence in the face of mystery and suffering that separates these texts in genre and tone, if not in content. Job eventually confronted God and negotiated with Him. Abraham silently acquiesced. Jonah silently fled. Each use of speech – the holding back and the holding forth – makes its own theological statement about the nature of the relationship between God and human beings, providing a spiritual variety that is not as much judged as it is offered for us to digest. We cannot blame Abraham for his silence. We cannot fault Job for his speech.

---

5. Klitsner, *Subversive Sequels*, xxii.
6. Ibid., xxiii.

The Final Word

REPENTANCE AND FORGIVENESS IN EZEKIEL AND DANIEL

A chief difference is, of course, that Abraham and Job were able to neatly tie up their stories and redeem their ends. No such literary luck awaits the reader of Jonah who wonders what happened to this prophet and his theology. In his book, Jonah never had a moment of atonement or an old age characterized by redemption. As readers, we ponder how speech might have changed everything. Jonah never expressed real repentance the way that it is clearly explained in Ezekiel: those who repent of sin will be forgiven and not punished:

> "If the wicked one repents of all the sins that he committed and keeps all My laws and does what is just and right, he *shall live*; he shall not die. None of the transgressions he committed shall be remembered against him because of the righteousness he has practiced, he *shall live*. Is it My desire that a wicked person shall die?" says the Lord God. "It is rather that he shall turn back from his ways *and live*." (18:21–23)

The conditions articulated here, that a person who sins must regret his past and reconfirm his commitment to God's laws, will result in his transgressions being erased from the accounts of good and evil. That person shall live because God does not desire death. This, however, must not have been an obvious understanding of God's ways because in each of these three verses the term "live" is used; it stresses that God desires life for His flawed and failed human beings, and that they too shall seek life in the richness of the covenant. Yet, mired in guilt, shame, or indifference, this may be hard for a human being to digest, integrate, and believe.

Ezekiel's message translated into the lives of heroic biblical figures, shaping the way that they prayed and developed, from the time of Moses onward. God was identified as just but also and primarily as merciful. It was to this sense of compassion that penitents pleaded their case, as did Moses after the Golden Calf or David after the sin of Bathsheba. We see strains of this thinking in Daniel when he realized that the prophecy of doom and exile predicted by Jeremiah was fast approaching. Daniel put on sackcloth and ashes, fasted, and prayed. His confessionary language was later borrowed by the sages for liturgical purposes; it forms the spine of our Yom Kippur prayer script:

> We have sinned; we have gone astray; we have acted wickedly; we have been rebellious and have deviated from Your commandments and Your rules and have not obeyed Your servants the prophets who spoke in Your name to our kings, our officers, our fathers, and all the people of the land. (Dan. 9:5–6)

The confession of sin creates the readiness for God's mercy because it is hard not to pity someone who humiliates and shames himself through such a difficult reckoning. Only then, once wrongdoing has been established and the pain of it is described almost as if it is relived, could Daniel move to the next phase in the trajectory of repentance: "To the Lord our God belong mercy and forgiveness" (v. 9).

Daniel then drilled down further into his sin and the sin of his people; his prayer culminated in a request that God listen to his supplication, not because of its inherent worthiness but because of God's compassion: "Not because of any merit of ours do we lay our plea before You but because of Your abundant mercies" (v. 18) – another verse we recognize from High Holiday petitionary prayers.

This trope may sound familiar to us, having internalized penitential prayers and their meaning. But it was not necessarily obvious to ancient readers. This may explain Jonah's outrage in chapter 4. Kugel, in *How to Read the Bible*, writes that although one cannot mistake Ezekiel's message, in the ancient world, it was a "relative novelty."[7] More than God's mercy, Jonah demanded – indeed, expected – God's consistency. Jonah was not prepared to live in a world without it even though, on the face of it, Jonah was a wildly successful prophet. Yet he did not see it that way. Jonah, Kugel argues,

> feels his reputation as a prophet has been ruined. After all, the most basic thing about prophecy is that God is supposed to let the prophet's words "fall to the ground" (I Sam. 3:19); in other words, everything a true prophet says must come to pass. Indeed, the very definition of a false prophet is one who announces something "but the thing does not take place or prove true"

---

7. Kugel, *How to Read the Bible*, 629.

(Deut. 18:22). Jonah therefore feels betrayed: God ought to have destroyed the people of Nineveh just the way He said He would.[8]

As nearly every commentary points out, when Jonah finally spoke directly and provocatively to God in chapter 4, he described all of God's attributes of mercy but neglected – in the formulation known to us from Exodus – the one that ends with *emet*, "truth." This is a different kind of prayer from Jonah's first, which expressed deep yearning for intimacy with God. This second prayer sounds little like the prose prayer with which we are familiar. Instead of intimacy, Jonah suddenly longed for distance. Finally reconciled with his mission and in close proximity to God, Jonah was disappointed in the God he remembered, a God who was more merciful than just. As a result, while Jonah prayed for his life in chapter 2, in chapter 4 he was ready to have God take his life, indeed pleaded that He do so. With an urgency he did not express previously, Jonah recalled the sentiments that may have explained his first escape. He intimated as much: "O Lord, is this not what I said when I was still at home? That is why I was so quick to flee to Tarshish" (Jonah 4:2). Jonah was well aware of God's tendency to grace – to mercy – and was only touched by it briefly when he required mercy as seaweed encircled his head and his body, near lifeless, sank to the sea's bottom. But the momentary and deep contact Jonah had with divine mercy was not able to erase a lifetime of acting and thinking differently about God's ways. Suddenly in Nineveh and then on its outskirts, Jonah returned deep, deep inside to a place that negated this expansive and, for Jonah, irritating feature of God's relationship with flawed human beings. Stop forgiving, Jonah begged. If God could not help but accept contrition, then Jonah had no place of theological safety in this world.

THE SON OF TRUTH

If God did not represent truth, then the son of truth could not live. "For I know that You are a compassionate and gracious God, slow to anger, abounding in kindness, renouncing punishment. Please, Lord, take my life, for I would rather die than live" (Jonah 4:2–3). Virtually every commentary cites Exodus 34, the original formulation offered by Moses when seeking only God's compassion after the sin of the Golden Calf. Early in the

---

8. Ibid., 628.

morning, Moses climbed Mount Sinai, perhaps the most strenuous ascent of his career, burdened as he was by his people's infidelity. "The Lord, the Lord, a God compassionate and gracious, slow to anger, abounding in kindness and faithfulness, extending kindness to the thousandth generation, forgiving iniquity, transgression, and sin; yet He does not remit all punishment" (vv. 6–7). Moses bowed low to the ground and asked to excuse the unacceptable behavior of his people: "If I have gained Your favor, O Lord, pray, let the Lord go in our midst, even though this is a stiff-necked people. Pardon our iniquity and our sin, and take us for Your own!" (v. 9).

> God's answer to Jonah, stressing the supremacy of compassion, upsets the possibility of looking for a rational coherence of God's ways with the world. History would be more intelligible if God's word were the last word, final and unambiguous like a dogma or an unconditional decree: once wickedness had reached its full measure, punishment would destroy it. Yet, beyond justice and anger lies the mystery of compassion.[9]

In a contemporary use of the Jonah story, Pope Francis during Mass at the Casa Santa Marta told the faithful not to put their own beliefs before God's mercy, citing Jonah's initial resistance and then his eventual submission to God's will. He said, "It really was a miracle, because in this case he abandons his stubbornness, his rigidity, to obey the will of God, and he did what the Lord commanded him."[10] Jonah even rebuked God. In the first chapter Jonah resisted his mission. In the second, he became obedient. In the third chapter, "There is resistance to God's mercy." For Pope Francis, the ministers of God might become the most rigid to God's message of mercy, but he concluded, "Where the Lord is, there is mercy." He even coined a term for piety without love: the Jonah syndrome.[11]

---

9. Heschel, *The Prophets*, 368.
10. "Pope Francis: God Wants His Ministers to Be Merciful," Vatican Radio, October 6, 2015. See: http://en.radiovaticana.va/news/2015/10/06/pope_francis_god_wants_his_ministers_to_be_merciful/1177174.
11. Elise Harris, "Pope Warns against 'Jonah Syndrome' of the Pharisees," Catholic News Agency, October 14, 2013, http://www.catholicnewsagency.com/news/pope-warns-against-jonah-syndrome-of-the-pharisees.

God had to explain forcefully to Jonah that there can be no piety without love, no truth without mercy, and, most importantly, that human beings will never have a vast enough perspective and context to know when to apply justice and when to offer compassion. We almost long for the speeches God gave Job, who could have listened carefully and responded, more mature as a result of the dialogue between him and his Creator. Not so Jonah. His silence seems to have brought out God's silence. There are no speeches here, just questions. And when Jonah confirmed that, yes, he did wish to die, perhaps God saw that there was no room in Jonah's mind to evolve the prophet's thinking, as God aimed for with Job. And thus, unlike the Job narrative, we have no happy ending or resolution. We have only a question. We must look elsewhere in the Hebrew Bible to find a more compelling theology of change than what existed in Jonah's limited and rigid mindset. We find it in Joel:

> "Yet even now," declares the Lord, "return to Me with all your heart, with fasting, with weeping, and with mourning; and rend your hearts and not your garments." Return to the Lord your God, for He is gracious and merciful, slow to anger, and abounding in steadfast love; and He relents over disaster. *Who knows whether He will not turn and relent,* and leave a blessing behind Him, a grain offering and a drink offering for the Lord your God? Blow the trumpet in Zion; consecrate a fast; call a solemn assembly; gather the people. Consecrate the congregation; assemble the elders; gather the children, even nursing infants. Let the bridegroom leave his room, and the bride her chamber. (2:12–17)

Who knows whether He will not turn and relent? asks the prophet Joel. One of the compelling reasons for human beings to repent in the theology of the Hebrew Bible is that God may change a human's fate as a result of penitence. Sadly, Jonah did not abide by this theology. It put him into crisis, a crisis he left and returned to at the book's end.

Chapter Eleven

Nature as Teacher: A Hot Sun, a Blistering Wind, a Gourd, a Worm

Now Jonah had left the city and found a place east of the city. He made a booth there and sat under it in the shade, until he should see what happened to the city. The Lord God provided a ricinus plant, which grew up over Jonah, to provide shade for his head and save him from discomfort. Jonah was very happy about the plant. But the next day at dawn God provided a worm, which attacked the plant so that it withered. And when the sun rose, God provided a sultry east wind; the sun beat down on Jonah's head, and he became faint. He begged for death, saying, "I would rather die than live." (Jonah 4:5–8)

There is a pleasure in the pathless woods,
There is a rapture on the lonely shore,
There is society, where none intrudes,
By the deep sea, and music in its roar:
I love not man the less, but Nature more.[1]

---

1. Lord George Gordon Byron, "Childe Harold's Pilgrimage."

The Final Word

Lord Byron, a leading Romantic poet of the nineteenth century, regarded nature as music, as a balm to the soul and an ecstatic escape from the tug of humanity. The woods, the shore, the sea drew him in, inspired him, expanded him. We find such sentiments common, even if not always expressed with Byron's lyricism. And yet nature as a subject – as a character – is not always a place of poetry and comfort. It can be indifferent to human travesty or be the source of calamity itself. It can wreak terror in the heart of man. And in our story it becomes the abiding horror of one prophet in his fruitless attempt to avoid God. Nature is the central instrument in God's repository of reformation when it comes to Jonah.

Jonah's quixotic persona and the book's engaging plotline can draw all of a reader's attention to the foreground of the story and ignore the fascinating background: the natural landscape that propels the actions in the story forward, and in some instances, backward. The natural landscape is not merely a matter of the sea and the dry land, although much must be said of these large expanses and their role in the narrative (and has been said in an earlier chapter). In the first two chapters of Jonah, maritime images dominate: roiling waves, uncontrollable winds that can capsize large ships, big fish, seaweed, and sand bars. "The Lord provided a huge fish to swallow Jonah, and Jonah was inside the fish three days and three nights" (Jonah 2:1). The fish was his savior, his sanctuary – "Jonah prayed to the Lord his God from the belly of the fish" (v. 2) – and his torture. The animals of chapter 3 behave strangely. Strange climatic changes bookend the chapters, from the storm that seems to identify Jonah as the culprit to a hot, easterly wind that burns with such intensity that it prompts Jonah to beg God to be released from life itself. "And when the sun rose, God provided a sultry east wind; the sun beat down on Jonah's head, and he became faint. He begged for death, saying, 'I would rather die than live'" (4:8). Creatures great and small poke through the verses, turning Jonah's self-understanding inside out. The fish that saved Jonah, temporarily trapping him and then spitting him out in exactly the right location to make good on his mission, occupies no more a significant place in the story's unraveling than the small worm that consumed Jonah's special tree.

ANIMALS IN SACKCLOTH

The role of the fish and the worm are not even the strangest animal behaviors in Jonah:

> When Jonah's warning reached the king of Nineveh, he rose from his throne, took off his royal robes, covered himself with sackcloth and sat down in the dust. This is the proclamation he issued in Nineveh: "By the decree of the king and his nobles: Do not let people or animals, herds or flocks, taste anything; do not let them eat or drink. But let people and animals be covered with sackcloth. Let everyone call urgently on God. Let everyone turn back from his evil ways and from the injustice that is in his hands." (Jonah 3:6–8)

Some medieval commentators were troubled by the oddity of the king's command that animals not eat and that they wear sackcloth, a command he extended with a royal proclamation. Since the king cried out, one might think that he was irrational with grief and consternation, and this propelled his foolish demand that cattle fast and wear sackcloth. Yet this was no casual throwaway line but a thought-out, intentional request. Ibn Ezra explains that the inclusion of the word "decree" means just this: "from his wisdom, his knowledge, and his common sense."[2] Nothing seems less commonsensical than depriving animals of their food, especially because, as domesticated creatures, they were instruments of labor whose work would be compromised without food. It is one thing to obligate human beings who can make conscious decisions to repent, but what is the wisdom of enforced fasting for animals that would, even in this fantastical story, have been unlikely candidates for personal transformation? Rashi, if he finds anything odd here, does not comment on it, offering the impression that this was normal or acceptable behavior. This is also true for other classic medieval commentators like Ibn Ezra and Radak, who feel a need to define "proclamation" but do not deal with the substance of these verses, only their linguistic nuances.

Gaster believes that the animals here are merely part of the flavor of activity, a not uncommon feature of ancient Near Eastern life:

---

2. Ibn Ezra to Jonah 3:7.

> Animals are part of the "topocosm" – that is, of the aggregate of living beings and inanimate objects which together constitute the corporate entity and "atmosphere" of a place. Hence, in popular belief, they participate in its fate and fortune. It is in this spirit, for instance, that cattle as well as men are victims of the plagues inflicted upon Egypt at the time of the exodus, and that the prophet Joel can declare, when disaster befalls his country, that "the flocks of sheep too are held guilty."[3]

Animals, thus, were swept up in national mourning, but only as a manifestation of human mourning and not expressly because they sought repentance or understood the significance of the rituals in which they participated.

Only in the nineteenth century do we see any attempt at an explanation that highlights the animals as more than background music, so to speak, in Nineveh's atonement process. The rationale for the sackcloth and fasting of animals is filled with immense power and tenderness. The *Metzudat David* observes that "because of the anxiety, he [the king] commanded that food not be given to the animals in order to move the hearts of men."[4] Human beings may fast and dress in sackcloth and yet not be inspired to change at all. These may be perfunctory rituals to achieve a "look" of repentance rather than an authentic act of change. But human beings who lack compassion for each other may still have compassion for their animals, especially when they witness them in a state of suffering. This view is supported by a passage in the Jerusalem Talmud:

> R. Yehoshua b. Levi said: This was a deceitful repentance. What did they do? ... they placed nursing calves inside and their mothers outside, nursing donkeys inside, and the mothers outside; these [the suckling offspring] were crying from their side [from hunger] and these [the mothers] were crying from their side. They [the people of Nineveh] said [to God]: If you will not have mercy on us, we will not have mercy upon these [animals]. (Y. Taanit 2:3)

---

3. Gaster, *Myth, Legend and Custom in the Old Testament*, 656.
4. *Metzudat David* to Jonah 3:7.

Withholding food from a domesticated animal that has no control over its food supply unless it scavenges in the wild would generate mercy and sadness in its human owners who might otherwise have hardened their hearts to the difficult task at hand. What future potential they could not see in each other would be resolved by, at the very least, addressing the harm they were doing to their animals. This impulse would also be self-serving, since they required their animals to work on their own behalf. The king, by putting obstacles in the way of Nineveh's citizens lest they reject the prophet's cause, was ensuring a smooth and collective commitment to a new and improved city.

There may be an explanation even more profound than animal suffering inspiring the repentance of their owners. Animals in the ancient world were often put on trial for "crimes" as if they were conscious of and accountable for wrongdoing. We have instances of this recorded in the Talmud.[5] Aristotle mentions that animals were tried, but the first recorded document of such a trial – a pig that killed a child – does not appear until the fourteenth century.[6] J. J. Finkelstein contends that such show trials had an educational purpose: "The ox is to be executed, not because it had committed a crime, but rather because the very act of killing a human being – voluntarily or involuntarily – had rendered it an object of public horror."[7] Such trials would showcase the primacy of human life and induce animal owners to be more scrupulous about supervising their cattle and flocks.[8] Because the Book of Jonah is populated by animals that save humans and invest in human reformation, it

---

5. See, for example Bava Kamma 90a, where an ox that committed a capital offense was put on trial.
6. See W. W. Hyde, "The Prosecution and Punishment of Animals and Lifeless Things in the Middle Ages and Modern Times," *University of Pennsylvania Law Review* 64 (1915–1916): 696–730. Available online: http://scholarship.law.upenn.edu/cgi/viewcontent.cgi?article=7589&context=penn_law_review.
7. J. J. Finkelstein, "The Ox that Gored," *Transactions of the American Philosophical Society*, 71, no. 2 (1981): 1–89.
8. For more on this subject, see Jeremy Brown, "The Prosecution and Punishment of Animals" on the blog site Talmudology.com, Aug. 29, 2016. See: http://www.talmudology.com/jeremybrownmdgmailcom/2016/8/28/bava-kamma-90a-the-prosecution-punishment-of-animals.

would seem only reasonable in this fairy-tale universe to have animals that engage in other human behaviors.

Not all the animals in Jonah have a specific moralizing purpose. The cattle mentioned in 4:11 deserved pity because they did not know their right from their left hand. Animals do not have right or left hands, and if they did, they would not know that they did, making this verse one of the strangest in the book. This forces us to focus not on what the humans or animals are capable or incapable of doing but on God's vast mercies that extend to creatures that are not conduits for God's plan. They are sentient beings and they exist, and this was enough of a reason to save them. And this was enough of a reason for Jonah to care about them, just as God did.

NATURAL FORCES AND THE *KIKAYON*

When we move beyond chapter 3, whose dominant landscape is the city itself, we find that chapter 4 of the Book of Jonah offers the highest concentration of natural phenomena that, in the prophet's mind, persecuted him: a sweeping wind, a burning sun, a sudden tree, a ravenous worm. To Jonah, three of the four were there to torture him and taunt him to death. Whereas animals did aid in change in chapter 3, they impeded change as it related to Jonah's welfare. Where winds pushed the story forward in chapter 1, they had a deleterious effect on Jonah in chapter 4. In chapter 4, the hot sun was joined by another peculiar climate change: a vehement east wind (Jonah 4:8). The adjective *harishit*, "vehement," is strange. The sages felt it necessary to define it. R. Yehuda relates it to the Hebrew word *horeshet*, "plow," explaining that "at the time it blows, it forms many furrows in the sea," giving the illusion of plowing. (Gittin 31b). The wind created a chopping motion on the sea, generating foam on its crests. From a distance, it offered the appearance of digging.

As long as they are discussing the wind, the hot sun mentioned in the same verse seems to also require rabbinic attention. If the wind blew and the sun beat upon Jonah's head such that he fainted, this kind of wind, they believe, was a cool rather than a hot wind. Rabba chimes in, understanding the root as H-R-SH, to quiet: "At the time that it blows, it silences all the winds before it" (ibid.). Since it was only this wind that blew, quelling all others, it became very hot. Rabba uses a proof text from Job: "You swelter in your clothes even as the earth is hushed by the south wind" (37:17). In explaining this verse, R. Ḥisda observes that "when the earth is still by reason of the south wind, as at the time that the wind blows, it silences all the winds before it" (Gittin 31b). East wind or south wind, the rabbis are trying to understand the exact conditions that contributed to suffering so intense that it prompted thoughts of death. The combination of the sun and the specific type of winds would have burdened Jonah with intense heat and unbearable cold, reminding us of Robert Frost's short yet potent poem, "Fire and Ice":

> Some say the world will end in fire,
> Some say in ice.
> From what I've tasted of desire
> I hold with those who favor fire.
> But if it had to perish twice,
> I think I know enough of hate
> To say that for destruction ice
> Is also great
> And would suffice.[9]

The poem presents two terrible options and the unlikely predicament that its narrator might actually get to choose his demise should the world come to an end – as Jonah imagined his was.

Then there is the strange tree. Botanists curious about the kind of tree that could grow overnight and die the same night are of different minds about the identity of this tree. The tree was Jonah's only salvation, but the loss of it pushed Jonah over the edge. The death that he had contemplated earlier he longed for once again with his precious tree gone:

> The Lord God provided a ricinus plant, which grew up over Jonah, to provide shade for his head and save him from discomfort. Jonah was very happy about the plant. But the next day at dawn God provided a worm, which attacked the plant so that it withered. And

---

9. Robert Frost, *Frost: Collected Poems, Prose, & Plays* (New York: The Library of America, 1995), 204.

> when the sun rose, God provided a sultry east wind; the sun beat down on Jonah's head, and he became faint. He begged for death, saying, "I would rather die than live." Then God said to Jonah: "Are you so deeply grieved about the plant?" "Yes," he replied, "so deeply that I want to die." Then the Lord said, "You cared about the plant, which you did not work for and which you did not grow, which appeared overnight and perished overnight. And should I not care about Nineveh, that great city, in which there are more than 120,000 persons who do not yet know their right hand from their left, and many beasts as well?" (Jonah 4:6–11)

The Talmud and Modern Hebrew identify the *kikayon* as a ricinus, gourd, castor-oil, or castor-bean tree, which offers many medicinal properties in addition to growing at a rapid pace – though perhaps not nearly as quickly as it did in the biblical text. They can reach heights approximating forty feet. There are plants – like corn and bamboo – that can grow as much as one and a half to three feet in twenty-four to thirty-six hours with the right water, soil, and sun conditions, but this is still not sufficient to fit the description in the text; the *kikayon*'s life and death presumably occurred within a twelve-hour-or-less time frame. Scientifically, this would not be enough time to produce a plant with enough shade to provide Jonah the happiness he described. (Certain species of insects, however, could fell a tree overnight. Corn borer insects could accomplish this.)

The Talmud, in its discussion of permitted wicks and oils for candle-lighting on the Sabbath, forbids the oil of this tree. In the process, the Talmud discusses the properties of this special tree that grew up over Jonah.

> Shmuel said: I asked all seafarers about it and they told me that this is a certain bird in the sea towns called *kik*. R. Yitzḥak b. R. Yehuda said, It is cotton seed oil. Resh Lakish said: Oil from Jonah's *kikayon*. Rabba b. Bar-Ḥanna said: I myself have seen Jonah's *kikayon*; it resembles the ricinus tree and grows in ditches. It is set up at the entrance of shops. From its kernels, oil is manufactured, and under its branches rest all of the sick of the West. (Shabbat 21a)

Nature as Teacher

Identifying the plant was not only of interest to Jewish interpreters. Jerome, in a letter to Augustine, 404 CE, also attempted to figure out the kind of plant that could grow with this speed, and, interestingly, did not limit it to a tree, which largely diminishes the problem with speed since a tree would take much longer to provide shade:

> I have already given a sufficient answer to this in my commentary on Jonah. At present, I deem it enough to say that in that passage, where the Septuagint has gourd, and Aquila and the others have rendered the word ivy (κίσσος), the Hebrew manuscript has ciceion, which is in the Syriac tongue, as now spoken, ciceia. It is a kind of shrub having large leaves like a vine, and when planted it quickly springs up to the size of a small tree, standing upright by its own stem, without requiring any support of canes or poles, as both gourds and ivy do. If, therefore, in translating word for word, I had put the word ciceia, no one would know what it meant; if I had used the word gourd, I would have said what is not found in the Hebrew. I therefore put down ivy, that I might not differ from all other translators.[10]

Ivy is a fast-growing plant and with an aggregate of leaves, and it may have provided the shade that Jonah claimed was such a great relief.

These two passages demonstrate the curiosity of our sages and Christian scholars as they attempt to identify the plant images as a key to understanding the biblical text. Of all the trees God could have sent Jonah, why this one? Perhaps the last detail in the talmudic discussion is most significant. This was a healing plant, well-known as having medicinal properties in the ancient Near East. Jonah, sick of his existence, was in desperate need of healing. It was clearly fragrant and appealing if merchants would place it in front of their shops to attract customers, and it was a tree that gave oil, an important and valuable commodity. No wonder Jonah experienced such joy over this tree. Being in its proximity made him feel nourished and taken care of by a God who had compassion.

---

10. "From Jerome to Augustine," the letter is available online at http://www.newadvent.org/fathers/1102075.htm.

The Final Word

With this tree, Jonah felt God's love. Who but God would bestow upon him something of such value instantaneously? If Jonah wondered why so many aspects of nature were at the ready to serve him, he never expressed it in the text. He took it all in as if it were his due.

In Modern Hebrew, *kikyoni* means "crazy" or "temporal," suggesting that something can rise and fall quickly; it has been used to describe both start-ups and political parties that enjoy a meteoric rise and an equally fast decline. God might have been castigating Jonah for thinking that something that required no investment of time, like this tree, could ever be permanent.[11] Or God might have been teaching Jonah the opposite lesson. Nineveh repented with tremendous speed, a speed that would have made anyone suspect their motives and sincerity, especially a Hebrew prophet. Jonah could not believe their superficiality, nor did he trust it. Building a small booth outside the city's parameters was his way of signaling that the once-promised destruction coming to the city would soon be realized when the shallowness of their repentance showed its telltale signs of their recidivism. Once Jonah was given a plant that grew rapidly and withered just as quickly, God was better positioned to admonish Jonah because he did find value in its fragile and temporal existence. He did not question its existence. He rejoiced in it. He never contemplated for a moment that the speed of its growth meant that there was something wrong with it.

The Book of Jonah offers a fast pace of actions and reactions. We do not know how long it took Jonah to run away from God's word nor how long he spent on the boat nor how many hours he spent under the sea until salvation arrived in the guise of a fish. But the story is narrated in such a way that makes the reader feel this all happened almost instantly. Jonah spent only three days in the fish, one day of the three-day journey in Nineveh, and presumably one day and night out of Nineveh. The entire narration could have taken place in less than a week.

---

11. I am grateful to Josh Klein for this reading and for his help in identifying the *kikayon* in shared correspondence. He reads this meaning into using this tree as a symbol: "God seems to prefer stasis, or at least a tendency to stability. Thus, He wants Nineveh to return to proper religious and moral practice, and He doesn't want Jonah to rely on instantaneous deviation-from-the-mean-of-experience salvation or even answers, even though such may be provided miraculously from time to time."

Compassion tends to surface in the book with a similar presentism. While justice seems to operate within complex and often bureaucratic systems that offer slow processes and even slower judgments, mercy tends to be a more instinctual, immediate emotional response to a situation. God was not asking Jonah why he felt happy and then subsequently saddened by the tree. He simply wanted him to state his emotions and through this articulation validate them, enabling God to highlight Jonah's rigidity when it came to others and his fluidity of feeling when it came to the mercy extended to him. The gourd was an educational prop to God's message.

ELIJAH, JONAH, AND THE LESSON OF THE TREES

Simon points out that this is not dissimilar to God's use of an animal to serve a prophet in the story of Elijah and the raven, mentioned in section one. God told Elijah to run away and hide from King Ahab; he was instructed to travel to a wadi at a time of famine. A wadi is a dry place, and in a drought, it would not be a desirable location for either refugee or pursuer. God told Elijah not to fear: "You will drink from the wadi, and I have commanded the ravens to feed you there.... The ravens brought him bread and meat every morning and every evening, and he drank from the well" (I Kings 17:4, 6). Elijah's rescue by the ravens is not the only similarity to the Jonah story, where animals served as saviors. The two texts also describe a palpable fear and escape. Elijah ate and drank again after fleeing Ahab two chapters later when he had another encampment in the desert:

> He was afraid and he fled for his life. When he reached Beer-sheba, he left his servant there and himself went a day's journey into the wilderness. He came upon a broom tree and sat down under it and prayed for death. "It is enough," he said, "now, Lord, take my life, for I am no better than my fathers before me." (19:3–4)

Like Elijah, Jonah sought refuge under a tree, a place that temporarily brought relief but would soon become the site of a death wish. Jonah and Elijah had had enough and asked God to free them from their wretched existence. In Elijah's case, the difficulties were pervasive and obvious. Elijah was a refugee from an evil king and the malice of a queen who thought nothing of taking a human life. Elijah preferred to die at God's hand. In Jonah's case, the reason for his death wish is so elusive it stumps the reader. The reader has no sense that Jonah is ever in mortal danger beyond his own control or that conditions like drought and famine dogged him.

Each time Elijah escaped into the wilderness, God nurtured him with a meal. In the second passage, an angel touched him and said, "Arise and eat" (v. 5). When Elijah rose, there was a cake and a pitcher of water at his head. Like God's gift of the *kikayon*, the gift of food signaled nurturing and compassion at a time of deep and injurious pain. In Jonah's case the gift was quickly removed; he was not sufficiently worthy of it. In Elijah's narrative, the gift of the tree kept giving. According to Nogah Hareuveni's *Tree and Shrub in Our Biblical Heritage*, the *rotem* or "broom tree" that Elijah sat under has this name because its leaves are shaped like brushes, and they have a remarkable insulating capacity.[12] Thus, Elijah took refuge under the tree's spiky leaves and then arose to see the cake baked on the tree's embers. The tree nourished him in more than one way.

Jonah's tree too had many wonderful properties. Shade was its most important feature for the immediate time, the only time Jonah seemed to find himself in. But Jonah could not hold on to his special tree, a symbol of his own instability, since trees throughout the Bible represent stability and security, blessing and nourishment. "She is a tree of life to those who lay hold of her; those who hold her fast are called blessed" (Prov. 3:18). Human beings were created in a garden and meant to be nourished by trees, except for the tree which was off-limits. That tree then became a temptation.

Fruit-bearing trees are to be protected during war and are likened to human beings: "For is a tree a man that should be besieged by you?" (Deut. 20:19). Tree fruit is not to be taken in the first three years of a tree's growth to maximize its energy expenditure on the development of deep roots, critical to vegetation vitality in the Middle East. In the very first Psalm, the image of a tree near water is a metaphor for piety

---

12. Nogah Hareuveni, *Tree and Shrub in Our Biblical Heritage* (Kiryat Ono: Neot Kedumim, 1984), 27–32.

and is redolent with images of life thriving and flourishing: "He is like a tree planted beside streams of water, which yields its fruit in season, whose foliage never fades, and whatever it produces thrives" (Ps. 1:3). Hope itself is tied into the image of the tree: "Hope deferred makes the heart sick, but a desire fulfilled is a tree of life" (Prov. 13:12). The hope is literally an outgrowth of the capacity for a tree to grow and regenerate: "For there is hope for a tree, if it be cut down, that it will sprout again, and that its shoots will not cease" (Job 14:7).

God likened His investment in the city of Nineveh to Jonah's tree because the city was old and living and stable and necessary. But Jonah's understanding of the world was temporal, as were his urgent needs. He could not see a long-term picture. So God removed from him something that he had never invested in: "You cared about the plant, which you did not work for and which you did not grow, which appeared overnight and perished overnight" (Jonah 4:10). Tossed about by water, spat out by a fish, perambulating in Nineveh, and then leaving, Jonah would no doubt be ecstatically happy over a tree that represented everything that his life was not. Yet it was not meant to be, because Jonah's tree behaved the way trees never behave. And when nature – the storm, the wind, the fish, the cattle, the worm, the tree – consistently behaved against their nature, Jonah should have realized that as a prophet he was behaving against his destiny. But he did not.

God analogized Jonah's feelings toward the tree with God's own feelings and obligations toward the city of Nineveh. And yet, upon careful examination of the word ḥos, or "pity," we find more satire in this comparison than logic.[13] Jonah did not actually express pity for the plant, nor did he invest in its care or nurturing. When the plant withered, there was, not surprisingly, no active response from Jonah. There was grief at its loss, but it was only for himself, not for the plant. When God compared the absence of Jonah's pity for Nineveh with the pity that Jonah experienced over the plant, perhaps God was subtly suggesting that even then, Jonah's pity was only a narcissistic sense of personal loss and not the wash of sadness that comes with the loss of any living thing.

---

13. For comparative uses of ḥos as compassion, see Gen. 45:20; Jer. 3:14; 21:7; Ezek. 9:5; 16:5; 24:14.

The Final Word

Nature bent itself to God's will throughout the Book of Jonah – but the prophet did not. Nature, like the human beings in the Book of Jonah, changed. The sailors changed. The king changed. The king's subjects changed. God changed. Cattle changed. But Jonah did not change.

Chapter Twelve

To End with a Question

> Then the Lord said, "You cared about the plant, which you did not work for and which you did not grow, which appeared overnight and perished overnight. And should I not care about Nineveh, that great city, in which there are more than 120,000 persons who do not yet know their right hand from their left, and many beasts as well?" (Jonah 4:10–11)

We close in an open-ended manner, as voyeurs to God chastising Jonah for his pitiful emotional attachment to a plant in which he made no investment. It is a response to the way that Jonah chastised God for His abundant mercy and lack of true justice. And it is so much more.

Jonah is the only biblical book to end with a question.[1] Just as the beginning of the story is filled with oddities and unexplained

---

1. Not everyone concludes that the last verse of Jonah should be read as a question. Alan Cooper advises a declarative rather than interrogative reading, suggesting that while God retracted punishment for the moment, Nineveh would ultimately be ruined because its ignorant inhabitants, human and animal, had insufficient moral scruples to sustain enduring change. Thus, Nineveh would be destroyed, as it actually was as reflected in the prophecies of Nahum. See Cooper, "In Praise of Divine Caprice: The Significance of the Book of Jonah," in *Among the Prophets: Language, Image and Structure in the Prophetic Writings*, ed. P. R. Davies and D. J. A. Clines (Sheffield: JSOT Press, 1993), 158.

tensions, so does the end leave the reader unsatisfied, curious, unfulfilled. Did Jonah learn his lesson, painstakingly delivered by God as a "teaching moment" in the form of a miracle tree and a very determined worm? Did Jonah turn around, leave his makeshift hut on the margins of Nineveh, and step back into the city, spitting himself out as the fish spat him out two chapters earlier?

Phyllis Trible believes that the form of a question is an important literary flourish here, stressing that "rhetorical eloquence is theological eloquence."[2] God's rhetoric hides a not-so-subtle jab at the prophet about the nature of his job and the nature of divine work. Trible also believes that this way of concluding has other benefits: "By stopping with a question, the book of Jonah remains open-ended. By stopping with a question, the rhetorical analysis of Jonah remains open-ended. The reader may want no more, the writer carries on."[3] Perhaps we can invert her statement: the writer wants no more and chooses to end mid-point in Jonah's strange journey – but the reader is not yet done.

Jonah's strength was his weakness. His rigid desire for consistency – God's and Nineveh's – matched the harsh judgment he placed on himself. Contemporary writer Michael Ben Zehabe redeems the flawed prophet Jonah in a half-hearted way:

> Whatever criticism we may have for Jonah, at least it can be said that Jonah was consistent. This legalistic, over-judgmental, young prophet will consistently proscribe the most severe form of punishment for the guilty – even when the guilty party is himself. The young Jonah hijacks written Torah to condemn everyone – even himself.[4]

JONAH'S PLACE IN YOM KIPPUR LITURGY

Jonah's scorching judgments led him to conclude that this world was no place for a man such as himself. He was angry unto death, and we feel

---

2. Trible, *Rhetorical Criticism*, 224.
3. Ibid., 227.
4. Michael Ben Zehabe, *A Commentary on Jonah* (CreateSpace Independent Publishing Platform, 2011), 25.

his burning desire to leave this world, to put an end to a universe that always disappointed with its shabby notions of justice and its half-baked transformations. Instead Jonah sought a place of extremity, an island of excellence in a sea of mediocrity. Jonah was not prepared, despite God's prompting, to make his peace with a world not to his theological liking.

But how are we to make peace with Jonah? What are we to make of the fact that we are mandated to read his story on the afternoon of the Jewish calendar's holiest day? This itself was decreed in the Talmud (Megilla 30a) in a lengthy and curious passage:

> On Yom Kippur we read, "After the death" (Lev. 16), and for the *haftara*, "For thus said the High and Lofty One" (Is. 57:14–58). At the afternoon service we read the section of forbidden sexual relationships (Lev. 18:1–30) and for the *haftara* the Book of Jonah. Wherever you find The Holy One, Blessed Be He [in the Bible], you also find His humility.

The paragraph continues to travel through the Pentateuch, Prophets, and Scriptures, identifying verses that suggest God's humility. There is no question posited about the inclusion of Jonah's story in the canon. Jonah's placement as the *haftara* for the Torah reading of forbidden sexual relationships in Leviticus enhances the bizarre coupling of biblical readings and cannot be ignored. What were the sages trying to accomplish on this somber day with these odd liturgical choices?

Jonah is a book about the power of God's grace and its extent. Mercy, true mercy, is not bounded by tribe or race or color, the way that kindness to one's own is less a form of tenderness than an expression of safety and security in one's own insurance policy. God's love has no such limits. The formulaic expression of God's compassion is written in Psalms – and the very same language is used by Jonah – and repeatedly includes all of God's creatures:

> The Lord is gracious and compassionate,
> Slow to anger and abounding in kindness.
> The Lord is *good to all*,
> And *His mercy is upon all His works*. (145:8–9)

The Final Word

When You are the Creator and Master of all of creation, all of creation interests You. And because of God's generosity, the Psalm continues with the relationship that this engenders: "All of Your works shall praise You, O Lord, and Your faithful shall bless You" (v. 10). The recipient of God's blessings and watchfulness takes part in a reciprocity of feeling that is returned in God's direction in the form of praise. "God-like attributes attach to all human beings; they are not a specifically Israelite property. Humans are the object of God's special care,"[5] Greenberg notes. To this end, Greenberg concludes that "the point of the Book of Jonah is God's impartial concern for the well-being of all of His creatures.... That the repentant Ninevites remain pagans matters not."[6]

The Exodus formulation of God's compassion is general and expansive. Malbim (Meir Leibush ben Yehiel Michel Wisser, 1809–1879), however, captures the subtlety of this mercy in his observation on the expression, *halo ze d'vari*, "is this not what I said" in Jonah's chapter 4 postscript. This trio of unexpected words throws the reader and mystifies exegetes. Jonah supposedly said something to God before he fled that is not recorded in our text. What exactly were Jonah's words? We seek them as an explanation for his odd behavior but not once do we hear Jonah say anything to God, not in prayer, not in rejection of God's assignment, not even tangentially in his conversation with the sailors. Malbim, whose commentary to Jonah, like Rashi's, is largely based on the *Mekhilta*'s reading of the text, fills in the blanks left open by our questioning:

> When I was on my land, in the Land of Israel, before I went to Nineveh this was my word, namely, that You would forgive Nineveh. He [Jonah] is trying to say, "I knew at that time that it was not in Your thoughts to bring evil upon them. You forgave them immediately at the time of the decree because of [Your] mercy and patience, even though they would not repent in a

---

5. Moshe Greenberg, "Mankind, Israel and the Nations in the Hebraic Heritage," in *Studies in the Bible and Jewish Thought* (Philadelphia: Jewish Publication Society, 1995), 371.
6. Ibid., 372.

proper way. Namely, they did not repent for the sin of idolatry, nevertheless You did not bring evil upon them because You had already forgiven them their wickedness. For a small improvement, You canceled the decree." (Malbim to Jonah 4:2)

Jonah was not only faulting God, in this reading, for the act that accompanied God's mercy; he was also faulting Him for forgiving Nineveh for their *incomplete* repentance. True, the Ninevites discontinued their corruption, whatever that technically means, but, Malbim astutely points out, there were sins not singled out here that were swept away in the fervor of compassion. Malbim specifically mentions idol worship, generally a troublesome thorn for the Israelites throughout biblical history; he neglects to say explicitly that by pushing this aside, God was willing to forgo His own honor if the Ninevites were able to reform their ways on earth toward their fellow humans, but not toward Him. Jonah could not contemplate how God could so easily and rapidly wipe away what Jonah may have regarded as serious transgressions, even were God to see a considerable measure of change in other arenas.

The text of the last verse of chapter 4 helps us understand just how expansive God's mercy is, and it is worth examining its details yet again to yield a surprising but obvious interpretation: "And should I not care about Nineveh, that great city, in which there are more than 120,000 persons who do not yet know their right hand from their left, and many beasts as well?" (v. 11). Note what God did not say here. God did not state that the reason for the divine investment in Nineveh was in response to their repentance, an obvious and logical conclusion. No; God cared about Nineveh regardless of its current moral state, it would appear, because these were inhabitants who did not yet know their right from their left hands, as if their ignorance itself was endearing. We would expect God to favor Nineveh because its residents were able to change themselves – but God extended mercy to them for simply existing and being His creatures. The message to Jonah is therefore more subtle: care about your tree and care about My people not because it or they give you something you need but purely because I created them and asked you to serve them.

This also points to an understanding of *teshuva* that differs for God and the prophet. In Jonah's rigid worldview, each sin was counted and must be accounted for. Transgressions were numbered and must be noted, one after the other, especially for a people whose sins mounted in an exasperating mountain of wrongdoing. Behavior, good and bad, was quantifiable. But for God, worthwhile living is not about this kind of micro-accounting. *Teshuva* in its broadest sense is the capacity to build or rebuild a relationship that transcends singular hurdles and labeled pitfalls. The crimes are still there but, with repentance, they do not serve as a barrier to the human/Divine relationship. God decided, as it were, to sidestep Nineveh's sins in pursuit of the relationship generally, offering us another way to understand the significance of reading this book on Yom Kippur.

Late in the day, when we are overwhelmed by the number of times we have beaten our chests in contrition and feeling deeply insecure about our fate in the coming year, there is one matter that we can be absolutely sure of: God's love. If we count every sin, as our liturgy and our tradition encourage, we might be paralyzed by self-loathing. Yet were we to realize that while we must do our best to name and make a reckoning for our misdeeds, these ultimately will not come between us and a loving God, our view of the world would be radically altered. Mercy takes us from the micro-view of sin to the macro-understanding of a world in which God's compassion reigns and goes far beyond our detailed lists of wrongdoing.

JONAH'S PARTICULARISM AND GOD'S MESSAGE

On the next expression in the verse, "that is why I was so quick to flee to Tarshish" (4:2), Malbim continues his theory:

> He [Jonah] is saying, "I did not flee because I thought they would engage in a complete repentance. If that were the case, I would not have refused to go on a mission to turn sinners from their path. I would not go only because I knew they would remain worshippers of idols and You would not destroy them. For that reason, I did not want to go on the mission." (Malbim to Jonah 4:2)

Jonah would have said yes in chapter 1 had he thought that God would hold the Ninevites accountable for the sins they continued to do, not those from which they would easily or readily depart. It was at this point in the chapter that Jonah told God he was deeply aggrieved to the point of actual death. In Malbim's reading of God's question to Jonah, "Are you that deeply grieved?" (Jonah 4:4), he offers a standard interpretation: the grief Jonah experienced was over being a false prophet who predicated doom erroneously; Jonah failed to understand his prophecy as conditional, in which case he could not ever be accused of false prophecy. Malbim turns this reasoning on its head: "For if the prophecy was for good tidings and it was not fulfilled, that would have strengthened the claim of false prophet. The positive promise that comes through the prophet must be fulfilled in any case, even if the people continue to commit sins through their actions."[7]

In questioning Jonah, God once again forced Jonah's introspection on what constitutes a worthy life – by having him consider what makes a worthy death. A worthy death is not the result of lame and rather pathetic anger at what others fail to do. Jonah did not see what the people of Nineveh did do; he saw only the negative spiritual space in the Ninevites' reformation. Like Cain whose anger toward his brother was hot and active, God too spurred this angry man into stating his true feelings; perhaps in that naming, he would realize the smallness of his feelings in light of the greater bonds of fraternity.

In the narrowness that was Jonah's worldview, his rigidity pertained not only to his role but to the confines of where Israelite love can extend. The reader senses Jonah's existential discomfort with reaching out to the Ninevites; he did not delight in their transformation nor did he authentically ask for it. The behaviors and inadequacies of foreign nations were not his business, or so he thought. Locked into the particularistic concerns of his own nation, Jonah found no reasonable justification for his mission. His interest in service was and remained within the thin geographic sliver of the Land of Israel alone. We find this stated explicitly about Jonah in II Kings where we reflect on his former responsibilities, which, not coincidentally, involved the enhancement and establishment of borders, a task that by its nature involves setting limits: "It was he who restored the territory of Israel from Lebo-hamath to the Sea of Arava, in accordance with the promise that the Lord, the

---

7. Ibid.

God of Israel, had made through His servant, the prophet Jonah son of Amitai from Gath-hepher" (II Kings 14:25). Expanding Israelite reach by restoring former borders was the perfect assignment for a prophet who valued his people above others or to the exclusion of others.

But God's message about the reach of the divine word knows no such artificial lines. There can be no boundaries in a world created in love by one God. If a prophet is the human embodiment of God's desires for the known world, then the prophet too must have boundless love for humanity. Yet particularism rarely casts the inclusive spiritual radiance captured beautifully by Rabbi Abraham Isaac HaKohen Kook in an oft-cited passage about the spillover of love:

> Some sing the song of the soul. Within their own soul, they discover everything, their complete spiritual fulfillment. Others sing the song of Knesset Yisrael, the community of Israel. They leave the restricted circle of the self and bind themselves to the soul of the community. They sing her songs, feel her pain, delight in her hopes, and contemplate her past and her future. Others allow their souls to expand beyond the people of Israel. They sing the song of humanity, reveling in the grandeur of humankind, the illustriousness of his divine image. They aspire towards humanity's ultimate goal and yearn for its sublime fulfillment. And some reach even higher in the expanse, until they unite with all existence, with all creatures and all worlds. With all of them, they sing the song of the universe.[8]

Jonah sang the song of his own soul. He also sang the song of *Knesset Yisrael*, "the Jewish people," at least for a time. He did not, however, allow his soul to revel in the grandeur of humankind. It came to a full stop with Nineveh.

Despite this, God continued to send representatives of the created world to protect, nourish, and nurture the prophet. Perhaps as the recipient of the universe's love, from great fish to insignificant worm,

---

8. Rav Abraham Isaac HaKohen Kook, *Orot HaKodesh* II:444. Translation found in *Rabbi Kook's Philosophy of Repentance: A Translation*, trans. Alter B. Z. Metzger (New York: Yeshiva University Press, 1978).

To End with a Question

from strange gourd to strange weather, Jonah might rethink his narrowness and fall in love with the world he had rejected that never rejected him. He would regard the way design operates in a thing so small, to quote Frost, and know that the world abounds in goodness.[9] Perhaps he would fall back in love with a God who could have but never rejected him. But Jonah could not. He did not. All that remained in God's education of the prophet was to teach Jonah that love and mercy are boundless if they are true. This He tried to accomplish with a question. God's question ended with Nineveh's cattle precisely as an illustration of this very boundless concern, this bovine love. It is not only directed to Jews or to humans. It extends to all and covers all.

THE JONAH COMPLEX

But there is one last mercy, the final great mercy that God had to convey to Jonah. Jonah may have had mercy on his paltry plant but he had little mercy for the powerless man living underneath it. As mentioned earlier, the word "great," *gadol*, appears fourteen times in the Book of Jonah, signaling to its readers how much larger the world was to a prophet cowed by its vastness and overwhelmed by his smallness. Abraham Maslow called it the Jonah Syndrome. André and Pierre-Emmanuel Lacocque wrote an entire book on it.[10] Jonah became, in psychological terms, the label for a certain type of human behavior, the fleeing from responsibility.

Jonah, having received a call to greatness, fled. God's call indicates a vocation, a nod to destiny, the idea that a person is destined for something extraordinary. Before even receiving the content of a call, the very act of calling is a validation of worth, an expression of affirmation and specialness. Such a designation is not for everyone; many shy away from the fanfare and the responsibility, preferring the life of the anti-hero or the ordinary. Extraordinary-ness, in Jonah's case, was thrust upon him.

---

9. Frost's poem "Design" begins with a "dimpled spider, fat and white" that has killed a moth. The intricacies of this miniature scene of conquest befuddle the onlooker:
    What brought the kindred spider to that height,
    Then steered the white moth thither in the night?
    What but design of darkness to appall?
    If design govern in a thing so small.
10. Lacocque and Lacocque, *The Jonah Complex*.

He did not seek it out. And because of this abrupt designation that was neither desired nor tolerated, Jonah saw only one choice before him: to run where God's reach could not extend so that he would be exempt from the weight of becoming extraordinary. But we are not free agents to relinquish God's plans for us. God told Jonah through nature, through entrapment, through the art of the well-positioned question. Everything pointed in one direction – a momentum toward Nineveh was also a push to actualization of the greatness within Jonah that he consistently refused to acknowledge.

For all of the reasons previously mentioned that explain Jonah's escape, from the fear of being labeled a false prophet to the worry that a reformed Nineveh would attack his people to the theological stress of believing your God to be one thing when He is another, none is more stirring and filled with more personal meaning than Jonah's fear of actualizing his calling. More nuanced than simply the fear of success, Maslow believed that the discovery of greatness could bring what he calls exhilaration, "but it also brings a fear of the dangers and responsibilities and duties of being a leader and of being all alone. Responsibility can be seen as a heavy burden and evaded as long as possible."[11] The calling singles out the prophet and forces him to pay attention to himself, to signs of potential grandeur and accountability; it demands that he see himself as different from all others. Jonah's attempt to mask this by depositing himself in a boat among sailors, to disappear into the ordinary tasks of swabbing decks and manning sails, failed. He soon realized that he could not hide from his uniqueness, particularly when questioned; his strangeness from others was a cause for both awe and alarm. One can only imagine Jonah looking up at the sky, speaking to God more than to those at his side: "I am a Hebrew...I worship the Lord, the God of heaven, who made both sea and dry land" (Jonah 1:9). I cannot run, he said in effect. At this, his would-be colleagues balked. "The men were greatly terrified" (v. 10).

This may explain the way Maslow specifically understood Jonah's anxiety. The Jonah complex "is partly a justified fear of being torn apart,

---

11. Abraham Maslow, *Toward a Psychology of Being* (New York: D. van Nostrand, 1968), 61.

of losing control, of being shattered and disintegrated, even of being killed by the experience."[12] The path to achieving greatness is littered with dangers, chief of which is the fear of failure that can paralyze all self-actualization. For Jonah these perils happened not when he answered God's call but when he absconded from it.

> But what is required of Jonah (and of humanity in general) is to go *beyond* his own limits ("toward the land I shall show you"),[13] because he has been chosen (like all other human beings created in the image of God) by one who is beyond all limits. While the calling does not make Jonah a superhero, one could say that it makes him leave his condition of subhumanity to become – in the image of his commissioner – bondless, liberated and free. The paradox is that Jonah, before he receives God's commandment and while fleeing from the commandment is *not* free. Only when one assumes responsibility for the commandment is one free, for the simple reason that it enunciates for the first time the *project* of a person, one's *raison d'etre*, one's ultimate meaning.[14]

Jonah's real project, however, was Jonah.

> For there is no last word. There is a *question*, framed by God in His dialogue with Jonah. The question remains suspended, resonant. It touches on God's pity for those who, in the most important sense, know nothing; who are themselves like cattle…. God's rhetorical question clearly invites Jonah's assent. But ambiguity hangs over this ending. Is this assent simply assumed, and therefore not narrated? Or is there a real question that remains?… Enigmas, stories never reach full closure, the place of no further interpretation.[15]

---

12. Abraham Maslow, "Neurosis as a Failure of Personal Growth," *Humanitas* 3 (1967): 165–166.
13. Maslow cites Abraham's journey in Genesis 12:1.
14. Lacocque and Lacocque, *The Jonah Complex*, 34.
15. Zornberg, "Jonah: A Fantasy of Flight," 82–83.

The Final Word

Perhaps the book ends with a question not to suggest that conclusions are elusive but to suggest that we must all live with the questions that most dog our human existence. And we must ask them again and again and not feel that we are entitled to clarity. As Jonah's non-linear journey suggests, there are questions of service, of selflessness, of mission and responsibility that we will ask ourselves again and again, opening ourselves up to hesitations, to confronting our demons, to addressing our deepest fears and anxieties. These questions do not get smaller. They may become magnified due to the importance of the task before us. But they also, over time and through trial and error, lessen in their intensity or in the fear that they generate within us unless we try, as Jonah did, to run away from them. In trying to escape our questions, they trail us with even greater ferocity.

The poet Rilke, in *Letters to a Young Poet*, tells his protégé to live his questions:

> Be patient toward all that is unsolved in your heart and try to love the questions themselves, like locked rooms and like books that are now written in a very foreign tongue. Do not now seek the answers, which cannot be given you because you would not be able to live them. And the point is, to live everything. Live the questions now. Perhaps you will then gradually, without noticing it, live along some distant day into the answer.[16]

Jonah too had to live his questions, rather than die as a result of them. Would he be able to muster sufficient compassion for those unlike himself? Would he be compelled by the troubles of those far away to risk all for them? Could he live in a world where God privileged mercy over justice or where truth was not spelled with a capital "T"? Can *we* ask these questions without toppling ourselves and compromising our identity but wrestling again and again with the same compulsions?

And so we read this short book on the afternoon of Yom Kippur as we think about accountability and all that we are trying to escape from. We read them after listing sexual indiscretions which hint to

---

16. Rainer Maria Rilke, *Letters to a Young Poet* (New York: Merchant Books, 2012), 17.

subversive and demonic impulses that often reside within the human being. We contemplate an ancient Hebrew prophet who tried to say goodbye and good riddance to greatness and a God who would not let him do so. We stand at attention on this holiest day of the year, with only a few hours remaining, and ask ourselves why we too run from greatness. Turn around, a little voice of holiness whispers. Turn around now and step into your life fully and wholly. Embrace the possibility of greatness before this year's gates shut tight. All awaits.

Epilogue

Jonah – Rebel or Revenant?

Having studied the four short and intriguing chapters of Jonah together, it is time to look retrospectively at the book as a whole, at the prophet as a man above and beyond the specific events that characterize him on the Bible's holy pages. Was Jonah ultimately a rebel or a revenant?

THE REBEL RISES

To Heschel in *The Prophets*, Jonah was a rebel. He rebelled because he did not understand God, nor did he trust God with the truth:

> God's change of mind displeased Jonah exceedingly. He had proclaimed the doom of Nineveh with a certainty, to the point of fixing the time, as an inexorable decree without qualification. But what transpired only proved the word of God was neither firm nor reliable. To a prophet who stakes his life on the reliability and infallibility of the word of God, such realization leads to despair. "O Lord, take my life from me, I beseech Thee, for it is better for me to die than to live" (Jonah 4:3), was his prayer.[1]

---
1. Heschel, *The Prophets*, 368.

Jonah

There are linguistic markers that hint at Jonah as rebel. The first appears in the very first verses of the book. When God gave Jonah his mission, the first words God used were *kum lekh*, "arise, go" or "go at once." One verse later Jonah did get up to go, using the very same verb to describe his actions but instead of going to his mission he rose and ran in the opposite direction, *vayakom Yona livro'aḥ*. The challenge of the vertical and horizontal directions of the Book of Jonah was mentioned initially in the introduction to this book. It is time to return to that theme.

The language of rising and fleeing is an assault on Jonah's judgment, indicating to some a direct statement of rebellion. Jonah twisted his assignment as if throwing it back on God, as if to say that he cared not a thing about God's request. He, in fact, rose as if to satisfy God's demand and then turned sharply away in the other direction. This last point is carried out quite literally; a cursory glance at a map of the ancient Near East and the Mediterranean Sea that frames it shows that Jonah descended from his home in Gath-hepher to the relatively close port at Jaffa and then went about as far from Nineveh as he could have in choosing a ship to Tarshish.[2]

The infinitive "to rise," *lakum*, is often used in the Bible as a statement of obedience, faith, or enthusiasm for the observance of God's word. It is a significant verb in the Bible, but the Book of Jonah suffers the exegetical neglect of classical medieval commentators who fail to note its repeated appearance and its meaning. This is not true elsewhere in the Hebrew Bible. At the binding of Isaac, although the word "to go," *vayelekh*, is utilized (and used repeatedly in the Abraham narratives), we also find the appearance of these verbs twinned, as in *vayakom vayelekh*, "*and he rose and set out*," for the place of which God had told him" (Gen. 22:3). No doubt, rising to sacrifice his son early in the morning showed Abraham's willingness to give up all for God and to do so with alacrity. One can imagine Abraham staying his feet, languishing or taking each step with hesitation.[3] The use of these verbs suggests the very

---

2. Tarshish, in the Hebrew Bible, is not only the name of a town but a personal name. There may be a connection between place and name but this is not indicated directly in any verse. See Gen. 10:4; II Chr. 7:10; Est. 1:14.
3. In his "Speech in Praise of Abraham," Kierkegaard makes this very point. We, as readers, would not be surprised if Abraham stayed his feet or hesitated, and yet, even

opposite. One midrash makes much of Balaam acting just as Abraham did, rising early and saddling his donkey himself, to curse the Jews: "Balaam *arose* in the morning and saddled his donkey," in order to curse the Israelites (Num. 22:21). Love dislodges the natural order as does hate, the midrash suggests, because individuals of this stature would not have ordinarily saddled their own animals.[4] Balaam, like Abraham, rose to perform an action, yet the very act of rising, normally not regarded in biblical literature as significant in and of itself, showed in these instances the protagonists' zeal to follow a course of action. Rising opens up possibilities. The very act of rising not followed by any verb turns the reader's attention to the momentousness of that gesture itself and the way it speaks volumes about the character of the biblical protagonist.

In the Book of Ruth – as we mentioned in the introduction – Naomi was left bereft of her husband, of her two sons, of her country, and of her co-religionists after the first five verses of chapter 1. Furthermore, according to rabbinic tradition, she was saddled in a foreign land with non-Jewish daughters-in-law and without heirs because her sons and daughters-in-law had no children. When she told the women who gathered at the gates of Bethlehem to "greet" her that she left full and returned empty, she could not possibly have communicated just how empty she was. And yet, in one verb, we are witness to her immense personal strength: *Vatakom hi*, "and she got up" (1:6). She awes the reader with a sense that the events that could have flattened her and laid her low would not stop her return. Soon enough her fortunes would reverse, but she was not to know that at the moment she left. And all this because she was able to rise out of the moment and out of the place which had brought such personal tragedy upon her.

---

this the knight of faith did not do. He would be a father but he would not then be Abraham, our father. Instead, he faced his task with religious zeal. See Kierkegaard, *Fear and Trembling*, 49–56.

4. Genesis Rabba 55:8. For more contrasts and comparisons between these two figures see Jonathan Safren, "Balaam and Abraham," *Vetus Testamentum* 38, no. 1 (1988): 105–113, and Ricky Novick, "Abraham and Balaam: A Biblical Contrast," *Jewish Quarterly Review* 35, no. 1 (2007): 28–33.

Jonah

The word *vayakom* is often paired with another verb, as it was earlier in Genesis 22, to suggest that the term "to rise" is a propaedeutic; it prepares the ground for the next verb of action. This is how Rashi understood what happened on the night that the last plague, the killing of the firstborn, hit Egyptian homes. "And Pharaoh *arose* at night, he and his servants and all of Egypt. And there was a great outcry in Egypt for there was no home in which there was no dead" (Ex. 12:30). Rashi here notes that Pharaoh's rising suggests the beginning of another action or series of actions which propels the plot forward. Rashi then turns our attention to the story of Cain and Abel: "And Cain *rose up* against Abel his brother and killed him" (Gen. 4:8). In Exodus, when Moses saved Yitro's daughters from the taunting of the shepherds, he too rose to take action: "And Moses *rose up* and saved them" (Ex. 2:17). In other words, this usage does not mean that an individual stood literally to rise but rather is a figurative way of suggesting preparedness to take action.

This verb is also significant in earlier narratives involving Pharaoh, particularly in the opening of Exodus where we read that a regime change had come to Egypt that would have significant consequences for the small Jewish population then living in Goshen: "A new king *arose* over Egypt who did not know Joseph" (1:8). Commentators question whether this was a new king or an old king with new policies who acted as if he had never met Joseph. This pharaoh forgot the way that Joseph had lifted him and all of Egypt out of economic peril. The fact that this new or old king had no relationship with Joseph suggests to the reader that he had no need to impress or protect Joseph's people either. Again, the verb portends future action or, in this instance, future inaction.

In Jonah's case, the verb is used in the same fashion. Instead of rising to proclaim judgment, he rose to flee. This contrast is amplified by two incidents. Several verses later, when Jonah fell into a deep sleep in the ship's underbelly, the ship's captain also prodded Jonah to rise and pray, using both meanings of the word. "The captain went over to him and cried out...'*Rise*, call upon your god!'" (Jonah 1:6). This imperative is the same language used by God. "Rise" here is both a literal command to rise from sleep and to rise and pray, suggesting that rising will lead to another action. Figures of authority stood over Jonah, demanding that he rise to the demands of an occasion.

Epilogue

No one, however, had to prod the king of Nineveh, who rose immediately and of his own initiative upon hearing of Jonah's prophecy: "When Jonah's warning reached the king of Nineveh, he *rose* from his throne, took off his royal robes, covered himself with sackcloth, and sat down in the dust" (3:6). Trible notes:

> The king's first act, "he-arose," recalls Jonah who twice made an identical response to YHWH's word, first in disobedience (1:3) and then in obedience (3:3). Heir to ambivalent uses, the third appearance of the verb needs explication. It comes through a particular structure and content not dependent upon repetition of balanced configuration,
>
> A And he arose from his throne
>   B and he removed his robe from upon him
>   B and he covered himself with sackcloth
> A and he sat upon the ashes.

Actions and counteractions produce an inversion of movement.[5]

The insertion of a third *vayakom* in the Book of Jonah by an outside party suggests a new meaning. Trible identifies the wordplay "from his throne," *mikiso* and "covered," *vayekhas*, as the mid-section reversal (indicated above by the letter B) – and the outer clauses of the verb, which also suggest a reversal, standing and then sitting, as yet another reversal. This verse holds in one sentence the total reversal which would be needed to engage God's mercy and the reversal of their fate. It is the ultimate play on the word "to overturn," *nehepakh*, as it appeared in Jonah's terse prophecy – namely, that Nineveh would be overturned in forty days. In Trible's words: "As an individual like unto his people, the king has humbled himself. He has 'overturned' in dwelling, dress, and dignity. Whether his actions precede destruction or deliverance awaits the telling."[6] What Trible does not say is that the king acted this way of

---

5. Trible, *Rhetorical Criticism*, 183.
6. Ibid., 184.

Jonah

his own accord. No one stood over him telling him to rise; this he did of his own initiative. The results spoke for themselves.

We do not encounter this verb again. Jonah did not rise to leave Nineveh. His leave-taking is announced with no drama; chapter 4 begins after he has already exited the city. One senses that with the disappearance of the verb "to rise" in the book, Jonah's opportunity to rise again also vanished. He tried and had a small window of triumph – but when re-acquainted with the mission, he returned to where he had always been, a disillusioned prophet.

DESTINATION: TARSHISH

Throughout this book, we have presented the theological difficulties that prompted Jonah to flee. But as we look back, Jonah may have risen to pursue a very different path, one quite far from the spiritual: the material. Tarshish, the place he rose to travel to, is mentioned in the Book of Ezekiel in a chapter dedicated to sailors and merchants who plied the high seas. Scholars believe it may have been an ancient city where King Solomon mined metals, a considerable source of his wealth:

> All King Solomon's drinking cups were of gold, and all the utensils of the Lebanon Forest House were of pure gold: silver did not count for anything in Solomon's days. For the king had a Tarshish fleet on the sea, along with Hiram's fleet. Once every three years, the Tarshish fleet came in, bearing gold and silver, ivory, apes, and peacocks. (I Kings 10:21–22)

It seems that Solomon's business relationship with Tarshish and his dominance over it was well established, as reflected in the Book of Psalms: "Let kings of Tarshish and the islands pay tribute, kings of Sheba and Seba offer gifts. Let all kings bow to him, and all nations serve him" (72:10–11). It is not hard to imagine one of King Solomon's fleet docking in Jaffa and emptying out its treasures for use in the king's various building projects. This particular chapter of I Kings stresses Solomon's opulent tastes with a nod to an excessiveness that betrayed the limitations on material wealth demanded of Jewish kings in

Epilogue

Deuteronomy.[7] This was not a city that kept its wealth to itself. Many verses that mention Tarshish do so in relation to its fleets, acknowledging a market dominance when it came to high-status bartering and business. "Tarshish traded with you because of your wealth of all kinds of goods; they bartered silver, iron, tin, and lead for your wares" (Ezek. 27:12).[8] It is also used as a term to refer to a precious gem, one located in the High Priest's breastplate, possibly mined in its eponymous location.[9] Yet, experienced as these sailors and merchants were, they too, suffered storms that tested their expertise, making the storm that tossed Jonah's ship a credible occurrence: "At the mere sight of it [God's mountain, Mount Zion] they were stunned, they were terrified, they panicked; they were seized with a trembling, like a woman in the throes of labor, as the Tarshish fleet was wrecked in an easterly gale" (Ps. 48:6–8).[10] If a Tarshish fleet could capsize, then this sight must have truly been wondrous.

Tarshish was known for its wealth, its fleet of merchant ships, and the strength of its sailors. It is not hard to understand why a rebel prophet would pick this city. When we read chapter 1 of Jonah, we may think that Jonah arbitrarily picked any ship traveling some distance to facilitate a swift getaway. His random lot fell on a ship going in the direction of Tarshish. But such a reading is not substantiated by the text or by the message offered throughout the book; there are no coincidences in the Book of Jonah.

> Jonah, however, started out to flee to Tarshish from the Lord's service. He went down to Jaffa and found a ship going to Tarshish. He paid the fare and went aboard to sail with the others to Tarshish, away from the service of the Lord. (Jonah 1:3)

---

7. See Deuteronomy 17:17, "nor shall he amass silver and gold to excess."
8. For Tarshish's specific connection to maritime trade and boats, see I Kings 22:49; Is. 2:16; 60:9; Ezek. 27:25; II Chr. 9:21; 20:36.
9. See Ex. 28:20; 39:13; Ezek. 10:9; 28:13; Dan. 10:6; Song. 5:14.
10. This Psalm seems to reflect a significant maritime disaster mentioned in I Kings: "Jehoshaphat constructed Tarshish ships to sail for Ophir for gold. But he did not sail because the ships were wrecked at Etzion-geber" (22:49).

Jonah

In one verse, Tarshish is mentioned three times. It is referred to specifically as a location of choice for Jonah *before* he arrived at the port city, almost as if he told himself – this son of a prophet – if God ever calls me again, I have a place to which I will escape. He then found a ship going in this direction and paid the fare to go there. One might conclude from a survey of biblical verses about Tarshish that Jonah selected this location because of the reputation of its fleet and sailors. To ensure that he would really get away from the Creator of the entire universe, he needed to rely on the best. But this would emphasize the journey over the destination, while the text stresses the final port.

The contrast of Nineveh to Tarshish in the mind of the prophet is critical to understanding Jonah's choice of city. Ackerman calls the two places "geographic antipoles":

> Nineveh, to the east, is the later capital of Assyria, the very nation that would destroy and carry off Jonah's people – the ten tribes of the Northern Kingdom – sixty years later. The Assyrians were renowned for their power and gross cruelty, and allusions in our story recall the Flood and the judgment on Sodom and Gomorrah. Thus we know Nineveh as a city whose power is a threat to Israel's existence and whose evil is antithetical to God's will. Tarshish, on the other hand, lies somewhere in the far west and is a place where YHWH is not known. Jonah, a servant fleeing his master's sovereignty, also sees Tarshish as a refuge beyond YHWH's domain. Strangely, Tarshish also connotes luxury, desire, delight…. For Jonah, therefore, Tarshish may paradoxically represent a pleasant place of security that borders on nonexistence.[11]

We understand and have abundant textual proof that Tarshish was associated with luxury of an almost mythic nature, but is there any rationale for believing, as Ackerman states, that it was a city where God was not known? We have only one biblical proof text that suggests this reading, a verse in the very last chapter of Isaiah:

---

11. Ackerman, "Jonah," in *The Literary Guide to the Bible*, 235.

Epilogue

> The time has come to gather all the nations and tongues; they shall come and behold My glory. I will set a sign among them, and send from them survivors to the nations: to Tarshish, Pul, and Lud – that draw the bow – to Tubal, Javan, and the distant coasts, that have never heard My fame nor beheld My glory. They shall declare My glory among these nations. (66:18–19)

Part of its mythical stature is that Tarshish was regarded as a distant place – so distant, in fact, that its residents were unaware of the presence of Israel's one God. In the future, Isaiah predicted that these remote nations would come to know God and articulate His glory.

Yitzhak Berger, in *Jonah in the Shadows of Eden*, regards Tarshish not as the material center of the ancient Near East but as a kind of mythic paradise, replete with abundant riches. All of the locations that the prophet sought out or occupied, Berger contends, "evoke suggestive associations with a divine abode reminiscent of Eden."[12] He suggests that Jonah was not merely running away from, but running toward a destination: "to attain the idyllic beauty – of a kind facilitated/signified by ships of Tarshish – that characterizes the exquisitely Eden-like kingdom of Tyre."[13] Berger extends this description to the belly of the fish, which he regards "not merely as a source of bliss but also as an Eden-like abode."[14] He also contends that Jonah's *kikayon* "embodies an Edenic domain,"[15] which explains why Jonah is crestfallen when the plant withers. A prophet in search of Eden despairs when associations with that idyll are compromised and lost.[16]

---

12. Yitzchak Berger, *Jonah in the Shadows of Eden* (Bloomington, IN: Indiana University Press, 2016), 3. This book was published within weeks of my initial submission of this manuscript. I was grateful that I was able to include some of its insights.
13. Ibid., 6.
14. Ibid., 20; see his discussion of the fish, 19–22.
15. Ibid., 46.
16. Berger's learned reading, which brims with compelling linguistic parallels, is narrowly focused on proving Jonah's search for Eden in verse after verse. But why was Eden Jonah's desired location? This desire is not self-evident. Berger's "study advances one core thesis" (p. 1). This minimizes other compelling themes in the book from getting sufficient interpretive exploration and can unintentionally suggest a literal reading which does not emerge holistically from the language itself. For example,

A more simple and pedestrian reading is that in choosing Tarshish, Jonah was telling God and confirming to himself that he wanted a material life of wealth and comfort over a life of spiritual service and hardship. By selecting a city of wealth with little spiritual promise, Jonah was, in effect, telling God he was uninterested in reforming a wayward city. He was interested in cities with gold and silver and precious stones. He could easily lose himself in so shallow a place, a place that represented the opposite of the lifestyle of an Israelite prophet. His location of choice represented in the ancient Near East a place of worldly pleasure and financial success, the ultimate rebellion for Jonah – and an insult to God. This conclusion may force us to ask a different question. What would a rebellion against God look like to an Israelite prophet? Would it be a direct confrontation about God's nature or an indirect escape to a place that represented the very opposite of what God asked a prophet to be in this world?

We understand how important comfort was to Jonah when we see how happy a small booth and a new tree made him in chapter 4. It is the only expression of happiness in the entire book: "The Lord God provided a ricinus plant, which grew up over Jonah, to provide shade for his head and save him from discomfort. Jonah *was very happy* about the plant" (Jonah 4:6). The lifestyle of the prophet was one of penury and self-sacrifice. Jonah was simply not interested; he had other plans in

---

to answer the rhetorical question Berger poses, "Might it be, then, that when the prophet asks the sailors to cast him out, he yearns for still another Edenic sanctuary by way of a divine salvation akin to the parting of the sea?" (p. 89) one might answer, "No." There is no textual proof that Jonah saw the ocean as an Edenic sanctuary and there is sufficient textual support from Jonah's prayer that he regarded the ocean as a terror and was grateful to be saved from its destructive waters. The fact that the fish saved him does not make it Eden-like either. The pursuit of Eden is a religious trope, perhaps best captured by a master of fantastic fictional landscapes, J. R. R, Tolkien, in one of his letters: "We all long for [Eden], and we are constantly glimpsing it: our whole nature at its best and least corrupted, its gentlest and most human, is still soaked with the sense of exile" (*The Letters of J. R. R. Tolkien*, ed. Humphrey Carpenter [Boston: Houghton Mifflin, 2000], 110). To write that "the prophet Jonah, profoundly troubled by God's response to the sins of humanity, persists in an escapist quest for an idyllic, Eden-like existence" (p. 1) is not obvious from the narrative. Neither is his supposition that "just when Jonah thinks he has attained such an existence, he finds himself banished from it" (ibid.).

Epilogue

mind. Had his plan been to self-destruct, he could have taken his own life in his own town as a way of refusing God's mission. Jonah did not do this. He actively decided to find another home in a place that offered a distinctively different orientation. Had he wanted Eden, he would have been trying to get back to God rather than away from God.

Pitting Tarshish against Nineveh in Jonah's mind takes the reader back to Genesis 10, where both are mentioned as offshoots of Noah's children who spread out to repopulate the world. Tarshish is a great-grandson of Noah's son Japheth: "The descendants of Javan: Elisha and Tarshish, the Kittim and the Dodanim. From these maritime nations branched out" (10:4–5). As early as Genesis, Tarshish the person was associated with Tarshish the place, a locus of maritime interest. Nineveh was a city created by the descendants of Ham, whose children and grandchildren spread out across Babylon and Assyria: "From that land Asshur went forth and built Nineveh, Rehoboth-ir, Calah, and Resen between Nineveh and Calah, that is the great city" (Gen. 10:11–12). Nineveh's immorality is not as surprising to the reader who is familiar with the story of Noah and Ham, the son who saw his father naked and drunk in his tent and exposed him to his brothers, who then covered him up. Noah cursed Canaan, Ham's son, when he awoke, hinting that this kind of licentious and inappropriate behavior would result in war and slavery and disrespect for authority that would subsequently travel for generations through Ham's line, as discussed in detail in a previous chapter.[17]

It is as if the early chapters of Genesis offered Jonah an almost primordial choice between the age-old city of Nineveh and the age-old city of Tarshish. Having himself thrown into the sea when neither option seemed realistic was a way to lose himself in a place of no boundaries, no name, and no history. Thus, we make the case for Jonah as a rebel who never truly came to terms with his mission because neither city of the mind was accessible – nor was death.

JONAH AS REVENANT

There may be another label to put on our struggling prophet. A revenant is one who comes back from the dead or a long absence,

---
17. See chapter 6.

sometimes merely as a ghostly apparition; it is derived from the French word *revenir*, "to return," and it seems an apt description for a prophet who disappeared and then made a spectacular reappearance right where he should have been all along. Jonah's return was naturally read by Christians as a prefiguration of Jesus, the one who died and came back. Augustine, in *City of God*, contends that Jonah did not prophesy Jesus' word as much as embody it in what befell him: "For why was he taken into the belly of the monster, and given back on the third day, except to signify that Christ would come back from the depths of hell on the third day?"[18] Jonah's near-death experience, his physical return and the return to God's word, and the timing of it all pointed in Augustine's worldview to a man-God who would follow much the same pattern.

But we would be mistaken to assume that Jonah's absence was only for three days – perhaps slightly longer, if we count his time in the ship in chapter 1. When Jonah left Gath-hepher for the port city of Jaffa, he disappeared from public view as a prophet of Israel. Because he was assigned a mission in another land, his family would not have been troubled by his time away. The sailors had no idea who he was and knew little about his land and people; the people of Nineveh knew even less. Letting go of attachments and not creating new ones puts one in psychosocial limbo. People cease to inquire about one's presence or absence. It is in this liminal state that one's mental equilibrium can come under serious challenge, since identity is a combination of nature and nurture. Stripped of context, personal identity can become a vexing conundrum. Who am I if I am not where I always was, doing what I know how to do and with people who know me? Michel Foucault captured this tension in *Madness and Civilization: A History of Insanity in the Age of Reason*. It is a strange coincidence for us as readers of Jonah that Foucault's madman is on a ship, a liminal space that is neither here nor there:

> Confined on the ship, from which there is no escape, the madman is delivered to the river with its thousand arms, the sea with its thousand roads, to that great uncertainty external to everything. He is a prisoner in the midst of what is the freest, the openest of

---

18. Augustine, *City of God*, 798.

Epilogue

routes: bound fast at the infinite crossroads. He is the Passenger par excellence: that is, the prisoner of the passage. And the land he will come to is unknown – as is, once he disembarks, the land from which he comes. He has his truth and his homeland only in that fruitless expanse between two countries that cannot belong to him.[19]

The interplay of freedom and prison is marvelously constructed in the contrast between the open seas that scream of possibility and the confines of a boat – a small, constricted space which mid-voyage one can only leave with the permanent exit of a gangplank or, in Jonah's case, by being thrown overboard. The openness is, on some level, a cruel illusion for Jonah, because while the expanse of the sea and sky indicated to the runaway that he was free, he was actually shackled to a destiny; the further away he ran, the tighter the chains on his freedom became. Nineveh and Tarshish are two cities that "cannot belong to him." He abides in the sea, the fruitless expanse between them.

When people go missing for weeks, months, or years at a time, it is not hard to wonder about the conditions that allow for such an absence. We do not know what happened to Jonah after our story ended. Perhaps he returned to Nineveh to complete what he started and to add greater commitment and depth to his mission. Alternatively, he may have returned home in shame, disgraced that he did not finish his task. Or his return may have included righteous indignation at God for privileging mercy over justice, for looking too kindly on the people of Nineveh in the immediacy of Jonah's visit instead of their long-term prospects for atonement and transformation. Here is how Michael Ben Zehabe regards Jonah's rebellion:

> Jonah can't see how Assyria could serve any useful purpose. How could this commission better Israel? Jonah might even fear that God will reverse His judgment against Nineveh. If that "unchanging God" changes His mind about Nineveh's destruction, then Jonah's personal religion won't make sense (Num. 23:19). The

---

19. Michel Foucault, *Madness and Civilization: A History of Insanity in the Age of Reason* (New York: Vintage, 1988), 9.

truth is, Jonah is not as overwhelmed by his new assignment as he is by his own small mindedness.[20]

In rabbinic law, there is a blessing recited upon seeing someone after a thirty-day absence – the *Sheheheyanu* blessing, in which God is praised for allowing the one who recites the blessing to have arrived at this special day. Thirty days away is a considerable time, and there is delight and possibly relief in the reunion that occasions a prayer:

> R. Yehoshua b. Levi said: One who sees a friend after a lapse of thirty days says: Blessed is He who has kept us alive and preserved us and brought us to this time. If after a lapse of twelve months, he says: Blessed is He who revives the dead. Rav said: The dead are not forgotten until after twelve months, as it says: "I am forgotten as a dead man out of mind; I am like a lost vessel" (Ps. 31:13). (Berakhot 58b)

In the ancient world, with scant means of communication across significant distances, there was an assumption that if an entire year had passed without seeing someone, there was a great likelihood that that individual was no longer alive: "I am like a lost vessel." This reunion necessitates an even stronger blessing. Here too a boat seems to feature; the lost person is like a lost vessel that drifted until its skeleton collapsed on itself and broke in pieces. The vessel became unrecognizable. Imagine being reunited after such a long absence. The Talmud assumes it is more than delight or even relief. It is astonishment, the kind of wonder and shock to the system that is almost frightening or awe-inspiring. It is the sudden encounter with the revenant, with the one who dropped out of one's mental universe such that one constructs an alternate practical and emotional way to function. This encounter demands a blessing, a verbal admission that this is for the good and that this person will once again be able to re-enter his earlier world. Rather than rejecting the returnee who may be fragile, humiliated, or otherwise vulnerable, we embrace

---

20. Michael Ben Zehabe, *A Commentary on Jonah*, 5.

him in prayer and welcome him with enthusiasm. With our blessing, in essence, we grant him permission to return.

> If anyone on the verge of action should judge himself according to the outcome, he would never begin. Even though the result may gladden the whole world, that cannot help the hero; for he knows the result only when the whole thing is over, and that is not how he became a hero, but by virtue of the fact that he began.[21]

RETURNING TO GOD

A revenant is not the same as a rebel. One who disappears and undergoes a radical change, an almost mystical experience that alters him and brings him back transformed, is not the same as one who fights against his role. It is too easy and reductive to label Jonah a rebel and dismiss his significant transformation. The transformation for Jonah was not that he was fully prepared to go to Nineveh and proclaim against it. For this he was willing but not completely committed. His great accomplishment as a prophet was his ability to be in dialogue with God, to come back with words rather than to flee without them. We do not celebrate this aspect of the prophet's development. Perhaps we even trivialize it. Yet this, arguably more than any other aspect of Jonah's life, is significant. When prophets respond to a call, there is the call and then there is the assignment. The call is the pause of intention before the action of the assignment. The call is about the relationship. The assignment is merely the task at hand, even if that assignment is immense and dramatic. For most prophets, one task follows another. A prophet's willingness to do the tasks, however, ultimately emerges from the strength of his relationship with God. Jonah may have failed or may have wildly succeeded at his task, depending on how we read this story, but what he was able to recover was the confrontation and intimacy with God.

Throughout this book, there have been oblique references to Cain and parallels, linguistic and thematic, that join these narratives. Berger notes many of these similarities – as do other scholars ancient

---

21. Kierkegaard, *Fear and Trembling*, 66.

and modern.[22] To suggest an alternative reading, perhaps Cain succeeded as a penitent and revenant where Jonah did not because Cain's deep remorse pushed him to come back into the narrative as a changed man after sin, whereas Jonah's lack of remorse prevented him, even when he was in the right place and doing the right things, from being a righteous prophet. Both men experienced and expressed anger at perceived injustice.

> Cain was much distressed and his face fell. (Gen. 4:5)

> But Jonah was greatly displeased and became angry. (Jonah 4:1)

God questioned the anger of each man:

> And the Lord said to Cain, "Why are you distressed and why is your face fallen?" (Gen. 4:6)

> Are you that deeply grieved? (Jonah 4:4)

> Are you so deeply grieved about the plant? (v. 9)

Both men left where they were originally stationed and moved eastward, further away from goodness. In both narratives, this flight was intentionally *milifnei Hashem*, "away from God," a relatively rare usage.

> Cain left the presence of the Lord (*milifnei*) and settled in the land of Nod, east (*kidmat*) of Eden. (Gen. 4:16)

> Jonah, however, started out to flee to Tarshish from (*milifnei*) the Lord's service. (Jonah 1:3)

> Now Jonah had left the city and found a place east (*mikedem*) of the city. (v. 5)

---

22. See, for example, Berger, *Jonah in the Shadows of Eden*, 13, 21, 42–45, 78, 83–85.

Epilogue

But Cain was not Jonah. Cain initially felt no responsibility toward his brother, a claim he baldly made to God directly. But after contemplating his actions and his punishment, he arrived at a penitent's conclusion: shame. "My sin is too great to bear," he confessed to God (Gen. 4:13). He understood that in seeking God's attention and intimacy by killing Abel, he paradoxically forced a greater distance between himself and God. He also created, through his impulsive and unchecked violence, the possibility in the new world that others too could act on their primal, brutal desires and destroy what and whom they did not like. Cain's remorse shaped him and prepared him for a different future. After he left God's presence and moved eastward, he became a new man: "Cain knew his wife, and she conceived and bore Enoch. And he then founded a city, and named the city after his son Enoch" (v. 17). Marrying, having children, building cities, and naming those cities after one's children are not acts of a punished wanderer. They are the accomplishments of the penitent, the fruits of total repentance.

When Jonah moved east of Nineveh, he achieved less intimacy with God than he had during his prayer in the fish. God questioned Cain *before* he acted; God questioned Jonah *after* he supposedly completed his mission. Cain's distress prompted him to transform himself and become the revenant, coming back a different man than the one he was. Jonah's distress made him more remote from God's service and unable to care about generational continuity the way Cain did. Cain finally responded to God's teleology, but only after Abel was dead: "Surely if you do right, there is uplift. But if you do not do right, sin crouches at the door. Its urge is toward you, yet you can be its master" (vv. 6–7). Cain did wrong but then, later, Cain did right. There was uplift. He finally understood that sin would be an ever-present seduction, but that he had self-control and could master his desires. So he built a family, and he built a city. Jonah could not even rebuild himself. Without remorse, without true repentance, sin crouches at the door and then pounces.

What difference is it to us if Jonah was a rebel or a revenant? There is a world of difference. Jonah did not flee God because he did not believe in God or because he rejected God. He fled because he believed in God too much, too much to actually confront God with his own paltry smallness. He was saturated with God, a God who, he felt, expected too much of him. Only in death, Jonah believed, could he could return to a God he could only disappoint with his measly human failings, with his poor judgment, with his cowardice. Jonah was daunted by a God who displayed forgiveness for the evil with which Jonah could not live. The revenant wants to find home, is distressed by the distance, suffers alienation and confusion. He or she is a person lost. The temporary passage out of convention and accustomed space eventually turns into a strong yearning for home accompanied by the insecurity that perhaps one cannot ever go home again. The rebel's intent is to leave and to leave for good, to fight, to reject, and to reinvent. The revenant is lonely. The revenant is existentially tired. The revenant wants to come back even if the return is desperately hard, is not linear, and will be punctured with mistakes and spiritual switchbacks.

Maybe, just maybe, ending with a question tells us that although Jonah had not been tasked again, he was, however, still engaged in a meaningful dialogue with God. Jonah finally overcame the silence and arrived at speech. He spoke few words to Nineveh but more words to God. Jonah did change, though not early enough or deeply enough to warrant his call. His repentance may have taken place after our book formally ends. We, as readers, will never know. What we do know is that God has the capacity to change and expects the same of those God creates, especially those designated for divine service.

The fonts used in this book are from the Arno family

Other books in the
Maggid Studies in Tanakh series:

Genesis: From Creation to Covenant
Zvi Grumet

Joshua: The Challenge of the Promised Land
Michael Hattin

I Kings: Torn in Two
Alex Israel

II Kings: In a Whirlwind (forthcoming)
Alex Israel

Isaiah (forthcoming)
Yoel Bin-Nun and Binyamin Lau

Jeremiah: The Fate of a Prophet
Binyamin Lau

Ezekiel (forthcoming)
Tova Ganzel

Nahum, Habakkuk, and Zephaniah (forthcoming)
Yaakov Beasley

*Haggai, Zechariah, and Malachi:
Prophecy in an Age of Uncertainty*
Hayyim Angel

Ruth: From Alienation to Monarchy
Yael Ziegler

Nehemiah: Statesman and Sage
Dov S. Zakheim

*Maggid Books
The best of contemporary Jewish thought from
Koren Publishers Jerusalem Ltd.*